D0842980

CRITICAL SOCIAL WORK WITH CHILDREN AND FAMILIES

Theory, context and practice

Steve Rogowski

First published in Great Britain in 2013 by

The Policy Press
University of Bristol
Fourth Floor
Beacon House
Queen's Road
Bristol BS8 1QU
UK
t:+44 (0)117 331 4054
f: +44 (0)117 331 4093
tpp-info@bristol.ac.uk
www.policypress.co.uk

North America office
The Policy Press
c/o The University of Chicago Press
1427 East 60th Street
Chicago, IL 60637, USA
t: +1 773 702 7700
f: +1 773-702-9756
sales@press.uchicago.edu
www.press.uchicago.edu

British Library Cataloguing in Publication Data
A catalogue record for this book is available from the British Library.

Library of Congress Cataloging-in-Publication Data
A catalog record for this book has been requested.

ISBN 978 1 44730 502 6 paperback
ISBN 978 1 44730 503 3 hardcover

Cover design by Qube Design Associates, Bristol
Front cover: image kindly supplied by www.alamy.com
Printed and bound in Great Britain by Hobbs, Southampton
The Policy Press uses environmentally responsible print partners

FSC
www.fsc.org
MIX
Paper from responsible sources
FSC® C020438

'Can you remember when we just did social work? It wasn't all about assessments and filling in forms.'

Quote from a manager of a children and families social work team

'And did you exchange a walk-on part in the war for a lead role in a cage?'

'Wish You Were Here', Pink Floyd, 1975

Contents

List of case studies

About the author

Steve Rogowski is a qualified and registered social worker who has been practising, mainly with children and families, for approaching 40 years. He has a particular interest in young offending and obtained his PhD in 2002. He has published widely in the social work/policy fields, his recent work including the book *Social work: The rise and fall of a profession* (2010, The Policy Press).

Acknowledgements

Perhaps surprisingly, during the thinking and writing of this book there are two managers I want to mention – Justine Hughes and Martin Murphy. There may have been discussions about, for example, whether it was right that the *quantity* of paperwork and the speed it took to complete should be the overriding goal, rather than *quality*. When it came to child protection/safeguarding they may have made comments about, for instance, 'worrying' about my concern to rely on minimum intervention in terms of child protection procedures unless there were *clear and unmistakeable* child protection/safeguarding issues. Or again they may have questioned what might be considered my 'unorthodox' views about social work more generally. However, they 'put up with'/'turned a blind eye' to attempts to work more preventatively and/or anti-oppressively on issues and concerns as defined by children and families.

Preventative social work has had to be restrained and limited over recent decades because of government-imposed 'modernisation' agendas involving managerial and financial constraints, and the need to protect social work organisations 'if things go wrong'. Then again, the controlling aspect of social work, rather than care, tends to predominate in the current neoliberal world, this leading to the dangers of oppressive practice. However, such managers show that it is possible to allow some limited discretion in specific cases, despite the fact that at times it might have seemed I was a thorn in the local authority's side. Quiet challenges to working in a managerial-dominated, neoliberal system were just about tolerated, and my argument is that all social workers need to do their best to avoid what can be the managerial straitjacket.

Other colleagues who merit a mention for various reasons are Nahara Begum, Cameron McPhearson, Stuart Hannah, Peter Hanlon, Richard Irving and Jill Richardson. No doubt there are others who, unfortunately, I have omitted – my apologies to them.

Finally, thanks to Paul Michael Garrett, Ray Jones, Bill Jordan and David Smith who read earlier drafts of this book and made helpful comments, with additional thanks to Bill Jordan for writing the Foreword.

Foreword

Capitalism has been in crisis worldwide since 2008, and government finances lie in ruins in many European countries. In Slovenia, a group of social workers have signed a declaration in support of the Occupy movement, declaring that they want to serve people, not computers or paperwork. In Spain, they march through the streets and camp in city squares; in Jerez they protest about not being paid for more than four months.

In the UK, despite the efforts of the Social Work Action Network and, on occasions, the British Association of Social Workers, social work continues to play the low-key role it has done for over 30 years, keeping its head down and hoping not to attract adverse media attention. It does the bidding of the government of the day, be it New Labour with its targets and checklists, or a Conservative-led Coalition government bent on putting 120,000 'problem families' on the straight and narrow, and getting them into work despite the fact that there are few meaningful jobs.

All this belies social work's origins in humanitarian and radical movements, and its involvement in social action and protest as recently as the 1970s. It is now a far larger and arguably better equipped profession from a technical standpoint; but is it merely willing to serve authoritarian and coercive political masters in an age of austerity?

This book argues that social workers should be active in forging their own destinies, not passively wait for the next round of policy guidance and management instructions. They should be aware of what is happening to poor, disadvantaged, minority and marginal citizens, and social work's own part in their situations. The 'critical' social work in the title implies that this awareness involves an independent-minded approach to practice, and a willingness to take some risks.

Above all, social workers should look at the big picture, and avoid becoming bogged down in organisational tasks. They should see how economic and social forces are bearing down on the communities they serve, and recognise in outbreaks of disorder – like the riots of August 2011 in England – the signs that official control, discipline and punishment can be counterproductive. Young people are disillusioned with the old order and the old political parties. After the Arab Spring of 2011 and the Bradford Spring of Respect candidate George Galloway being elected MP and overturning a large New Labour majority in 2012, where next? And how will social workers respond, wherever it is?

Steve Rogowski supplies a very interesting, motivating and scholarly, but accessible, analysis of the factors which have been missing from many social work textbooks. His cogent arguments are enriched by examples drawn from his many years of practice, mainly in a gritty urban setting. He shows how social work with children and families has evolved in a number of specialist fields against a background of neoliberal ideology, managerialist organisational reform and a contract culture that emphasises marketisation and privatisation. All this is far away from what can be seen as the heyday of social work some 40 years ago. Then, public services, including social work, were administered (as opposed to being managed) in order to ensure need was met, this being on the basis of progressive taxation and collective provision for all.

The book, however, does not simply look back through rose-tinted glasses; rather it is a call for a critical response to the current situation faced by both practitioners and the children and families they work with. This involves resistance to the managerial orthodoxy of rationing and risk assessment/management, instead working alongside users on the issues they face. It has a vision of a better, more socially just and equal world.

I first met Steve Rogowski when I worked as a consultant to his local authority's children and families services some 30 years ago, and was immediately impressed by his knowledge, understanding and commitment to social work. Before then, and increasingly since, he has published widely, all of which has been of great value to students, practitioners and academics. I commend this book, in the certainty that it will be of similar value for years to come.

Bill Jordan, Professor of Social Policy
University of Plymouth
December 2012

1

Introduction:
Critical social work and why we need it

> Many, many years ago you helped my family, [my children are] Jean
> and John Smith. We had a lot of problems with neighbours and the
> council trying to evict us. You stood up against the council even
> though you did not really know us that well. Luckily I won the case
> and eventually over the years the weird gang left us alone.
>
> I saw an article in the newspaper about a book you wrote on social
> work, and I have been writing this little letter since, just to let you
> know. Jean is now 28, she went to Sheffield Hallam Uni and has a
> degree in tourism/business management. She has now got her own
> photography business.... John finished Uni this year and has a degree
> in design.
>
> So, after all the bullying/upset caused by these sad people many
> years ago, Jean and John have done really well – I just wanted to let
> you know, many years on, and to say thank you for all your help....
> You were our guardian angel when we needed one.

During December 2010 I received the above comments in a letter from a former
client/service user.[1] They are not reproduced here out of self-indulgence, but
rather to show that critical practice is possible, even to the extent of being 'in
and against the state' (London-Edinburgh Weekend Return Group, 1980), in this
case the local authority. It reminds one of the possibilities arising from 'street-
level bureaucracy' (Lipsky, 2010 [1980]), the potentialities of which still remain.

I cannot recall the details of my work with the family and the council, but the
comments of Jean and John's mother clearly point out that such practice is valued
by the people social workers are there to serve. Social work is not simply about
ensuring that people accept and adjust to their social and economic circumstances
by changing their behaviour or lifestyle so as to avoid consequences, such as losing
their house (as was the case here), or even, in some scenarios, their children and
liberty. It is not, as some would have us believe, solely about rationing and risk
assessment/management; nor is it just about child protection. Critical social work[2]
involves a broader, political project aimed at making small steps at changing society
on more socially just and equal lines, notwithstanding the difficulties that can
be encountered in day-to-day practice dominated by managerialism (Rogowski,
2010b, 2011a). There are continuities with the 'first wave' of radical social work
(Bailey and Brake, 1975a; Corrigan and Leonard, 1978; Langan and Lee, 1989)
and the 'second wave' of the late 2000s (Ferguson and Woodward, 2009; Lavalette,

2011a) in that the focus is on how structures dominate, while recognising that there may be multiple and diverse constructions of ostensibly similar situations. This is where critical social work comes in (Fook, 2002; 2012), amounting to emancipatory social work, a practice that 'is person centred, empowering, critical of power structures and systems of resource distribution that undermine the well-being of many' (Dominelli, 2010, p 2). Although perhaps not familiar with the finer detail of such theoretical considerations, I am sure Jean and John's mother would agree with such sentiments, as would the vast majority of children and families with whom I have come into contact over the years.

A major difficulty confronting social work is the influence of managerialism, which has developed as a result of political, economic and ideological changes over the last three decades, coinciding with marketisation, the commodification and bureaucratisation of the individual and the subsequent demise of relational practice (Ruch et al, 2010). What social workers do, and how, is now set by managers who are focused on organisational goals rather than meeting service users' needs. My contention is that this lies at the root of the current crisis facing social work, because the imposition of such neoliberal practice means practitioners can find it hard to resist the negative impact on social work itself and, more importantly, the people they work with. For example, it is all too easy to feel the effects of what John Pitts (2001) has referred to in relation to social work with young offenders, namely 'zombification' – merely filling in assessment forms/computer exemplars almost unthinkingly and as quickly as possible to meet targets and performance indicators. Put simply, it also includes a 'practice' of telling young offenders and/ or their parents/carers to 'do this or that, or else!' Such comments equally apply to much current social work practice more generally. However, the argument throughout this book is that such managerial orthodoxy can still be countered by resilient practitioners in their individual work with users, by building alliances with other like-minded professionals, and by working collectively through trade unions, professional associations and wider social movements. It is about resisting the neoliberal tide that causes so much anxiety and suffering for so many, while simultaneously ensuring that those with wealth and power are allowed to continue their exploits unabated. The obvious example is the banking and financial sector-created economic crisis of 2007 to date, which has shown the remarkable resilience of capitalist formations; they have recombined the public and private spheres to bring ever more advantages to those who are already wealthy and committed to profit making (Sinclair, 2010). As well as resisting, and having a view of the possibilities of a changed neoliberal world that is at the root of most people's difficulties, social work is about alleviating individual difficulties in daily practice.

In this introductory chapter, I begin by arguing that when considering social work practice and the wider organisational, policy and societal context, social workers need to move beyond the 'how to do' or competency-based level towards a critical analysis, and hence critical practice concerning the situations that users face. In pursuing this, I look at critical social work, why it is important and why it is needed, before commenting on the book's structure and organisation.

The need for critical social work

The antecedents of critical social work have some foundation in the late 19th century, but more significant was the height of the postwar social democratic and welfare state consensus during the late 1960s and early 1970s. Professional social work was in the ascendency during a period which accepted that the state, through the government of the day, had a key role in ensuring the basic needs of its citizens. Any social problems that remained were the remit of the new social work profession which, both in terms of working with individuals, families and communities, as well as ensuring various agencies were fulfilling their responsibilities and meeting people's needs, would alleviate the situation. However, simultaneously the social sciences produced many critical texts, coinciding with the influence of the 'counterculture' and the New Left.

In relation to critical social science, Barbara Wootton's work (1959) was perhaps the first call to arms for radical/critical social workers, arguing that, despite the welfare state, the root of many social problems was sheer inequality and social injustice. This was particularly pertinent as poverty was 'rediscovered' in the 1960s (see, for example, Titmuss, 1965; Abel-Smith and Townsend, 1966; Kincaid, 1973). In the fields of critical psychology and psychiatry respectively, Herbert Marcuse (1964) and R.D. Laing (1965) were important influences; the former looked to social change as a means of preventing and treating psychological ills, while Laing challenged the core values of psychiatry by stressing the role of society and the family in the development of mental illness. Feminist thought, in the form of second wave feminism, addressed a wider range of issues relating, for example, to the family, the workplace, sexuality and reproductive rights (see, for example, de Beauvoir, 1964). And new deviancy theorists (for example, Becker, 1963, 1967) stressed the importance of deviant motivations, as well as the fact that official reactions to deviant behaviour could actually amplify deviance.

Although there was some convergence between the counterculture and New Left, the former referred to the values and norms of behaviour of many young people during the 1960s and early 1970s who wanted a non-materialistic, more expressive and meaningful alternative to a consumer society. In the UK there was a focus on issues such as women's and gay rights, as well as a permissive attitude to sexual activity more generally. Similarly, the use of recreational drugs and alternative styles of dress was accepted and encouraged. The hippie movement epitomised much of this and led to experiments with alternative ways of living, such as communes and exploring spirituality. Meanwhile, the New Left thinkers and activists of the 1960s and 1970s became disillusioned with orthodox communism as it had developed in the Soviet Union, advocating more democratic and participative strategies. The Marxist historians E.P. Thompson and Ralph Miliband were influential in the UK, along with the work of such institutions and scholars as the Frankfurt School, Antonio Gramsci and Louis Althusser.

Such developments in critical social science, together with the influence of the counterculture and the New Left, helped lead to Bailey and Brake's (1975a) seminal book, *Radical social work.* This pointed to the deficiencies in the welfare state, and that, paradoxically, while social workers were dealing with people's difficulties, actually the justification of social work lay in its maintenance of a social and economic system, namely capitalism, which was the cause of the ills that it had to confront. The charge was that social workers were the 'soft', sometimes even the 'hard', cops of the welfare state. This initial outbreak of radical social work occurred, however, just as the social democratic settlement was to fall apart and neoliberalism took hold. Ironically, the critiques of the most ardent supporters of the welfare state opened up a space that, as we will see, was colonised by the New Right.

The mid-1970s saw an emerging consensus that saw society as best served by a free market economy with limited state intervention, resulting in fundamental changes to British society. The Labour Prime Minister at the time, James Callaghan, started with major public expenditure cuts at the behest of the International Monetary Fund, and this was the precursor of more fundamental changes initiated by the New Right Conservative governments of Margaret Thatcher (1979-90) and John Major (1990-97). Such changes have been ongoing ever since, first under the stewardship of New Labour's Tony Blair (1997-2007) and Gordon Brown (2007-10), and now under the Conservative-led Coalition government of David Cameron (2010-to date). One of the most profound results has been the dramatic increase in inequality that, in turn, has had significant and deleterious effects on social problems such as poverty, mental health and drug misuse, as well as worries about the happiness and well-being of young people, teenage births, youth crime and child abuse (Dorling, 2010; Wilkinson and Pickett, 2010). Importantly, a United Nations report (UNICEF, 2007) noted concerns about the health and well-being of children and young people in the UK. Less obvious perhaps, but no less serious, there has been increased feelings of anxiousness and insecurity for the majority of people (Young, 2007).

Neoliberalism, a critique of the social democratic consensus, as well as a political and economic philosophy and ideology, has now been adopted throughout most of the countries in the largely capitalist, globalised world. It is a theory of political economic practices based on the belief in individual freedom and of liberating individual entrepreneurial skills within an institutional framework characterised by strong property rights (Harvey, 2007). It has even managed to capture and accommodate some of the vocabulary and aspirations of the counterculture, including the trend towards more individualist expressions of identity. More fundamentally, perhaps, the major concern, as Bourdieu (1998, p 94) points out, is that neoliberal arrangements amount to a 'utopia of unlimited exploitation' leading to vast inequalities in wealth and power. It involves 'accumulation by dispossession' (p 340), this being the way neoliberalism and neoliberalisation has constantly aimed to redistribute wealth in favour of the rich (see Garrett, 2010a, for a discussion). Linked to this is the fact that self-interest, self-responsibility and individualism are key values, ones which advocate that everyone should stand on their own feet, supported by families, friends, the local community and charities if necessary, with the state having only a minimal role. Such views were initially adopted by Prime Minister Margaret Thatcher in the UK and President Ronald Reagan in the US, both of whom propagated the belief that free markets and free trade would best achieve human well-being. A result was that unbridled selfishness and greed was unleashed, leading to the banking and financial crisis of 2007/08, and the resulting and continuing worldwide recession. In the end the banking sector has been saved while the public sector has amassed huge deficits to pay for it, a consequence being that ordinary people are now facing reduced services, attacks on workers' wages and terms of conditions, and many losing their jobs – 'accumulation by dispossession' aptly describes this process. Despite all this, and as already commented on, it currently seems unlikely that societal arrangements will be changed in any meaningful, positive way, one that works for the benefit of everyone. It is no exaggeration, therefore, to refer to the 'debacle of neoliberalism' (Lambie, 2011, p 25).

There has often been much talk about the need for a 'moral compass' in issues of governance, but the fact is that the austerity measures being carried out by the Coalition government have led to massive cuts to public services and affected the most vulnerable in society. Even if the need for the deficit to be reduced is accepted, there are alternatives in the form of progressive taxation, a clamp down on the multi-billion pound tax-dodging industry, harnessing the banking system to play a positive role in stimulating the economy, and investment in public services such as council housing. It should be remembered that Britain built its way out of recession with a far higher debt following the Second World War, while currently there has been a craven failure to rein in the financial system, indicating how business and economic policy is dictated by multinational conglomerates (Crow, 2011). I believe that we should have an economy geared to producing goods and services that meet our shared human needs rather than securing excessive financial gain for the few.

Neoliberalism and social work

Returning more explicitly to social work, what has been the effect of these changed political, economic, social and ideological circumstances? In brief, the belief in the free market and minimal state has led to the gradual dismantling or, at the very least, the changing nature of, the welfare state. Individuals must increasingly rely on themselves, families, friends or charity (the latter euphemistically often referred to as the voluntary or third sector) if they fall into difficulties. And what remains of welfare has increasingly involved more coercive aspects, particularly under New Labour (Broadhurst et al, 2009).

The Conservative governments of the 1980s and 1990s were never happy with so-called self-serving professions, particularly social work, because it was viewed as encouraging welfare dependency. Private sector managerialism was introduced to control social workers, as well as to limit public expenditure (see, for example, Clarke and Newman, 1997; Harris, 2003; Clarke, 2004; Rogowski, 2010b, 2011a).

This eventually involved a concern with social workers' 'competencies' rather than their knowledge and understanding of social problems and how they should be responded to. Care management in relation to adults was the first example of such managerial changes, before New Labour, for many having morphed into a neo-Conservative party (see Powell, 1999, 2002, 2008, for a comprehensive account of New Labour and its legacy), continued with such strategies concerning practice with children and families. There were ever more bureaucratic performance indicator hurdles, prime examples being assessment forms having to be completed within specified timescales. Numerous inspection and regulation regimes were also introduced in order to ensure this was happening. The overall intention was that all public services, including social work, should look and be managed like the private sector; it was an attempt to create the 'social work business' (Harris, 2003). These changes have meant that users' needs, along with social work practice, have been subordinated to the needs of managers and their organisations, transforming a relationship-based service into a bureaucratic one.

Neoliberal governments have always been wary of social workers 'going native' by forming relationships with users because it can mean issues being seen from users' points of view rather than how the 'powers that be' would like them to be viewed. Being close to users means that there is more likelihood of victims not being blamed for their predicament, with structural issues instead, such as inequality and social justice, being far more to the fore. The introduction of managerialism and all the associated bureaucracy and preoccupation with performance indicators works against the building of meaningful relationships with users.

Another, and linked, aim of social workers having to comply with centrally imposed bureaucracy and performance indicators is to ensure that managers and organisations cannot be criticised if 'things go wrong'. The result is a defensive practice predominating, one that can be defended rather than one genuinely aimed at meeting need. Further, whereas once social workers had a wide repertoire of methods of working at their disposal when dealing with people's problems and difficulties, these have been reduced and narrowed, so that they are now largely restricted to being bureaucratic people-processors aimed at rationing resources and risk assessment (Harris and White, 2009). It amounts to a situation where social work's possibilities are a limited version of what they once were. In addition, the increasing coercive nature of welfare, particularly under New Labour, has resulted in social workers being increasingly involved in the responsibilisation and remoralisation of children and families (Broadhurst et al, 2009), something that is taken up further in Chapters 5 and 6.

In addition, the results of the imposed managerial and bureaucratic changes mirror the changing form of knowledge in social work over the past 30 years, something that Nigel Parton has usefully summarised (see Parton, 2008). The impact of 'modernisation' systems relates to a range of new information and communication technologies, and highlights the shift from a narrative to a database way of thinking and operating. This raises important questions about how far social work is still primarily concerned with subjects and their social relationships, the danger being that social work theory and practice is in danger of operating less on the terrain of the 'social' and more on the terrain of the 'informational'. One result is that although social workers working with children and families are involved in much intrusive information gathering in order to produce their various assessments, unless there are serious child protection concerns, often little or no help and support is offered.

The effect of these changes on social work and social workers has been well demonstrated (see, for example, Jones, 1999, 2004). They include feelings of disillusionment and demoralisation as an increasing gulf has arisen between the reasons why they came into social work and what has happened to their profession.[3] Even Lord Laming (2003), the person largely responsible for the way that child protection and safeguarding services are currently organised, has pointed out that the overemphasis on bureaucratic processes and targets is ruining social workers' confidence. Such feelings are also highlighted in the work of one of New Labour's key social policy advisers, Julian Le Grand.

Le Grand (2007) pointed out that social workers were frustrated because of the procedures, bureaucracy and managerialism that took them away from direct work with users. He also commented on their initial strong moral purpose, idealism and commitment to rectifying injustice when they enter the profession. However, once into the job, they are often overwhelmed with meaningless targets and deprived of autonomy. Unfortunately, such a situation is then 'blamed' on local authorities, notwithstanding that it was New Labour that inflicted private sector managerialism on to them. Disingenuously, this is not acknowledged; instead, the way forward is seen as establishing social work practices for looked-after children, which would enable practitioners to be given the autonomy and freedom from a complex management structure to prioritise children and young people. Professional decision making would replace decisions by managers. The problem, however, as always with New Labour spin, is that the situation is much more complex. The high moral tone of Le Grand is less than sincere because although the frustrations of social workers are real and significant, there is no acknowledgement that they have been caused by the neoliberal context in which they have to operate. They simply cannot be solved by inflicting even more neoliberalism on to social work, with its belief in the market and the private sector. The obvious charge is that social work practices mean local authority children's services for looked-after children are to be privatised and that such children are to be commodified. Le Grand even concedes that such practices could eventually take over child protection/safeguarding and children in need services. Further, after the establishment of pilot practices for looked-after children, note that there are current proposals for similar practices for adults.

Given the changes that have taken place over recent decades, both at the societal and social work level, it is not hard to see the need for critical social work. In short, and bearing in mind previous comments, such practice aims to be emancipatory and has some view of a better, more equal and socially just world, one without power structures that do not meet the needs of everyone. As stated on Marx's epitaph, 'The philosophers have only interpreted the world in various ways; the point, however, is to change it.' Social work is unlikely to be at the vanguard of fundamental societal change, but critical social work's emphasis on critical analysis and practice that is person-centred, with work wherever possible focusing on problems and difficulties as defined by users, makes a small contribution to making the world we inhabit a better place.

Structure and organisation of the book

At the outset, it is important to emphasise that this book concentrates on the UK, and England in particular. Things may well be different for readers elsewhere, because social work and neoliberalism are different in different places, and in addition, the neoliberal project learns to 'speak the local language' as it pursues its goals (Garrett, 2009b). An example of this is in relation to social work practices – social workers are certainly fed up with bureaucracy and managerialism, but, as stated, this will not be rectified by inflicting even more neoliberalism on to them (Garrett, 2010b).[4] Having said this, I want to emphasise, perhaps belatedly, the fact that I am not against management per se. After all, management can be implemented in democratic, accountable (to practitioners as well as service users) and progressive ways. It is the new public management, introduced by Conservative and New Labour governments to control public services, that is the concern (Clarke and Newman, 1997; Harris, 2003; Clarke, 2004; Harris and White, 2009). Such management is driven by the dictates of neoliberalism and geared to, using the current jargon, 'getting more for less' rather than genuinely meeting the needs of children and families, something that is, of course, antithetical to critical social work.

There are two other points to note. First, although this book is about critical social work with children and families, what follows can be applied to social work more generally. It is also written by a practitioner who has been embedded in the field for approaching 40 years, this hopefully providing insights that are not often accessible or apparent to many of those in academia. Second, I do not aim to provide a complete 'how to do' critical social work book; rather, I want to question and unsettle current dominant neoliberal ideologies and resulting social work practices which focus on assessments aimed at rationing resources and risk assessment/management. It is this, sometimes unquestioned, currently more conventional practice that I want to interpellate, and in so doing, point some ways forward.

The book is divided into two parts. The first features two chapters dealing with the theory and context of critical social work, while the second consists of five chapters dealing with practice considerations in relation to child protection and looked-after children, children in need and those with mental health issues, young offenders, asylum-seeking and refugee children and families, and disabled children and families. Practice examples are included as well as suggestions for further reading. The Conclusion looks at future possibilities for critical social work.

Chapter 2 provides an overview of the key theoretical and conceptual concerns of critical social work. Critical social work's antecedents go back 150 years, but, as stated, it was the critical turn and resulting radical social work movement of the late 1960s/early 1970s that heralded its more substantial beginnings. In addition to this 'first wave' of radical social work, there is the 'second wave' of the late 2000s, with other important issues to consider being critical theory, feminist, anti-discrimination/oppression, empowerment and advocacy perspectives. I also comment on community development, an aspect of which is community work, this initially forming an important part of radical/critical practice. Critical social work itself is then considered, in particular Fook's (2002; also see Fook 2012) work. All these developments took place over the postwar social democratic era and subsequent neoliberal decades.

The challenges and opportunities for critical social work in current neoliberal times are the focus of Chapter 3. The neoliberal project's initiation by Margaret Thatcher and subsequent continuation by Conservative, New Labour and now Conservative-led Coalition governments, has had profound effects. In particular, there have been significant changes to the welfare state as, most recently, the 'Big Society' is supposedly about to unfold. These changes have had a negative impact on social work, notably the introduction of managerialism, marketisation and bureaucratisation (Ruch et al, 2010). As a result, practising critical social work is now much more difficult, reflected in the loss of influence of radical social work during the 1990s. Nevertheless, social work theory has managed to progress, particularly in relation to what has become critical social work (Fook, 2002; 2012). Then there was the return of radical social work towards the end of the 2000s (Ferguson and Woodward, 2009; Lavalette, 2011a). Despite the challenges, critical social work plays an important part in resisting neoliberalisation, thereby staying true to its emancipatory and social justice potentials.

Part Two addresses practice considerations, and begins at Chapter 4. This chapter looks at critical social work in relation to child protection and looked-after children, these being the 'heavy end' focus of much current social work with children and families. The critical possibilities of practice in these areas includes working on issues as defined by children and families, and relating these to wider structural issues such as poverty and inequality, along with 'race' and gender. Concerning child protection, interventions are targeted at the poor and women, with personal inadequacies being the focus rather than the wider, structural factors. Furthermore, if changes are not made quickly to parents' lifestyles and behaviour, then consequences have to be faced including the child(ren) being removed and quickly placed for adoption. Again, concerning looked-after children, the reasons why most are actually looked after, namely, their family's relationship with poverty and deprivation, are often neglected. Instead, parents are often blamed for their inadequacies by having to attend parenting classes that tend to neglect or dismiss their views and experiences.

Critical social work with children in need and those with mental health issues feature in Chapter 5. Children in need are now often given the least attention by social workers, particularly as the Common Assessment Framework (CAF) is supposed to deal with the vast majority of children with additional needs. Such a framework is what preventative social work used to be entail, albeit these days it amounts to filling in a CAF form, something which 'anyone can do', with little in the way of extra help and support being provided to service users. Meanwhile, the number of children with mental health issues is increasing, but are these increases real or do they reflect social constructions around 'normality'? If it is the former, then issues in relation to happiness and well-being need to be considered, especially as it seems that increased affluence has not led to increased positive feelings (Layard, 2005). Then again, interventions with children with mental health issues can simply relate to the policing of the poor, in this case by the medicalisation of what are social, political and economic issues. Critical considerations regarding both user groups are considered here.

Chapter 6 examines critical social work with young offenders, an area where the authoritarian state makes no bones about rearing its head (Wacquant, 2009). Youth justice has seen a move away from the welfare/treatment of young offenders to one of punishment, and the creation of Youth Offending Teams has led to a diminished social work role (Smith, 2007). What remains is largely controlled by managers, leading to the 'zombification' of workers, although critical possibilities still endure. Listening to and heeding what young people and their parents say is required, linking this to factors of class, 'race' and gender. My research with young offenders, for instance, suggests that the youth justice system focuses on 'people like us', namely, poor and black young people, with young women being treated disproportionally harshly, rather than administering fairness and justice to all (Rogowski, 2000/01). Social workers need to engage in a critical practice, one that questions dominant discourses and associated social practices (Rogowski, 2003/04). This involves more than merely aiming to ensure young offenders play by the rules of present society given that these rules, and the inequality of wealth and power they support, lie at the root of youth crime.

Part Two ends with chapters on two relatively neglected areas of critical social work with children and families, namely, practice with asylum-seeking and refugee children and families, and disabled children and families.

Work with asylum-seeking and refugee children and families can be a contentious area, with practitioners increasingly having to confront practical, ethical and political challenges (Fell and Hayes, 2007). This is the subject of Chapter 7, with the important point to stress being that practice can often amount to the policing of users and checking their immigration status before help and support are offered. This is because such children and families are caught up in the moral panic fuelled by many politicians and the media suggesting that the country is being overrun by 'undesirables'. Consequently, if they are not entitled to benefits, too often parents can be told to 'go home' or that if they are not providing 'good enough' care for their children, the children could be accommodated in children's or foster homes and, in effect, the family torn apart. Instead, there is a need for social workers to seriously consider their role in this area, with the aim of developing critical practice. Such practice means more than simply complying with what managers, policy makers and politicians stipulate because on occasions, this can amount to oppressive practice. Instead, more positive critical approaches are required, ones that emphasise working in collaboration with users on issues defined by them.

Chapter 8 looks at critical social work with disabled children and families. In order to work effectively with this user group, an understanding of disability is needed, including practitioners questioning their own assumptions, views and experiences. The social model of disability is a key aspect of this, with practitioners having to acknowledge that physical and social environments create barriers which can preven disabled people from becoming full members of society (Oliver, 1996). It also is important that practitioners have a critical understanding of the legal and policy framework together with practice issues concerning the particular problems disabled children face in relation to, for example, poverty, educational attainment and well-being. The resulting critical practice includes recognising that if society has created the problems that confront disabled children and families, then it is society that should un-create them (Crow, 1996).

Chapter 9, the Conclusion, looks at critical social work and its future. The future for social work, and for critical social work, remains uncertain in the globalised neoliberal and, for some, postmodern world (Dominelli, 2010). Some argue that we have witnessed the 'rise and fall' of social work (Rogowski, 2010b) because of the encroachment of other 'professionals' or of it being out of tune with a no longer social democratic era in which collectivism has given way to neoliberalism, where values of individualism and self-responsibility dominate. Equally there are more sanguine views of the situation because social work, particularly in its critical form, does make a make a contribution to humankind's well-being and advancement (Webb, 2010). Such views emphasise the need to form and sustain collaborative relationships with children and families, which chimes with the feminist-based ethics of care. They accept that social work is not simply a technical activity but depends on an appreciation and application of core values, all of which are inherent in critical social work. It also involves the application of knowledge and understanding. This final chapter discusses such issues and, even if rather tentatively, ends on a optimistic note, arguing that social work must remain true to its value base in the current difficult, ever-changing, times (see also Rogowski, 2011b).

Conclusion

As this introductory chapter was being written, the leader of the Labour Party, Ed Miliband, announced that he was concerned that the next generation would fare worse than previous ones (BBC, 2011a). Looking at the financial cost to students of university education, the uncertain employment situation, the difficulties they will face in buying their own homes, and threats to their pensions, he has an important point. Then there is the increasing privatisation of health services, and the threat of individuals having to bear the costs of their own treatment. However, what Miliband did not acknowledge was that it was New Labour's embracement of the neoliberal project that now lies at the heart of such difficulties. Free markets have been 'softly' or 'lightly' regulated, people at the top have been allowed to accrue what they can while simultaneously those at the bottom are living with increasing job insecurity, and public services have been subject to marketisation and privatisation. What remains of a robust welfare state is nowhere near what it was or, even close to, the goals of its makers. And what remains of professional social work is nowhere near what its aspirations once were (Rogowski, 2010b), another key reason why critical social work is needed now more than ever.

The reduced and limited discretion that social workers retain in the current neoliberal, managerial world must be defended and fought for, leading to the critical thinking and practice outlined throughout this book. This can mean engaging in seemingly 'deviant' activities, potentially coming at great cost to individual practitioners, including disciplinary action, loss of reputation and job loss (Carey and Foster, 2011). Nevertheless, my argument is that such critical social work is needed simply because it critiques the present social order and the social control activities of social workers, while simultaneously offering a distinctive analysis of social issues that will help social workers think creatively about their practice and respond to concerns about oppressive practice. Paraphrasing Fook (2002, p 168), it is not what type of power (structural or personal) that individuals have at their disposal that is important, but how they use, engage with and create the opportunities that become available. Each social position that people have carries challenges and opportunities for the exercise of different types of power, and the promise of critical and (some) postmodern perspectives on practice is that they provide access to these opportunities. From a more overtly radical view, the neoliberal form of social work that we currently endure has led practitioners to disillusionment and discontent, but in turn, it has created a space for the rebirth of radicalism (Lavalette, 2011a). Such radicalism, along with critical analysis and practice more generally, are necessary because otherwise the way is left clear for those who see social work as a means of social control increasingly exercised in an authoritarian manner. Such a situation aims to ensure the status quo, a free market society consisting of inequality and injustice. In contrast, and as utopian as it may seem, critical social work is about small steps towards creating a society in which all humankind's needs are met, and where all are encouraged and enabled to fulfil their potential rather than to be simply workers and consumers.

Key point

Social work is ever-changing and faces considerable challenges in the neoliberal, globalised world. This includes children and families being less able, through social workers, to turn to the state for help and support, having to rely instead on themselves, family, or charity. Critical social work is needed to resist this, and in so doing remains true to its transformative potential by aiming to ensure equality and social justice for all.

Further reading

The best introduction to social work, including critical social work, is the trilogy edited by Robert Adams, Lena Dominelli and Malcolm Payne: *Social work: Themes, issues and critical debates* (3rd edn, 2009); *Critical practice in social work* (2nd edn, 2009); *Practising social work in a complex world* (2009); all published by Palgrave Macmillan (London).

Harris, J. and White, V. (eds) (2009) *Modernising social work: Critical considerations*, Bristol: The Policy Press. This is a critical commentary on New Labour and social work, one that provides an antidote to managerial, market-driven approaches, including introducing the concept of 'quiet challenges'.

Notes

[1] There are difficulties in categorising the people social workers work with. 'Clients', 'service users', simply 'users' and even 'customers' are all used. The latter term reflects the current neoliberal consensus and the emphasis on free markets. As critical social work rejects this orthodoxy, such a term is not used in this book. As for the others, they remain contested terms. For example, parents who have their children taken away because of child protection concerns, young offenders subject to youth justice measures, and people with mental health difficulties subject to compulsory admission to hospital, are unlikely to consider themselves as 'service users'. And 'client' implies a rather unequal relationship with the social worker. Given these caveats, and if only for convenience sake, I tend to use 'service user'/'user' in this book.

[2] I tend to use the term 'critical' social work as opposed to 'radical' social work unless specifically referring to the latter. This is because initially radical social work referred to the more overtly Marxist, class-based analysis of the 1970s. Over subsequent decades, issues of 'race', gender and other aspects of diversity came into play, hence the move to the now generally accepted use of 'critical' social work. This is not to say that class no longer matters (see Ferguson, 2011), thus the re-emergence of radical social work towards the end of the 2000s.

[3] Anecdotally, however, from my own experience, some recently qualified and student social workers seem to embrace the changed social work role, which often entails domination by managerial diktats and a resulting emphasis on the social and moral policing of children and families, rather than the role of helping and supporting.

[4] Another example is the right wing think-tank, the Centre for Social Justice. It is hard to accept that social justice can result from the inequalities caused by neoliberalism.

PART ONE

Theory and context

2

Critical social work:
Theory and concepts

As alluded to, the origins of critical social work can be traced back to the beginnings of professional social work in the 19th century. Many of the pioneers such as the Charity Organisation Society and Octavia Hill were influenced by the prevailing values and ideologies of the time that were dominated by liberalism (Rogowski, 2010b). These included values of self-responsibility and self-help, with the focus being on individual, moral failings such as laziness or lack of thrift that were seen as leading to problems such as poverty and destitution. However, this was not always the case, with the problems of the poor sometimes being linked to more structural issues such as the selfishness of factory owners and slum landlords. The social work pioneers might not have gone so far as to agree with Engels (1973 [1892]) who saw the misery of the Britain's poor as caused by class inequality and exploitation, but many did begin to question, and to have some understanding of, the links between the structure of society and societal ills. In particular, two leading Fabians, Sydney and Beatrice Webb, argued that the cause of the difficulties faced by the poor lay with the moral failings of exploitative employers and the greedy rich rather than with the poor themselves.

The development of social work slowed down in the first half of the 20th century, but accelerated after the Second World War when social democracy took hold and the welfare state was established (Fraser, 2002). This era of optimism in the political, economic and social spheres included agreement on the state's role in terms of economic regulation and planning, and meeting the needs of all its citizens. There was a feeling that, according to the Conservative Prime Minister Harold Macmillan of the late 1950s/early 1960s, that people had 'never had it so good'. In many ways those words had a ring of truth because people could live their lives and plan for the future in a way that a generation earlier could only have dreamed of (Timmins, 1996). It was in such a climate that social work came of age following the Seebohm Report (1968) that led to local authority social services departments being established and staffed by qualified social workers. They worked within an administrative ethos (as opposed to the managerial ethos of today) whereby an element of professional discretion and autonomy prevailed (Harris and White, 2009), and this is when radical social work first appeared. It was a time when social workers were seen as being able to deal with social problems by including the 'other' by working directly with them, as well as ensuring that other agencies were meeting their needs (Marshall 1996 [1950]; Young, 1999). This inclusive society saw the deviant as someone who could be socialised, rehabilitated or cured until they became like 'us'. Unfortunately the ideological, political and economic changes initiated by Margaret Thatcher after 1979 resulted in a neoliberal consensus, leading to the current exclusive society of change and division (Young, 1999), despite New Labour's emphasis on tackling social exclusion.[1] For some the move to the neoliberal world corresponds with the move from a concern with the modern to the postmodern, especially as it affects welfare (see O'Brien and Penna, 1998, for a discussion).

This chapter deals with some of the main theoretical and conceptual issues affecting initially radical and then critical social work as it developed from the 1970s to the current time. The importance of theoretical and conceptual issues cannot be overstated, simply because *all* our action, whether acknowledged or not, is guided by theory (for example see Garrett [2013] regarding the relevance of social theory to social work). Social work is not, and cannot be, common sense, despite what parts of the media and some politicians would have us believe. I begin with a comment on the social construction of welfare and social work, prior to consideration of broad social work perspectives and related social work practice theory. This encompasses the move from radical to critical social work that occurred between the 1970s and the 2000s (see, for example, Bailey and Brake 1975a, and Fook, 2002; 2012 respectively). Initially, radical social work focused on class before embracing such issues as 'race' and gender (Langan and Lee, 1989), and re-emerging at the end of the 2000s (Ferguson and Woodward, 2009; Lavalette, 2011a). In pursuing the development of critical social work, I consider critical theory, feminist and anti-discriminatory/oppressive perspectives, empowerment and advocacy (see Payne, 2005). I also comment on what was a key element of radical/critical social work in the UK, namely, community development, before outlining Fook's (2002; 2012) critical social work that draws on some postmodern influences.

Theory and concepts

Although it may be stating the obvious, social work is a contested area because people do not often agree on what social work is or what it should consist of. Similar comments apply to what are, or are not, considered as social problems. Moreover, what social workers do in their actual day-to-day practice creates what social work is. Such contestations are related to ideological, political, economic and social factors (covered in Chapter 3), but the point can be made here that social work, together with the social problems it aims to address, amount to *social constructions* because social work and social problems, rather than being existing realities, emerge from ideas. The idea of social construction derives from the sociologists Peter Berger and Thomas Luckmann (1971 [1966]) who maintained that in social life, as opposed to the natural world, reality is based on the social knowledge which guides behaviour, despite individuals often having differing ideas. Such knowledge can be seen as historically and culturally specific, with people arriving at their views of reality by knowledge being shared or inculcated through various social processes that eventually make it seem objective or 'common sense'. The influence of the media and education are obvious examples of such processes, although in earlier times, religion dominated this process.

In relation to social work, what the profession actually consists of, along with what theories guide and indicate how it should be carried out, emerge from differing ideas, debates and actions. This is an important reason why there are different theories and perspectives. Similarly when it comes to social problems, the definitions of these vary over time, meaning that certain situations may have to be addressed as problematic during one period of history, although accepted as part and parcel of 'normal' life in another. The converse, needless to say, is equally true. Again it is crucial to emphasise that theory itself is not a word game carried out by academics; it is a dimension of action, giving direction and meaning to what we actually do.

The idea of social construction raises some significant issues, but one important point is that Marxism's method of historical analysis and debate is *the*, or at the very least *a*, legitimate, form of study. Despite the collapse of communism in the former Soviet Union and the subsequent triumph of neoliberalism, you only have to look at the work of, for example, Miliband (1977, 1973 [1969], 1994) and Hobsbawm (2011), to see the continued relevance of Marxist theory, even to the extent that it can be argued that 'Marx was right' (Eagleton, 2011). Significantly, Marx's work is an important inspiration for social work and its resistance to neoliberalism (Garrett, 2010b). More broadly, critical theory argues that positivist science maintains ruling hegemony by accepting and promoting the present social order. From such a view, all theory, including that of social work, represents ideological positions, ones that are usually in support of the ruling class or elite. The important point about radical, and indeed critical, theory is that it works away at the weaknesses of such conventional wisdom and practice, and in so doing aims to make small steps towards a better world, one involving a more just and equal society.

Turning more specifically to social work theory, Malcolm Payne (2005) provides a useful overview, helpfully outlining three views of social work. First, *reflexive-therapeutic views* see social work as seeking the well-being of individuals, groups and communities in society by promoting and facilitating growth and self-fulfilment. Interaction between workers and users leads to both the latter's ideas being modified by the former, as well as users affecting workers' understandings of their world as they gain experience of it. It is a process of mutual influence and it is what makes social work reflexive. It expresses in social work the social democratic view that economic and social development should work hand in hand so as to achieve individual and social improvement. Second, *socialist-collectivist views* see social work as seeking cooperation and mutual support so that oppressed and disadvantaged people can gain power over their own lives. Here elites in society, or the ruling class in Marxist terms, are seen to accumulate and perpetuate power and resources in society for their own benefit, thereby creating oppression and disadvantage that social work seeks to supplant by more egalitarian relationships in society. It amounts to emancipatory practice because the aim is to free people from oppression (Dominelli, 2009a, 2010) by transforming society on more just and equal lines, with planned economies and robust social provision seen as promoting this. Value statements about social work represent this view by proposing social justice as a key value of social work. Third, *individualist-reformist views* see social work as an aspect of welfare services to individuals in society. These are 'maintenance approaches' as social work concerns itself with ensuring social order by maintaining people during difficult times (Dominelli, 2009a). This concern with maintaining social order and the social fabric of society reflects a concern with liberal or neoliberal political ideology/philosophy whereby free markets and the rule of law is seen as the best way of organising society. All such perspectives are applicable to social work practice with children and families.

The three views of social work are often at odds with, or offer critiques of, the others.[2] For instance, seeking personal and social fulfilment, as in reflexive-therapeutic views, is difficult to reconcile with those of a socialist-collectivist persuasion because the interests of the ruling class/elite work against those of the poor and oppressed, unless significant social change takes place. In addition, merely working within or accepting the current social order, as reflexive-therapeutic and individual-reformist views do, actually supports the interests of those with wealth and power, this being a key point that socialists/collectivists make. As we will see, this is not to say that working within and yet against current society, as is the case with the socialist-collective view, is not without problems and difficulties, with many seeing a gap between the theory and its practical implementation in day-to-day social work. This is what critical practice continually seeks to address.

Despite the three differing views, there are also some affinities between them with, for example, reflexive-therapeutic and socialist-collective views being essentially about change and development. It can be argued that at times there is no clear dividing line, with social work practice theories often including elements of each and sometimes acknowledging the validity of elements of the others. Nevertheless, broadly speaking, practice theories can be placed within one of these views. Existentialist, humanist (for example, Gestalt therapy) and social psychological (for example, solution-focused therapy) theories are linked to reflexive-therapeutic views, while task-centred theory is linked to individualist-reformist views. Critical social work theory and practice is linked to socialist-collectivist views, an important component being radical social work.

Radical social work

Radical social work draws on Marxist thought (see, for example, Marx and Engels 1967 [1848], 1970 [1845-46]; Garrett, 2010c), as well as the counterculture and the New Left, which provides an understanding of the development of welfare in society and of the state. It uses an approach to social work that involves a concern not only with theory but a 'political practice that confronts capitalism with an alternative model of social order' (Leonard, 1978, p xiv). This includes a materialist understanding of society whereby how the materials of life are produced through the economic system is a crucial determinant of the social system in which we live. Importantly, radical social work sees the myriad of problems confronting people in society being defined as social and structural rather than arising from individual failings. Furthermore, inequality and injustice in society arise from people's working-class position (Bailey and Brake, 1975b) together with oppressions based on 'race' and gender (Langan and Lee, 1989). From all of this, the focus of practice is political action and social change while at the same time attempting to address the immediate needs of users.

At the heart of radical social work is an antagonism to the neoliberal view that economic markets, where individuals compete to accumulate wealth, are the most effective organisation for societies. Neoliberals argue that rational individuals seeking to benefit their own economic position thereby contribute to economic growth and social development which benefits everyone in society. However, this neglects the fact that it leads to economic and social inequality, together with the oppression of the poor and disadvantaged more generally. Recall the restricted life chances for those children and families living in deprived areas (see Bradshaw, 2011).

The work of Freire (1972) and his notion of *conscientisation* is a significant component of radical social work. It refers to the consciousness of oppressed people being raised, becoming aware of, and resisting, the process of oppression rather than accepting it as inevitable. It is about learning to perceive the real essence of economic, political and social situations and contradictions, and about taking action against the oppressive elements of reality (Leonard, 1984). Participation in dialogue and praxis, that is, implementing theories in practice so that practice reflects on and alters the theory, is important; it is a process whereby people can take action to lose their fear of freedom and some of their powerlessness.

This is not to say that radical social work was or is homogeneous because there were clear differences of emphasis. Classical Marxists saw social workers as agents of class control enhancing the oppression by capitalist societies of the working class, although more positive views were also taken. Such views address the contradiction that, while social workers were enforcers of (capitalist) state legislation and policy, equally they had had an imperative to protect, support and advocate on behalf of the vulnerable. Then there is the view that social work is an agent of change, connecting more general bourgeois society with the representatives, and thus the demands, of the working class. Another, and linked view, is that social work is an agent of capitalist control yet can undermine capitalist society by increasing working-class capacities to function; it can also offer some knowledge and power of the state to service users in the working class. The existence of this contradiction in social workers' roles, the argument continues, leads to other contradictions that can eventually contribute to the overthrow of capitalist society (see, for example, Bailey and Brake, 1975a; Corrigan and Leonard, 1978; Brake and Bailey, 1980; Rojek et al, 1988).

Perhaps the major current statement of radical, indeed Marxist, social work is Mullaly's *Structural social work* (2003). Drawing on Canadian theoretical traditions, it argues that as social problems are inherent in present society, the focus of change should mainly be on social structures, not individuals. In pursuing this Mullaly compares Marxism's paradigm of political social thought that underlies social work with those of neoconservatism, liberalism and social democracy. Marxism's class analysis seeks a planned economy based on the collective effort of everyone, and has a progressive view of welfare and social work. Neoconservatism sees welfare as having a residual role in current society, while liberalism has an individualistic view of welfare. Social democracy seeks a participative and humanitarian social system, and has much in common with Marxism, also having a progressive view of welfare and social work.

When it comes to 'structural' practice, Mullaly highlights a number of examples. First, *consciousness raising* involves promoting the understanding of dehumanising structures and how to overcome their effects. Second, *normalisation* refers to helping users to see that their problems are not unique, and linking them to others who share them. And third, *dialogical relations* means a dialogue of equals should be maintained, including practitioners demystifying their own activities and providing inside information.

Radical social work was influential in the UK for much of the 1970s and into the 1980s, admittedly more often at the level of theory rather than practice. However, this influence waned as the New Right gained power and dominated during the 1980s and 1990s. The collapse of communism was another factor in its apparent decline. This led to a re-examination and recasting of radical ideas, including, as noted, the integration of 'race' and gender issues into the original class-based analysis. There were also other factors to consider as a 'looser', critical theory became incorporated.

However, prior to considering critical theory we must consider the 'second wave' of radical social work (Ferguson and Woodward, 2009; Lavalette, 2011a, 2011b). This arose because of the introduction of a form of neoliberal managerial social work that emphasised an increased concern with bureaucracy and targets aimed at rationing resources/services and risk assessment/management, with resulting practice often merely amounting to moral policing. The resultant disillusionment and discontent within social work created a space for the rebirth of radicalism (Lavalette, 2011b). The restrictions of managerialism, as well as those arising from marketisation, left many practitioners, in both adult and children's services, feeling they were no longer able to do the job the way it should be done (Unison, 2009, 2010), resonating with what academic studies also show (White et al, 2009). As the Social Work Task Force (2009) has commented (see Chapter 3), the social work profession is certainly not flourishing.

Radical social work now helps practitioners frame solutions to the current global economic crisis as well as drawing on resources of hope that include a view of a better world. First, echoing aspects of the counterculture and the New Left of the 1960s/1970s, the end of the 1990s saw the birth of a new social movement, namely, the 'anti-capitalist' or global justice movement. This was against the impact and consequences of neoliberalism including third world debt, the privatisation of public services and the effect on working conditions as well as on state welfare provision more generally. Then there was the effect of market deregulation on the environment and the plight of refugees across the globe. Resulting campaigns and protests broadened and deepened, merging with, for example, global anti-war and climate change protestors. They questioned Fukuyama's (1993) 'end of history' thesis that there was no alternative to global capitalism, and opened up the possibilities of alternatives. This spawned intellectuals such as Naomi Klein, Alex Callinicos and George Monbiot who developed critiques of neoliberalism, the meaning of equality and social justice, the environmental crisis and the possibilities of an alternative world. Recent protests have included the Occupy movement in New York and London, focusing on the banking and financial sector, its role in causing the worldwide economic crisis, and the fact it is ordinary people who are having to pay the price for the catastrophe.

A second resource for hope is revitalising existing collective organisations such as trade unions, as well as social workers and service users coming together to campaign on specific social work and service user issues. This latter grouping is evidenced by the Social Work Action Network (SWAN), working in conjunction with the main trade unions by campaigning and organising conferences. SWAN is committed to anti-racist and anti-oppressive practice, service user engagement, and participates with all movements aiming for a better and more humane world. Importantly, it is engaged in rethinking the radical social work project for the 21st century, and asserts that 'another social work is possible', one that rejects managerialism and marketisation, along with the retrenchment of social welfare services and substantial cutbacks (Lavalette, 2011a).

This 'second wave' of radical social work leads to a more positive view of aspects of critical social work. The focus of critical social work per se was often on identity and difference, admittedly leading to positive developments in relation to feminism, anti-racism and anti-discriminatory/oppressive practice. However, a problem was that whereas commonality provided a basis for joint, collective action, the stress on identity and difference led to a fragmentation that is part and parcel of neoliberal policies that accentuate the belief in individualism. Importantly, these new emphasises led to a retreat from class analysis and politics, together with the possibility these offer for collective action. It also meant the sidelining issues of poverty and equality, and the resultant 'politics of redistribution' (Fraser, 1997). In practice, much of critical social work, at least in its broadest sense, sought to overcome fragmentation and make links between oppression and material inequality. But it is the return of radical social work itself that highlights the continued relevance of class.

Class still matters because of three distinct but related aspects (see Ferguson, 2011). The first aspect is that it is a social division and a determinant of life chances. Second, it provides an explanatory framework by helping make sense of both the experience of people who use social work and practitioners themselves. Third, it continues to have the potential to promote social change with the politics of class still having relevance. Such comments resonate with Bailey and Brake's

(1975a, 1975b) work, and have direct significance as far as current social work is concerned. This is because, for example, managerialism can be understood as a class-based project aimed at applying neoliberal ideas and practices to the public sector, and 'getting more for less'. Resistance through trades union activity and building alliances with user groups offers the hope of protecting services and making a new kind of social work.

An example of the continued relevance of class and Marxist ideas more generally is provided by Garrett (2008, 2009c) in relation to the Italian Marxist, Antonio Gramsci, and his notion of cultural hegemony. This refers to how modern forms of economic and political power include the active and practical involvement of hegemonised groups, meaning that it is actually a form of consent. It occurs because those with power maintain a social order that benefits them, this being done by integrating key social beliefs into cultural life through the influence of the media and education. Such a situation can be contrasted with the concept of dominant ideology which is about a more passive, static subordination involving, for example, the use of force (Joseph, 2006). Garrett promotes a more Gramscian way of thinking about, and acting in, social work, involving a practice of hegemonic critique that can help free individuals' minds from the distortions of bourgeois ideology.

This is not to say, of course, that resistance to managerialism and neoliberalism is easy, but radical and critical ideas can be pursued in practice by, wherever possible, working with individual users on issues defined by them, by building relationships with them, and by always being attentive to their needs and rights. It involves recognising the oppression and discrimination that users continually face. Such practice has to go hand in hand with the more collective strategies outlined previously.

But there is another issue to consider. A concern with values, although essential, is not sufficient merely because the vagueness and ambiguity of words such as 'empowerment' and 'respect' means they can be appropriated by forces that are directly opposed to social work values and objectives (Ferguson, 2008). Often, for instance, changes in practice may seem to have a semblance of loyalty to social work values, whereas, in actual fact, it entails doing the bidding of managers and policy makers who have a very different agenda. The concern with values, therefore, has to be underpinned by a critical analysis of the political context in which social work is taking place. In pursuing this it is possible to assert the possibility of a different, radical or critical social work (Lavalette, 2011a). This is necessary because to do otherwise means we capitulate to a social order based on selfishness, greed and inequality rather than one based on social justice and equality.

Critical theory

Moving to critical theory, during the 1930s-1950s many on the political left in Europe felt that the moment of socialist revolution had passed. The rise of fascism in Germany, Spain and Italy, the totalitarian communism of Russia, and the Second World War were all factors in this critical pessimism. Many turned away from direct involvement in workers' movements and socialist political parties, turning instead to ideology critique. Rather than a concern with revolutionary strategy and mobilisation, the lines of political engagement moved towards a strategy of exposing the negative ideology of capitalism. Such ideology, as Lenin, Lukács and Gramsci had recognised, blocked the way for a true understanding of its exploitative nature, so freedom from capitalist oppression required an intellectual analysis of the ideological and cultural superstructures of modern society (see Ransome, 2010). The result was the critical theory of the Frankfurt School of Social Research which first opened in 1923 under Max Horkheimer, other leading members being Theodore Adorno, Herbert Marcuse and, later, their second generation representative, Jürgen Habermas.

Critical theory aims to understand and be critical of current society with a view to bringing about positive change (Callinicos, 1999). It can be counter-posed to traditional theory that merely serves to legitimate the status quo. Critical theory strives to imagine alternatives to traditional theory, of getting beyond it so as to look back at social reality from a fresh perspective. With echoes of Marx, it is geared to achieving a superior, more civilised society, one that humanity should strive to achieve. It is hard to argue against the view that if one cannot envisage a better society than exists at present, then surely humanity has lost something. At critical theory's heart, therefore, in achieving such a goal there lies an 'attempt to achieve a unity of theory and practice, including a unity of theory with empirical research and both with an historically grounded awareness of the social, political, and cultural problems of the age' (Calhoun, 1995, p 13). Adorno and Horkheimer may have become pessimistic about the possibility of human emancipation by the working class, but Habermas, through his theory of communicative action, retained a sense of optimism for what has been and is the emancipatory project of Enlightenment and modernity (Habermas, 1981a, 1981b). Communicative action emphasises that dialogue between social actors is fundamentally shaped by their mutual desire to reach understanding and agreement, and this can eventually lead to humankind's emancipation. Importantly, his theory involves the principle of *immanent critique*, the idea that criticisms emerging from within a particular paradigm or cultural tradition demonstrate the capacity of the paradigm to turn its own critical and explanatory power against itself. Despite postmodern challenges such as the questioning of 'grand narratives', and the emphasis on language and identity, Habermas' (1987) *The philosophical discourse of modernity* is an 'extraordinary attempt to pursue the questions which have been constituitive of social theory since Hegel' (Callinicos, 1999, p 287).

In looking at critical theory in relation to social theory more generally, it has had three significant influences (Ransome, 2010). First, it emphasises that social theory cannot do without its critical dimension. This is because to understand social reality, one must penetrate the surface of things to discover discrepancies between appearance and actuality. In so doing, it is possible to discern those elements of social reality that can lead to the transformation of reality. The second influence is that of the Frankfurt School which legitimated the use of basic Marxian concepts like alienation, reification and praxis for the purposes of ideology critique, rather than as solely tools of revolutionary strategy. Such concepts have been refined for new purposes in the sense that their revolutionary potential is used not to mobilise the revolution, but to revolutionise perceptions of social reality itself. Third, the Frankfurt School, despite its tendency to work in the abstract, also had a grounded dimension by identifying some novel features of modern society as it entered its consumption-oriented stage; as touched on, one example is an acknowledgement of the role of the mass media in shaping or crafting public opinion.

When it comes specifically to social work, it is Jan Fook (2002; 2012) who provides the most significant attempt to develop critical theory and social work practice (see below). She provides an analysis of social issues that helps social workers think creatively about their practice and respond to concerns about oppressive practice.

Feminist perspectives

Feminist perspectives on social work focus on explaining and responding to the oppressed position of women in society. This is particularly important because much social work is done with women, and practitioners must understand their roles and position. There is also the fact that, although most social workers are women, they do not tend to reach the higher echelons of management. Such issues mean that a feminist practice often focuses on collaborative and group work in order to achieve consciousness of the issues that affect women in their social relations within society. There is also an emphasis on dialogical, egalitarian relationships between users and practitioners. Such practice often seeks radical change in societies, along with equality and mutual help and support, although there is also a concern with personal and social growth and development. As a result, the influence of feminist perspectives on practice can embrace socialist-collectivist and reflexive-therapeutic views of social work, depending on the actual practice emphasis.

Feminist thinking has a long history with many differentiated perspectives concerning the political, social, cultural and other forms of domination of women and their social relations by patriarchy, which is a system of thought and social relations that privileges and empowers men (Beasley, 1999). It also creates relationships between genders that disfranchise, disempower and devalue women's experience. As we will see, the different perspectives are united by common concerns, but they are fundamentally divided in their analysis of the reasons for women's unequal position and in strategies for correcting it.

The 'first wave' of feminism dates back to the late 19th century and was related to gaining legal and property rights. 'Second wave' feminism became influential in the 1960s and 1970s, being concerned with inequality of opportunity in work, political influence and the public sphere more generally. All this is linked to attitudes towards women in the private sphere and in interpersonal relationships. Five feminisms now can be distinguished, each having a different focus, and it is worth briefly elaborating on them here (see Dominelli, 2002a). First, *liberal feminism* is concerned with equality with men, of both having the same opportunity in terms of work, caring and family responsibilities. Second, *radical feminism* focuses on patriarchy, the social system that is characterised by men's power and privilege, and instead emphasises valuing and celebrating the differences between men and women. Third, *socialist/Marxist feminism* sees oppression as part of social inequality in a class-based structure, with women being seen as helping in the reproduction of the workforce for the benefit of capitalism through their domestic tasks and childcare. Fourth, *black feminism* begins with racism and points to the diversity of women and the different kinds and combinations of oppression that affect them. Finally, *postmodern feminism* looks at the cultural and social discourses in society that limit conceptions of women and the possibilities for development.

It was in the 1980s that major feminist social work texts began to appear (for example, Hanmer and Statham [1988] 1999; Dominelli and McCleod, 1989). They raised the relevance of feminist thinking on many social work issues such as domestic violence and sexual abuse, as well as examining social categories where women are strongly represented because of gender difference such as mental health, care givers and older people. More recent work focuses on feminist social work from a socialist perspective (Dominelli, 2002a), feminism and critical practice (Fook, 2002; 2012), and feminism and postmodernism (Healy, 2000). When it comes to feminist practice, as indicated it aims to take place within dialogic, egalitarian relationships whereby women's experience and diversity are shared and valued. There is also a focus on the division and relationship between private experience and public problems, and how social workers' intervention on behalf of the public within the domestic arena can potentially be oppressive. One obvious example is in relation to domestic violence/abuse where there can be a tendency to blame the victim, that is, the woman, for failing to protect her children from the possibilities of physical and emotional harm.

Feminist perspectives have had three significant influences on social work. First, feminist, non-sexist, social work is vitally important to many women, also offering lessons to men in understanding and approaching women users. This, in turn, can lead to new and less judgemental stances towards women's sexuality and lives. Second, feminism has clearly given greater priority to women's issues and makes the important point that there would be social value in replacing patriarchy in social relations. It has also raised the policy context of welfare as it affects women, by its concern for the effects of gender on expectations for caring, and on services for women who suffer violence. Relatedly, there is the emphasis on ethics of care, taken up later in Chapters 6 and 9. Finally, the distinctive practice contributions referred to – attending to gender issues, group consciousness raising and dialogical, egalitarian relationships – have had a significant impact on critical social work practice.

Anti-discrimination/oppression and cultural and ethnic sensitivity

Anti-discrimination/oppression approaches arose largely as a result of developments in relation to 'race' and gender which have occurred since the 1970s, but they were also influenced by work in relation to gay and lesbian rights, disability, ageing and the like. Feminist perspectives/approaches have been dealt with, so here I look at 'race' and briefly, the other social groupings.

Anti-discrimination/oppression and cultural and ethnic sensitivity approaches originate from a concern about racism and ethnic conflict. For instance, recall the inner-city riots during the early 1980s in England and further riots in Burnley, Oldham and other northern towns in the early 2000s. Anti-discrimination/ oppression theories mainly take a socialist-collectivist view, while sensitivity approaches, although incorporating some structural aspects that are socialist, apply these in a more reflexive-therapeutic way (Payne, 2005). Thus, rather than seeking broader social change, sensitivity approaches seek to make the social order more responsive to the problems that 'race' and ethnicity issues raise. In brief, anti-discrimination/oppression perspectives focus on fighting institutionalised discrimination in a society that represents the interests of powerful groups, while sensitivity perspectives advocate positive responses to cultural and ethnic diversity in societies. It is also worth noting that multiculturalism, despite being questioned by the political right, remains the dominant paradigm; it affirms ethnic diversity and seeks to incorporate this into societies by valuing cultural contributions to the whole.

Racism itself consists of ideologies and social processes that discriminate on the basis of an assumed different racial membership, often based on colour, although increasingly focusing on cultural factors. Anti-racism, the precursor of anti-discrimination/oppression and sensitivity approaches, can be seen as having five perspectives (Ely and Denney, 1987) and it is worth noting these here. First, assimilation assumes migrants to a new country will take in the culture and lifestyle of that country, with social and personal difficulties seen as a failure to adapt, 'blaming the victim' if you will. Second, liberal pluralism focuses on equal opportunities for immigrants. Third, cultural pluralism accepts various ethnic and racial groups, wanting them to be encouraged and valued, with a policy of multiculturalism. A problem, however, is the encouragement of different cultures without coming to grips with the element of discrimination that is crucial to developing an anti-racist stance. Fourth, the structuralist perspective sees capitalist societies affecting groups within them differently, with ethnic as well as class division recognised as the basis for economic and social domination of particular groups by the ruling class. Finally, black perspectives emphasise the requirement to include the point of view of black communities themselves. From a critical perspective, structuralist and black perspectives are particularly important in that they involve social workers exploring their own racism, being careful to work with black people in ways that accept their values, moving social work away from controlling to supportive mechanisms, and working in alliance with black communities (Dominelli, 1997).

Anti-discrimination/oppression and sensitivity approaches stress the importance of responding to discrimination and oppression as part of all social work. Dalrymple and Burke (2006) provide a comprehensive account of anti-oppressive practice emphasising an empowering approach, working in partnership with users and minimal intervention. Thompson (2003) provides a theoretical rationale for practice across a range of social divisions, including class, 'race' and gender, but also ageing, disability, sexual orientation, religion, language, nation, region, and mental illness and impairment. He sees structural explanations of oppression as central to anti-discrimination/oppression, these providing a clear view of the social objectives of such theory, while sensitivity approaches focus on cultural and social relationships is a way of incorporating these issues into other approaches to practice. Both anti-discrimination/oppression and sensitivity approaches seek to influence all forms of social work rather than create specific models of practice, although they do see empowerment approaches in particular as a way forward.

Empowerment and advocacy

Empowerment and advocacy relate to critical, feminist and anti-discrimination orientations, and aim to enable people to overcome barriers in achieving life objectives and gaining access to services. It is important to emphasise initially that empowerment is often used by neoliberals to mean placing responsibility on individuals for providing for their own needs with the aim of limiting state services. One should therefore be wary in using the term as, like advocacy, it does not necessarily relate to critical social work.

Despite the qualification, empowerment seeks to help people gain power over decision making and action in their own lives, while advocacy seeks to represent the interests of the powerless to powerful individuals and social structures. Empowerment is geared to ensuring the social justice aspects of social work, with Rees (1991) providing a comprehensive account, seeing its objectives being that of social justice, giving people greater security and political and social equality through mutual support and shared learning. Adams (1996, p 8) adds that 'Marxist socialist perspectives generally seek empowerment as a means of promoting contradictions in society, with a view to eventually seeking change.'

Advocacy originates from legal skills and involves promoting social change for groups and their causes as well as advocating individually for individuals. Regarding the latter, an obvious example is acting and arguing for people's interests in the field of welfare rights (Bateman, 2000).

Importantly from a critical perspective, empowerment and advocacy, especially in the form of groupwork as in, for instance, Mullender and Ward's (1991) self-directed groupwork model, have the potential to promote solidarity and consciousness raising. Such approaches also provide practitioners with useful ideas for including issues of oppression, critical thinking and joint working with users into their practice. Beresford and Croft (1993), for example, show how users can become involved in seeking changes in services through group activity and campaigning. They draw attention to the possibility of seeing power positively, as being available in society for people to use.

Community development

Community development theories (see Payne, 2005) have a theoretical base that is more sociological and less psychological, as well as having links with empowerment and advocacy. Community work is an aspect of this and involves helping people come together to identify issues of concern and to take action to resolve them. It is not necessarily related to radical/critical practice, however, because it can be used by those with power to ensure that people accept the status quo or do what 'authority' deems desirable. However, it does have radical/critical possibilities, including aiming to consciousness raise and emphasise equality. Unfortunately, such practices were among the reasons why the community development projects of the early 1970s were wound up (Rogowski, 2010b); the government disapproved of practitioners and researchers, arguing that multi-deprivation should be redefined and reinterpreted in terms of structural constraints rather than being the result of individual, psychological failings.

Nevertheless, community work theory and practice remained influential in the 1970s until the 1980s, latterly under the guise of community social work (Barclay Report, 1982; see Chapter 3 in Rogowski, 2010b, for some practice examples), although sadly, it is no longer a significant part of social work in the UK. This is because both the New Right and New Labour were never happy with semi-autonomous professionals working with residents, helping them to organise in pursuit of their own goals, engaging in, for example, tenants/residents groups, squatter groups, claimants unions and the like. Bill Jordan (personal communication, 2012) initially saw aspects of the 'Big Society' (see Chapter 3) as a means of reinvigorating community social work, although having seen the extent of the Coalition government's austerity measures, he has revised his optimism.

Despite its removal from social workers' toolboxes, Henderson and Thomas (2002) provide a useful guide to neighbourhood work and hence community work. They argue that local communities need help to escape from isolation and marginalisation by becoming connected with resources in wider society. As far as it goes, this is well and good, although for the radical/critical practitioner, the focus becomes one of working with local groups and communities on projects aimed at social change rather than just accepting the current social order (see Ledwith, 2011). Teater and Baldwin (2012) also emphasise this latter point while lamenting the way 'community', as a focus for practice, has been disassociated from mainstream social work.

Critical social work

As stated, perhaps the most comprehensive exposition of critical social work is that of Fook (2002, 2004; 2012), who includes features of critical theory, post-structuralism and postmodernism into her analysis (Payne, 2005).

From critical theory a number of points are incorporated. First, *domination* is created structurally but experienced personally. The powerful may directly exploit people but deceive themselves and others that inequality is unavoidable, which can result in self-defeating behaviour. Second, *false consciousness*, whereby people believe inequalities are natural, again can be self-defeating. Third, *positivism* is seen as an ideology about how knowledge is created, leading to passivity because social facts cannot be changed. Instead, critical theory emphasises agency, the capacity to achieve social change. Fourth, knowledge does not reflect external reality but is actively *constructed* by researchers. The emphasis on the causal knowledge of the natural sciences is different from the knowledge of the social world that is created by self-reflection and interaction with others.

The points about positivism and reflection lead to the critical emphasis on awareness and agency. They also explain critical social work's scepticism of evidence-based and other positivist views of social work knowledge.

Fook's analysis starts by acknowledging the impact of globalisation, including the 'compression' of the world as a result of economic and technological changes. There are two points that follow from this. First, welfare states and the idea of *progress* in terms of the public good can be seen as modernist structures that will break down in postmodern globalised societies. Second, *professionalism* is questioned, along with the belief in reason and science being able to advance humankind. This means social work knowledge and skills are devalued, disaggregated into specific skill sets, and boundaries between social work and other professions are broken down. The focus is on services becoming targeted at specific behaviour and lifestyles rather than there being an emphasis on a more holistic, professional social work practice. Management skills are more valued than professional practice, with social workers becoming separated from policy, and even practice, development and change. Much of this corresponds with the neoliberal view of, and influence in, the world or, put another way, it is the cultural logic of late capitalism (Jameson, 1992).

Fook goes on to rethink ideas about social work practice in four ways. First, when it comes to knowledge, critical practice questions where it has come from and how it is used, particularly by professionals. She advocates a critical reflexive approach, challenging domination in social structures, social relations and personal constructions. Second, there is the question of who has power and how they use it. Critical social work analyses and reflects on the power in people's situations, trying to reconceptualise it and negotiate experiences of new power relations that are less disempowering. Third, following Foucault's work, discourse, language and narrative are important. Language is not seen as neutral but influences how we think and what we know; the narrative we tell about something chooses between possible alternatives so our discussions convince others that what we say is true. We can rethink all of this and in so doing different interpretations may become true. Fourth, identity and difference are emphasised – instead of thinking in terms of dichotomies (what we are and what we are not), we should see ourselves with more complexity and diversity.

Critically reflexive practice has links with the idea of social construction, and focuses on deconstruction, resistance, challenge and reconstruction (Fook and Gardner, 2007). Resistance and challenge resonate with radical theory, while other key components of critical social work are feminist and empowerment approaches. Of particular importance is the rejection of the authoritative 'therapist' practitioner in favour of a more complex relationship between social worker and user that reflects the ambiguities of their relationship. In sum, critical social work is concerned with a practice that furthers a society without domination, exploitation and oppression. It focuses:

> … on how structures dominate, but also on how people construct and are constructed by changing social structures and relations, recognising that there may be multiple and diverse constructions of ostensibly similar situations. Such an understanding of social relations and structures can be used to disrupt understandings and structures, and as a basis for changing these so that they are more inclusive of different interest groups. (Fook, 2002, p 18)

Conclusion

The Thatcherite governments of the 1980s inflicted vastly expensive and socially divisive defeats on many workers, their families and communities in the steel, printing, dock working and, most significantly, mining industries. Social work similarly came under attack from government ministers and the media because of its links with welfare dependency, 'political correctness', being soft on crime and failures in relation to child abuse (Penketh, 2000). Such developments contributed to the gradual demise of radical social work's influence, even though it had helped leave a legacy that included anti-oppressive and advocacy perspectives.

The introduction of managerialisim and marketisation by both Conservative and New Labour governments ushered in a form of neoliberal social work that hindered the potential of social work to be a positive force, both at an individual and societal level, and increased the alienation of practitioners. Social workers were increasingly faced with carrying out repetitive tasks aimed at rationing and increasingly risk assessment, which clashed with their and social work's value base (Jones, 2004). Indeed, like social work with adults, practice with children and families can now often be 'characterised [as] high-volume, low-intensity practice' (Lymbery and Postle, 2010, p 2510). But there is another important factor to consider.

It is worth repeating that following the financial crash and global economic recession, the people who had nothing to do with causing the economic crisis – the deprived and vulnerable, along with those employed in the public sector – are precisely the ones expected to pay the price for the unbridled greed and casino gambling of the few. The head of the Church of England, Archbishop Rowan Williams, alluded to this in his Christmas Day message of 2010, saying that the rich had to play their part in dealing with the country's economic woes.[3] In June 2011 he was further concerned about the 'radical' nature of the Coalition government's cuts and privatisation policies in relation to health, education and welfare, no doubt a factor in the riots in London and other northern cities in England during August 2011. However, the Archbishop's remarks, as well as the protests inherent in the riots, have been ignored as swinging public expenditure cuts continue and affect social work and its users. What has happened to the oft-repeated Coalition's mantra of 'We are all in it together'? Such a situation re-emphasises why critical social work is needed and has theoretical and conceptual ideas that have the promise of moving things forward.

Critical social work is far more than complying with managerial and organisational demands that arise from political, economic and ideological changes over the last 30 years. At a theoretical and conceptual level, radical and critical perspectives highlight important aspects of social and economic life, including the importance of power, ideological/cultural hegemony, class and status, professionalisation, gender, 'race' and oppression more generally. There is therefore a need to promote issues such as consciousness-raising in relation to social inequalities, political action and social change. Critical practice helps confront a socially unjust and unequal order by making important theoretical and conceptual ideas available to social work more widely, as well as leading to the development of a specific emancipatory and transformational practice aimed at social justice (Payne, 2005).

Key points

Although marginalised over recent decades, the ideas of Marx and his successors in the form of those such as the Frankfurt School, Gramsci and Habermas, increasingly maintain their relevance. We need a more socially just and equal world, something that critical social work aims towards.

Radical and critical social work have made significant contributions to social work theory and practice, particularly in relation to anti- sexist/racist/discriminatory/oppressive practice.

Critical social work has theoretical and conceptual tools to resist neoliberal managerial and marketisation changes, as well working towards a better world.

Further reading

Fook J.(2002) *Social work: Critical theory and practice*, London: Sage Publications. This remains a comprehensive elaboration of critical social work, recently updated by 'Social Work: a critical approach to practice' 2012 London: Sage.

Garrett, P.M. (2013) *Social work and social theory*, Bristol: The Policy Press. This accessible book links social theory and critical thinking with social work practice, and focuses on key theorists including Bourdieu, Gramsci and Habermas.

Lavalette, M. (ed) (2011) *Radical social work today: Social work at the crossroads*, Bristol: The Policy Press. Written to celebrate the 35th anniversary of Bailey and Brake's seminal text *Radical social work,* this book examines the radical tradition by combining the first and second wave of radical social work.

Payne, M. (2005) *Modern social work theory* (3rd edn), Basingstoke: Palgrave Macmillan. This provides an impressive overview of social work theory, including those strands that make up critical social work.

Notes

[1] In relation to New Labour and child poverty, for example, Grover (2009) provides a damning critique of the failure to tackle growing social inequalities, of which the most unacceptable is poverty. The obvious comment is that if you seriously want people to be socially included, there needs to be far more equality (see, for example, Dorling, 2010; Wilson and Pickett, 2010).

[2] However, it is important not to be too schematic. Radical/critical perspectives see the causes of social ills as largely structural but individuals experience the 'pain' in various ways. There might well be a need for collective solutions, but in the meantime, people's pain has to be responded to. This might mean, for example, addressing therapeutic needs or work around particular 'tasks' to help and support a service user 'function' in society.

[3] Similar comments were repeated at the beginning of 2013 when both Rowan Williams and Pope Benedict XVI voiced concerns about growing inequality as well as the excesses of capitalism more generally.

3

Critical social work in the neoliberal world: Challenging times

> Stay in your agency or organization, but don't let it seduce you. Take every opportunity to unmask its pretensions and euphemisms.... In practice and in theory, stay 'unfinished'. Don't be ashamed of working for short-term humanitarian or libertarian goals but always keep in mind the long-term political prospects. (Cohen, 1975, p 95)

The words of Stan Cohen are as relevant today as they were in the mid-1970s, although the problems and difficulties faced by critical practitioners in the early decades of the 21st century are far more formidable. The 1950s, 1960s and early 1970s were 'the golden age of the welfare state' (Gough, 1979, p x), leading to the heyday of social work as a profession (Rogowski, 2010b). Keynesian economics provided the theoretical underpinning to high levels of government spending, leading to the welfare state being established and accepted by the major political parties of the time, Labour and Conservative. Those on the political left thought the situation could be a stepping stone towards socialism, while those on the right thought socialism could be avoided through the development of welfare state capitalism. Such a convergence of views was the foundation of the social democratic consensus of these initial postwar decades.

Until the early 1970s the political consensus had considerable economic success, together with progress in the social and political sphere (see Lambie, 2011). Its demise was linked to the financial and economic difficulties faced by the developed Western economies in the early 1970s. The sharp increase in oil prices and the resulting economic crisis of 1973 were key issues (Ferguson, 2008). The Conservative New Right, led by Sir Keith Joseph, argued that Britain's lacklustre economic performance was a result of the excessive powers of workers and trade unions. They were concerned about the size of the state, the growth of public expenditure and, echoing earlier comments, about so-called self-serving professionals in the public sector, especially those, like social workers, who were deemed to be on the side of the welfare dependent.

Margaret Thatcher's general election victory in 1979 enabled the New Right's ideas to be put into practice by introducing monetarism and, in due course, the hegemony of neoliberalism. Eighteen years of Conservative governments ended with the general election victory of Tony Blair in 1997. However, far from heralding a new dawn for the social democratic left, it led to an increase and intensification of the overall direction of ideological travel. New Labour had turned away from the transformative possibilities of the welfare state creating a more just and equal society. This was because free market ideas and practices had achieved a globalised status and the leaders of the Labour Party, including Tony Blair and Gordon Brown, argued that they had no choice but to adapt to the changed situation. The welfare state also had to change, including social work, along with all public services being reformed and 'modernised' by becoming more like the private sector. In May 2010 David Cameron's Conservative-led Coalition government came to power, again pursuing neoliberal policies. The emphasis is on the 'Big Society', one where the role of the state is reduced. The 'big idea', harking back to the 19th century, is self-responsibility and self-reliance rather than being able to count on collective help and support through the state. This involves the continued control and restriction of the role of social work, despite the rhetoric about 'bureaucracy-busting' so as to enable social workers to spend more time with children and families (Munro, 2011).

This chapter begins by looking at the rise of the New Right and neoliberalism and how they affected the welfare state and social work, followed by the ascent of New Labour together with its impact on the welfare state and the profession. The Coalition government, including the 'Big Society' and its influence on such developments, is then considered. The resulting neoliberal consensus means that there are ever more challenges for critical social work, but nonetheless possibilities remain.

The New Right, neoliberalism, the welfare state and social work

The New Right achieved power in the UK by providing an ideological critique that undermined the political and economic consensus of the postwar years. Similar ideas gained ascendency in the US, and by the 1980s the ideological move to the political right became known as neoliberalism, with its now global influence continuing to this day (Harvey, 2007). Essentially, both the New Right and ensuing neoliberalism involve a market-driven approach to economic and social policy that stresses the importance of private enterprise, and seeks to maximise the role of the private sector in determining the political and economic priorities of the world.

The New Right was influenced by Hayek's (1982) 'spontaneous order', namely, the market system, which ensures the welfare of members of society by supplying goods and services through competition and discovery (George and Wilding, 1993). They were against the Utopian belief that social problems could either be avoided or remedied, rather than being inherent in economic and social life. Opponents were seen as ignorant of economics because of their preoccupation with the social. Similar concerns related to opponents' understanding of concepts such as liberty, justice, need and social rights. For instance, the New Right saw liberty as simply the absence of coercion, rather than the presence of real opportunities involving the provision of resources and services. Then again, social justice had no real meaning because where outcomes were not intended, as in market relations, you could not talk of justice or injustice. Other key ideas include the view that people were fundamentally self-interested, with the forces that dominate them and society in general being economic rather than social. There was also a questioning of the sociological approach to social problems which tended to stress social and structural causes rather than personal factors or individual failings. This is reflected in the New Right and neoliberals' attitude to welfare and the welfare state that George and Wilding (1993, pp 20-35) usefully outline.

The New Right argued it was impossible to create a comprehensive welfare state because such a project ignored the nature of the 'spontaneous order', while simultaneously assuming the possibility of rational planning and of a common purpose in society. The 'spontaneous order' saw social institutions and social order arising from human action rather human design, with such planning and purpose being impossible because all the relevant facts could never be known. Welfare state supporters were seen as having mistaken views of human nature and social order because people were essentially individualistic, only responding to the prospect and possibility of individual reward and punishment; they were not primarily social beings who could be motivated by social concerns and social goals. Consequently, risk, uncertainty and the danger of failure were seen as necessary to human and social functioning.

Another argument was that the welfare state was based on mistaken ideas about welfare, especially the emphasis on equality and redistribution rather than on growth and wealth creation. 'Choice' was said to lead to individual satisfaction and the promotion of individual responsibility, rather than the state, through bureaucrats and professionals, not least social workers, 'knowing best'. This led to hostility to the state provision of services, instead preferring private and voluntary providers, including the need to see cash supplied to users, rather than services, so as to create a quasi-market. The overall emphasis was on responsibilities and obligations rather than rights, with the idea of welfare and the welfare state seen not as a positive force for change in society, but having negative effects such as trapping people in poverty or stigmatising them.

The welfare state was also seen as a threat to freedom because more government resulted in individual freedom and responsibility being eroded. In relation to social justice, for example, egalitarianism was seen as a particular threat to freedom because any redistribution was inevitably coercive. Welfare states were also seen as inefficient and ineffective because, without the spur of competition, there was no incentive to innovate or to become more efficient. Particular criticism was reserved for powerful bureaucracies and influential professional groups because services were said to be geared to their needs, and there were no corrective mechanisms to ensure services changed in response to changing needs or deficiencies; 'producer power' was seen to rule (Deakin, 1987).

Further New Right concerns related to the welfare state being economically and socially damaging because it interfered with the operation of the free market by reducing both the rewards for success and the punishments of failure. Such welfare collectivism was said to destroy independence, self-reliance, individual initiative and responsibility.

In terms of an ideal society (again, see George and Wilding, 1993), broadly the New Right wanted markets having a larger role, while the state had a reduced and different role. Markets were favoured because they provided a wider range of choice, and they did not depend for their success on the beneficent motives of service providers; instead they compelled providers to be sensitive to the needs of users in order to survive in business (Hayek, 1982). They also reduced producer power, and the fact of competition reduced the prices of goods and services. Market provision was also seen as more democratic because everyone counted in the market where the consumer ruled.

Despite faith in the market, this did not rule out all state action in welfare, with Friedman (1962) seeing, for example, the state setting out a limited legal framework for the efficient functioning of the market, as well paternalist provision for those not able to assume full responsibility for themselves such as those with severe mentally ill health or those with severe learning difficulties. Other guiding principles for the role of the state included it providing residual, safety-net services, but abandoning impossible goals of equality and social justice. In such situations, the state was envisaged as an enabler rather than a provider, and where public provision was seen as appropriate, then internal markets should be established. The state's overall role should be competitive and not monopolistic, including working in partnership with the private and voluntary sector, and with state provision itself being conditional, not simply a right.

The impact of the New Right on the welfare state

Despite the general election success of 1979, Margaret Thatcher did not initially embark on an all-out attack on the welfare state largely because 'One Nation' Conservatives still had some influence in Cabinet (Page, 2009a). However, the New Right's influence became increasingly apparent.

During her first term (1979-83) there were reductions in unemployment and sickness benefits, along with substantial spending cuts to housing and education. There were also curbs on the power of trade unions and the sale of council houses took place. Resistance, as well as rising unemployment, led to riots in places such as Brixton, Toxteth and Moss Side, but the successful Falklands War and a divided Labour Party led to further electoral success. Economic reform was a main focus of Thatcher's second government (1983-87), with privatisations of nationalised industries taking place. Efficiency savings were demanded from the NHS and performance indicators introduced, together with private sector-style management. Sales of council housing continued and rents were increased. In her third government (1987-90), even more radical proposals were introduced, including the introduction of an internal market within the NHS and the reform of community care by the NHS and Community Care Act 1990 (see below in relation to care management). Social security was reviewed to ensure spending was targeted at those in greatest need. The control of local authorities over schools was reduced together with the introduction of national tests that had to be made available to parents, both measures aimed at weakening producer power. There were further housing changes, with private landlords and housing associations allowed to take over the running of council housing if supported by existing tenants.

Following the successful resistance to the Poll Tax, Thatcher was replaced, but the John Major years (1990-97) saw the continued influence of New Right ideas. Citizen's Charters resulted in public services implementing performance targets scrutinised by independent monitors, dealing with complaints more robustly and providing redress as appropriate. Social security was again reviewed, with eligibility criteria for a number of benefits tightened. A more rigorous, external inspection regime for schools was introduced because it was felt a significant number were failing children and their families. A 'back to basics' campaign based on a populist approach to issues such as crime, health, education and social work was launched in order to challenge 'out of touch' welfare professionals.

In brief, the welfare state was transformed on New Right and neoliberal lines. The emphasis was on 'the injection of a private sector ethos into the delivery of public services, improved targeting, cost containment measures and greater "consumer choice"' to ensure that the welfare state was operating along New Right lines (Page, 2009a, p 128).

The New Right and social work

In many ways social work remained relatively untouched during the early years of the Thatcher/Major revolution (Rogowski, 2010b). Admittedly, there was an ongoing move away from the generic social work role. In relation to social work with children and families, examples include practice with disabled children and families, and fostering and adoption practice being hived off to form separate teams, while social workers working with young offenders had their own (youth justice) teams, although children and families social workers often played a key role. Overall, however, social workers working with children and families saw little difference as far as their day-to-day practice was concerned, and importantly, advances in relation to theory occurred (see Chapter 2). Significant progress was also made in relation to community social work and work with young offenders.

The Barclay Report (1982) was published when the new Thatcher government seemed committed to cutbacks in public expenditure as well as challenging much of what social workers did. However, for many the report amounted to a defence of social work, or more appropriately, 'community social work' (Jordan and Parton, 1983). At its heart lay decentralising and debureaucratising services so that social workers could build and maintain closer links with other agencies and the local community. Although the influence of community social work on practice during the 1980s was variable, there were a few areas where it had an impact and enabled progressive, even critical/radical, group and community work methods to be pursued (again see Chapter 3 in Rogowski, 2010b).

Social work's success in the1980's in relation to youth offending, by diversion from the youth justice system and developing alternatives to incarceration, has been well documented and was a factor in the decline of recorded crime by young people by the end of the decade (Thorpe et al, 1980; Pitts, 1988; Blagg and Smith, 1989; Farrington and Langan, 1992). It is arguably the most significant ever evidence-based social work achievement.

However, it was into Thatcher's third term and into the Major years that social work was to be affected in negative ways. The introduction of care management under the NHS and Community Care Act 1990 resulted in direct, relationship-based work with adult users being replaced by one where social workers were embroiled in bureaucracy aimed at rationing resources. Similarly, negative comments can be made in relation to the changes to education and training by the introduction of the Diploma in Social Work (DSW) in 1989, and the changes in relation to probation training in the 1990s whereby a social work qualification was no longer required. The DSW essentially allowed employers to shape social work education in their own interests, while probation training moved from 'soft' social work approaches towards offending, to more controlling and punishment-oriented methods.

When it comes to social work with children and families, the Children Act 1989 was significant, with resulting guidance and regulation including an emphasis on comprehensive assessments. However, despite its preventative and partnership ethos, it confirmed a move from child welfare to child protection (see Chapter 4). The 1989 Act addressed a key issue for the neoliberal state: formulating a legal basis for authority to intervene in family life in order to protect children, but also preventing all families from becoming clients of the state, while simultaneously presenting the legislation as applicable to all.

Despite the earlier social work successes with young offenders, from 1991 onwards 'populist punitiveness' (Bottoms, 1995) emerged as politicians of all parties became increasingly punitive in their pronouncements. Simply put, the Criminal Justice Act 1991 introduced court orders, *not* to help young people who had social problems and had offended, instead offering punishment and control in the community (Stewart et al, 1994).

Following the changes to social work under the Conservative governments of the late 1980s and 1990s, the welfare state and social work were to face even more challenges as New Labour swept to power in 1997.

New Labour, more neoliberalism, the welfare state and social work

Market socialism (Le Grand and Estrin, 1989), a version of democratic socialism (George and Wilding, 1993), dominated as New Labour adapted to, rather than challenged, the neoliberalism of the New Right. It formed much of New Labour's initial ideology, before the party moved ever more to the political right under Blair's leadership. Its central claim was that the economic system should be plural in nature, involving both the state and private enterprise, as well as, for example, cooperatives, but, importantly, nationalised industries were seen as inefficient and unsustainable.

Market socialism emerged as Labour, under Neil Kinnock (1983-92) and John Smith (1992-94), repositioned itself in an attempt to show it was 'fit' to return to office after the defeats by Thatcher (Page, 2009b). This included substantial policy revisions such as a retreat from public ownership, a rapprochement with industry, a firm commitment to fiscal and monetary orthodoxy, the abandoning of nuclear unilateralism, the retention of the curbs on trade unions and wanting an overhauled welfare state. These changes were taken further following Blair's election as leader.

Blair and the other 'modernisers' sought to rebrand the party as a non-sectarian party that would appeal to 'middle' England. This involved embracing the virtues of the market, the deregulation of financial markets and a reliance on employment growth in the service sector. Other issues included abandoning the previous attachment to public ownership, planning and deficit financing, together with state intervention and public spending more generally. It was a pro-market approach, one that had a relaxed view about inequalities of income and wealth. And this economic reappraisal had important ramifications as far as the strategy for the welfare state was concerned.

Instead of seeing the aim of social policy as challenging market imperatives, New Labour saw welfare policy as needing to support the market system and to contribute to the economic goal of competitiveness in the more open, globalised economy. There was a major concern about people of working age being dependent on benefits, resulting in encouraging paid work, if necessary by compulsion. This 'modernisation' of the welfare state was required because of defects in the original system relating to 'dependency, moral hazard, bureaucracy, interest-group formation and fraud' (Giddens, 2000, p 33).

Such changes in the economic and social policy spheres amounted to the 'Third Way', with Giddens (1994, 1998) proving to be Blair's guru. He argued that the demise of communism, globalisation, changing family and work patterns and more diverse personal and cultural identities made the left–right distinction in politics increasingly irrelevant. Instead the 'Third Way' had four core values (Blair, 1998). First, there was *equal worth* which equated to social justice in that it focussed on talent and effort being encouraged in all quarters of society regardless of an individual's background. Second, *opportunity for all* was a value seen as neglected by the right because they focused on freeing individuals from a coercive state, while the left downplayed the state's duty to promote the responsibility of individuals to advance themselves. Third, there was *responsibility*, this connected to rights in that without responsibility, selfishness and greed could result. Finally, there was *community* whereby voluntary activity was to be encouraged.

However, the New Labour repositioning amounted to veering to the political right. Despite at times trying to present itself as a 'progressive' left of centre government, at best the 'Third Way' was a softer variant of the New Right. At worst, it developed and took further New Right thinking and policy (again, see Powell, 1999, 2002, 2008). For example, there was a convergence with the New Right on the need for growth and wealth creation rather than an emphasis on equality and redistribution. Or again, the 'old' welfare state was regarded by New Labour as undermining responsibility and creating dependency.

The impact of New Labour on the welfare state

New Labour's welfare state strategy continued with many New Right ideas, and had six interconnected themes (Page, 2009b). First, a modern welfare state had to be *active* rather than *passive*. 'Welfare to work' programmes were established for those on benefits deemed capable of work; 'New Deals' were provided for young people under 25 years of age and subsequently for lone parents, disabled people and for those over 50 years of age. Involvement was voluntary in the first instance, although more coercive measures lay in wait, such as being required to attend regular work-focused interviews. Complementary measures were also introduced, including the statutory minimum wage, tax credits and a childcare strategy to increase substitute care for children. Later still, reforms to such as incapacity benefit confirmed the welfare to work ethos.

A second theme related to the *delivery* of publicly funded services. New Labour rejected the preference for publicly provided welfare services, instead encouraging the private and voluntary sectors, noticeably in health, education, housing and employment. The private finance initiative (PFI) of the previous Conservative government was expanded with more private sector contractors financing and building new hospitals and schools then leasing them back to the public sector. Private sector providers were given a share of NHS funding for routine procedures, and the number of 'independent', state-funded faith schools was allowed to increase, along with the encouragement of academies. In relation to housing, a mix of social landlords was encouraged rather than local authorities being the main provider. Private sector companies were allowed to administer benefits and to be paid extra bonuses according to their success in placing claimants in employment.

The third theme was emphasising the needs and preferences of service users. Rather than uniform, undifferentiated services, individually tailored services were favoured. Following the School Standards and Education Act 1998, failing schools could be closed and reopened under a new headteacher and governors, with parents being given a preference as to which school their child would go to. There was an emphasis on reducing waiting times for NHS outpatient and inpatient appointments, and in 2008, patients requiring non-urgent hospital treatments could choose any approved healthcare provider.

Fourth, New Labour was keen to extend opportunity by tackling socially constructed barriers to advancement in areas such as education, health and employment. Examples were Sure Start and the Children's Fund (preventative programmes for younger and older children and their families respectively; see Chapter 5), a national parenting helpline, and aiming to abolish child poverty and to increase the numbers of young people in higher education.

A fifth theme was the increased role individuals should play in advancing their own health and well-being. The emphasis was on personal responsibility, with individuals' rights to state support having to be matched by a responsibility to use such assistance effectively. Individuals were also expected to engage in neighbourly and civic activity because the state was no longer able to provide citizens with a guaranteed level of security and well-being.

The final theme was the stress on quality and performance being improved by rigorous targets set for service providers, and effective audit and inspection regimes being established. Ofsted, in relation to education and children's social care, is an example, as was the Audit Commission that monitored the overall performance of public bodies such as local authorities.

Under New Labour a modern welfare state was seen as having to work with, rather than against, the grain of market imperatives. Essentially New Labour allied itself with neoliberalism, evidenced by their failure to tackle embedded class inequalities or attempt to create an egalitarian society. Instead it focused on removing barriers to opportunity while accepting, even embracing, significant inequalities of outcome.

New Labour and social work

Perhaps surprisingly, social work fared even worse than it had under the New Right (Jordan, 2001; Rogowski, 2010b, 2011b). Admittedly there was the introduction of the Social Work BA degree, but the preoccupation continued with ensuring there was a reliable and compliant workforce to work at the will of employers through managers (Dominelli 2009b; Ferguson and Woodward, 2009).

Then there was the fact that social work was often subsumed under social care: the Care Standards Act 2000 resulted in the Central Council for the Education and Training in Social Work being replaced by the General Social Care Council to regulate social work training and the social work and care workforce. In addition, the Social Care Institute for Excellence (SCIE) was established to identify and disseminate evidence-based practice, with the subsequent demise of the National Institute of Social Work. Perhaps this reveals the disdain with which New Labour held social work as well as the continued desire to cleanse and remove any oppositional possibilities to the neoliberal project.

New agencies were created, all having a negative impact on social work. One example, together with the New Labour emphasis on interprofessional working, was the creation of Youth Offending Teams where the influence of social work declined. Then there was social work's absence from any real role in relation to Sure Start and the Children's Fund. As in other areas of public services, the overall result was work that was once the preserve of highly-trained professionals was increasingly carried out by less qualified support, outreach and other staff. Rather than this being done to ease the pressure on overworked social workers, the public were having to put up with cut-price services (Rogowski, 2010b).

Another point to note was the separation of post-16-year-old looked-after young people from children and families teams. Aftercare teams were established in the hope that this would remedy the fact that such young people came 'second best' because younger children were often prioritised. However, this change neglected the relationships that had been built up, often over many years, between social workers and such young people. Rather than further fragment the social work task, perhaps more attention should have been given to ensuring social workers had the time and resources to deal with both younger and older children and young people.

Significant changes followed the Victoria Climbié Inquiry (Lord Laming, 2003) into the death of a young girl who had died of injuries inflicted by her carers. *Every Child Matters* (DES, 2004) led to the Children Act 2004 aimed at transforming children's services and ensuring that every child had the support they needed, although offenders and asylum-seeking children (see Chapters 6 and 7 respectively) were largely conspicuous by their absence in such deliberations. The Act sought to enhance the integration of health, education, social services/care and others, and led to the demise of social services departments in 2006, with local government no longer providing a safe, supportive environment for social work. As we saw in Chapter 1, the establishment of pilot social work practices for looked-after children were seen as a way forward (see Le Grand, 2007).

However, New Labour's attempts at 'modernisation' and 'transformation' in relation to practice with children and families amounted to the increased proceduralisation, bureaucratisation and control of the social work task (see Garrett, 2003; Lymbery and Butler, 2004). In particular, there was the introduction of the assessment framework and the 'electronic turn' (Garrett, 2003, 2005), both evidence of social work's move from a concern with the 'social' to the 'informational' (Parton, 2008).

The standardised assessment framework (DH, 2000a) aimed to move social work from focusing solely on child protection, introducing instead an initial assessment for all children in need in the hope of developing an increased emphasis on family support. For more complex and/or child protection cases, in-depth core assessments were required. The assessment changes were an attempt to define out the indeterminacy, uncertainty and ambiguity in practice by introducing a 'techno-rationalist' method (Cleaver and Walker, 2004). However, it led to an over-focus on information gathering at the expense of genuinely meeting the needs of children and families. Such assessment processes, underpinned by the functional objective to manage risk and police the socially marginalised were used to screen out some needs, redefining them as someone else's problem, or saying they were insufficiently serious to warrant intervention (Smith, 2008).

Furthermore, New Labour seemed to give up thinking that social workers should work preventatively with children and families. This is because the

Common Assessment Framework was introduced, this being taken up further in Chapter 5.

The 'electronic turn' uses information and communication technologies (ICTs) that fulfil a crucial role in terms of technologising and marketising the public sector (Harris, 2003). The need for efficiency, effective targeting and ensuring the requirements of 'customers' dominate rather than those of service providers are the arguments put forward for the changes. However, the Integrated Children's System shows how disastrous the unthinking introduction of ICTs can be, with social workers having to spend most of their time simply inputting data required by the computer (Hall et al, 2008; White et al, 2010). A key question is how can social workers be expected to protect children when they are prevented from spending significant time with them or their families because of having to devote most of their time to the computer? More recent proposals to devise more practitioner and children and family-friendly systems following the 'Baby Peter' tragedy (see below) leave more questions than answers.[1]

As for young offending, New Labour's flagship Crime and Disorder Act 1998 continued with the punitiveness of the earlier 1990s (see Chapter 6), eventually widening to include anti-social behaviour – essentially, the criminalising of nuisance (Squires, 2008). Youth Offending Teams focused on correctional early intervention, deterrence and punishment, abandoning the well-established policies and practices of the 1980s. What remained of social work in the multidisciplinary teams was increasingly tied to a system primarily concerned with the management of risk by controlling the behaviour of young people who represented a threat to the wider community (Smith, 2008).

Children and young people with mental health issues, those who are asylum-seeking or refugees, and disabled children have all faired less than well under New Labour. For instance, there has been a failure to improve the capacity of Child and Adolescent Mental Health Services (CAMHS) (see Chapter 5), social work practice with asylum-seeking and refugee children became largely narrow and negative in relation to immigration control (see Chapter 7), and personalisation has been extended, including direct payments in relation to disabled children (see Chapter 8).

If there was anything positive for social work under New Labour, ironically it relates to the tragedy of 'Baby Peter' who died in 2007 in the London Borough of Haringey at the hands of his carers. This resulted in the establishment of the Social Work Task Force (2009) to look at the profession, and opened up spaces for a more progressive debate about social work for children and families (Garrett, 2009a). For example, there was an increased public awareness about the ICTs social workers were forced to use, including the inordinate amount of time spent on computers and bureaucracy in general. There was also a more sensible debate about what could and could not be achieved by social workers, namely, that although generally the child protection system works well (Smith, 2004; Pritchard and Williams, 2010), risk and child deaths cannot be *totally* eliminated. The subsequent Social Work Task Force report (2009) echoed much of this, thereby calling into question New Labour's 'modernisation' agenda. A Social Work Reform Board was established to improve social work, including the establishment of a College of Social Work to provide a voice for and to raise the status of the profession. Subsequently the Coalition government established the Munro Review (Munro, 2011) to look at reducing social work bureaucracy (see below and Chapter 4).

The Conservative-led coalition, the 'Big Society', the welfare state and social work

David Cameron's general election campaign of 2010 and subsequent Conservative-led Coalition government emphasised the 'Big Society' and the devolution of power and control to local and voluntary organisations (Jordan, 2010), which is in tune with the belief in the free market and limited state intervention. There is firm resistance to anything to do with ensuring the collective good by means of the state. Furthermore, the ongoing global financial and economic crisis provided an opportunity to impose swinging cuts to public services. As Farnsworth (2011, p 260) notes, 'the Conservative-led Coalition [was] determined not to let a good crisis go to waste.' The June 2010 Emergency Budget led to 'the longest, deepest sustained period of cuts to public services spending at least since World War Two' (IFS, 2010), and the pain of the cuts fell disproportionately on the poorest. Bearing in mind that the previous increase in public expenditure had been amassed to defend, boost and bail out the private sector generally, and the financial sector specifically, this amounted to a major redistribution of resources from the poorest to the wealthiest in society. It is no wonder that these developments have been referred to as the 'alchemy of austerity' (Clarke and Newman, 2012). In short, the financial and economic crisis was used to cut welfare provision and to reshape politics so as to cement the whole neoliberal project.

In this section I do not dwell on the Coalition government's political ideology or philosophy; suffice to say that, broadly speaking, it is in the same vein as, and a continuation of, the New Right and New Labour's embracement of neoliberalism. It was and is the continuation of the 'Conservative Revolution', one that favours the rich and powerful while at the same time causing insecurity and precariousness for the majority of people in society (Garrett, 2010a). There may now be little difference between the major political parties in the UK, but perhaps the most significant one has been Cameron's emphasis on the 'Big Society'.

The 'Big Society': the big con?

Actually the 'Big Society' idea can be linked to the red Tory philosophy that originated in Canada and is against the welfare state monopoly but, perhaps surprisingly, also market monopolies (Blond, 2010). This view emphasises 'traditional' values such as freedom and liberty, as well as localism, small businesses and volunteerism in the hope of empowering social enterprises, charities and other elements of civil society with a view to solving social problems including poverty.

At the heart is the notion of relocalising the banking system and developing local capital, giving people new assets through breaking up big business monopolies. But does anyone really believe that the Coalition government will cut its links to big business and the financial system as a whole?

Surely the whole idea of the 'Big Society' is little more than a cloak for severe cuts in public spending, especially as it is often counter-posed to the 'Big State'. The nostalgia is for a paternalist past of, for example, the 1920s and 1930s, built around village shops, banks, churches and charities. It involves the view of better-off people, mainly married women, giving their time to help those less fortunate than themselves. But such volunteers are no longer available as most women now work and people in general have to work longer hours and longer into their old age. There is also the fact that individual lives are increasingly private and inward-looking, thus being less disposed to devote time, and income, to help others. New Right and neoliberal values of self-interest, 'looking after number one', are to the fore rather than those of a more collective nature. Consequently, volunteers and charities are not available to fill the space left by the dismantling of public services. Such notions, as well as that of a 'Broken Britain', results in policies that represent a form of moral regulation that justifies an assault on the welfare state (Jordan, 2010). And the savage cuts to public services, as well as the increased emphasis on private sector involvement and marketisation, will result in a bonanza for large commercial firms as well as being a blow to the well-being of vulnerable citizens; witness the current privatisation issues involved in the reforms to the NHS.

The problem is that if the state is pruned as drastically as the Coalition envisages, the effect will be a more troubled and diminished society, not a better one. The 'Big Society' is more about the 'sink or swim society', and woe betide the poor, the frail, the old, the sick and the dependent in such a scenario. By reducing the size of the state and expecting the void to be filled by charity, the government is simply washing its hands of providing decent public services, and using volunteers as a cut-price alternative. It is hard to disagree with the fact that public services must be based on the certainty that they are there when you need them, not when a volunteer can be found to help you. Adapting Marx's slogan 'From each according to his ability, to each according to his need' for the 'Big Society', it might well read 'From each according to their vulnerability, to each according to his greed' (Bell, 2011).

In short, despite the fact that neoliberalism is in crisis, the belief in free markets remains un-dented, with the system itself having to be propped up by sacrifices by those at the bottom of society who had nothing to do with creating the financial and economic crisis. Simultaneously, of course, apart from the odd scapegoat like the banker Fred Goodwin who lost his knighthood, those with wealth and power remain unscathed.

The impact of the Conservative-led Coalition on the welfare state

The Coalition government has been active in three particular areas of the welfare state: social security/welfare benefits, health and education.

As discussed earlier in this chapter, the New Right, and then increasingly New Labour, were against a robust welfare state, fearing that it would lead to dependency. Under the Coalition government we have repeatedly seen Iain Duncan Smith, Secretary of State for Work and Pensions, as well as other leading politicians, censuring people on welfare and stressing the need to tackle the 'culture of entitlement and dependency'. Consequently, the Welfare Reform Act 2012 results in contentious savings being made by the introduction of the universal credit, and changes to various other benefits, including a cap on the total amount any family can receive in benefits. The House of Lords, among others, were concerned about how the changes would affect those such as cancer patients and disabled people, including children. Such arguments, however, have fallen on deaf ears, with the emphasis instead being on people making more effort to find/being coerced into work, with private companies and charities being recruited to do this. Some of these companies, such as A4e, have been involved in scandals in relation to alleged fraud, while high unemployment itself continues following the double-dip recession. Then there is the fact that the value of benefits are being reduced by only increasing them in line with the consumer price index rather than the retail price index; the former excludes housing costs and typically runs far behind the latter. The overriding aim is to cut the welfare bill rather than a genuine concern with the welfare of individuals, including children and families.

Another controversial reform relates to health. As the Health and Social Care Act 2012 made its way through Parliament, it was condemned by virtually all the medical professional bodies. The legislation aims to promote patient choice and to reduce NHS administration costs, and includes general practitioners being given powers to commission services on behalf of their patients, the increased involvement of the private sector and more emphasis on competition. Major concerns are that it will lead to the widespread fragmentation of the health service and will work against integration with social care, not to mention the massive cost and destabilisation caused by yet another major reorganisation at a time of huge financial pressures. Overall, the reforms are about ever more marketisation and privatisation of the NHS, this being a threat to its very existence.

When it comes to education, we have already seen the introduction of university tuition fees, with universities in effect privatised since they will no longer be funded by the state. Instead, graduates have to pay their own fees. The Education Maintenance Allowance that supported students in higher education has also been scrapped. Both changes will inevitably deter those from poorer backgrounds from entering further and higher education. Meanwhile, there has been an expansion of the school academy programme, and 'free schools' have been established whereby parents and other providers are encouraged to set up schools using government money, although they are independent of local authority control. As with the health proposals, the obvious concern is one of increasing privatisation and the emphasis on competition and inappropriate sponsorship.

The Conservative-led Coalition and social work

The most significant development, at least as far as social work with children and families is concerned, was the publication of the Munro Review (Munro, 2011). The report rightly points out that earlier reforms led to too much bureaucracy and less of a focus on the needs of children. Instead, it argues for centrally imposed targets and bureaucracy being reduced, and for social workers being given more scope to exercise professional judgement. Paradoxically, however, it also recommends more 'determined and robust' management to achieve this. But surely it is precisely because of 'determined and robust' managerialism that we have the current crisis facing social work.

The report goes on to refer to the Hackney reclaiming social work model, notwithstanding that it is based on a management model developed by business consultants (Goodman and Trowler, 2012). The model has an emphasis on all staff sharing the values of the organisation, including having a similar 'outlook and approach' to working with children and families. I can think of at least two problems with this (see Rogowski, 2011c). First, given comments in the last paragraph, do we really want more private sector management/business consultants' recommendations involved in social work? Second, it is almost as if, first and foremost, social workers have to identify with the organisation and the way it operates, rather than the social justice values of social work. Where, for example, would having to adopt shared outlooks and approaches leave those practitioners who want to practice in more radical/critical, or even in just more innovatory, ways? There has to be some scope for individual social workers, working in collaboration with users, to practice as they see fit.

In any case, although Munro came up with some fine aspirations, the likelihood is that any resulting action is unlikely to live up to the expectations of practitioners. In the first place, some local authorities are actually increasing bureaucracy by focusing on risk (see Chapter 4). Second, although there are plans to drastically reduce child protection guidance, this is unlikely to lead to less bureaucracy for social workers (*Community Care*, 2012b). Third, at a time of austerity we should not underestimate the huge challenges to creating the paradigm shift the review aims to achieve (Parton, 2012: forthcoming).

The Coalition government might have been slow to react to Munro, but there are two areas that have seen some activity. First, at the Conservative Party conference in 2011 there were complaints about the lack of adoptions and of young children languishing in care. Cameron and other ministers complained about political correctness, including social workers' alleged fixation with getting ethnic matches, and of not approving people as adopters because of petty factors such as the fact that they smoked, were overweight or too old.[2] A review of the adoption process with a view to streamlining timescales was implemented, one result being that although the importance of ethnic matches was acknowledged, this should not be an overriding factor. One worry, however, is that the government might be more concerned with meeting the needs of white middle-class couples than those of looked-after children. The concerns about adoption delays, echoing Munro (2011), are perhaps due to the bureaucracy that social workers have to endure.

The second area concerns an example of the 'Big Society' in action and how it could have an impact on social work: the use of child protection volunteers to 'help children and save money' (Cooper, 2011a). Arguments for using volunteers focus on the families being hard to engage and being suspicious of social workers because their children might be taken away. These families see volunteers as being on their side, helping them to develop confidence in their own parenting. However, this fails to acknowledge that social workers have been 'forced' into a form of neoliberal practice that emphasises their controlling, authoritarian roles rather than that of care. Moreover, the use of volunteers again means that children and families have to put up with services on the cheap.

Conclusion

The current neoliberal consensus has undoubtedly had a negative effect on social work and its users. We now have a Coalition government that, despite Cameron's attempts to rebrand his party as compassionate Conservatives, has policies more in common with Thatcher's policies. There is little new or progressive as some might have us believe; instead we have the 'same old Tories' hiding behind an opportunist pact with the Liberal Democrats (King, 2011). We have only to see how they have dealt with the financial deficit following the bailing out of the banks/financial sector more generally, and the ensuing recession. They have taken the opportunity to further dismantle the welfare state and to force people to rely on the 'Big Society', which consists of themselves, family, friends, local community and/or charities. They are also committed to the continued marketisation and privatisation of services so as to compete in the globalised world.

Although 'globalisation' is a contested concept (see Sykes, 2009), the process has led to a drift by welfare states around the world to more neoliberal approaches to economic and social policy. Going further, it simply causes welfare retrenchment because of the dominance of capitalism (Mishra, 1999); ideologically and practically, policies prioritise economic competitiveness above welfare provision. This means that aims of equality, redistribution and collective provision are secondary to citizens having to find employment so as to alleviate their own difficulties. Again, as highlighted in this chapter, we can see links between the approaches of the New Right, New Labour and the Coalition governments.

Over 30 years of neoliberal hegemony has led to ever more challenges in pursuing a progressive, critical practice. More positively, as we saw in Chapter 2, during the last three decades social work was able to progress at the theoretical level with, for example, the development of anti-discriminatory/oppressive perspectives in the 1980s and 1990s, along with critical social work itself. Further, towards the end of the 2000s many radical/critical texts appeared and continue to do so (see, for example, Ferguson, 2008; Ferguson and Lavalette, 2009; Ferguson and Woodward, 2009, Garrett, 2009b; Rogowski, 2010b, Lavalette, 2011a; Lavalette and Ioakimidis, 2012). All point to the fact that social work's insistence on social justice is at odds with the neoliberal practice imposed on practitioners by policy makers via their managers. This is because social work values do not sit easily with the current neoliberal, market-driven agenda, and as such there has to be resistance. Spaces for the practice of critical social work may be hard to find, but all is not lost, with any tendency towards critical pessimism simply resulting in capitulation to the status quo. Recall Stan Cohen's words at the outset of this chapter: stay in your agency, do your best to obtain short-term gains for users, but remember the long-term goals. The call is to stay 'unfinished' so that 'the powers that be' are not always sure what you are up to, ensuring that when confronted with challenges arising from the neoliberal world, critical possibilities remain (Rogowski, 2011b). I turn to such practice considerations in Part Two.

Key points

The New Right ushered in a neoliberal consensus now embraced by all the major political parties in the UK. This entailed a belief that globalised free markets best led to human well-being, with only a limited role remaining for the state.

The welfare state has gradually been dismantled or changed so that it no longer aspires to meets citizens' basic needs 'from the cradle to the grave'. It has become more restrictive, more commodifying and more market-oriented.

Similarly, the role of social work has become more narrow and truncated, now largely limited to rationing and risk assessment/management. To the extent that a more proactive role remains, it is the controlling rather than caring aspect, particularly evident in relation to children and families.

As a result of the neoliberal changes, critical social work faces considerable challenges, but the opportunities that remain mean it continues to play an important part in resisting neoliberalisation, thereby staying true to its emancipatory and social justice potentials.

Further reading

Farnsworth, K. and Irving, Z. (eds) (2011) *Social policy in challenging times: Economic crisis and welfare systems*, Bristol: The Policy Press. A good account of how the financial and economic crash of 2007-to date is reshaping welfare systems.

Garrett, P.M. (2009) *'Transforming' children's services? Social work, neoliberalism and the 'modern' world*, Maidenhead: Open University Press. This is an excellent examination of New Labour's 'modernisation' and 'transformation' agenda for children and families social work, showing how an adherence to neoliberalism lies at its core.

Harvey, D. (2007) *A brief history of neoliberalism*, Oxford: Oxford University Press. The best account of the political and economic development of neoliberalism and its disastrous consequences.

King, P. (2011) *The new politics: Liberal conservatism or the same old Tories?*, Bristol: The Policy Press. An accessible analysis of the Conservative Party showing that essentially they are the 'same old Tories'.

Powell, M. (ed) (2008) *Modernising the welfare state: The Blair legacy*, Bristol: The Policy Press. The third book of Powell's trilogy of New Labour analyses the social policy legacy, highlighting continuities with the New Right.

Notes

[1] Current so-called attempts to reduce bureaucracy seem to ensure the needs of redesigned ICT technologies (and in turn managers) are met rather than those of children and families.

[2] Most recently in November 2012 we have seen social workers in Rotherham castigated because they removed some eastern European children from foster carers allegedly because the latter were members of the UK Independence Party.

PART TWO

Practice considerations

4

Child protection and looked-after children

Child protection, or as it is often referred to these days, child safeguarding, and working with looked-after children, are the 'heavy end' of social work with children and families. This is because social work has been forced into a more limited and restricted role as a result of the neoliberal changes outlined earlier. Most social work with children and families now relates to protecting children considered at significant risk of harm. There is an obvious overlap here with children who become looked after because many of them have also been the subject of child protection concerns, with younger children especially prone to being removed from their families. When it comes to older children and young people, particularly those with challenging behaviour, there is pressure to avoid the financial costs of them being admitted to local authority accommodation. The result is parents increasingly dealt with by being (often re-) directed to education and health agencies, that might implement the Common Assessment Framework (see Chapter 5), or other agencies dealing with specific issues. In both scenarios they are unlikely to be offered social work support. However, those children and young people who are accommodated have increasingly had to become a priority because of the allegedly negative aspects that can result from being looked after.

Recent decades have witnessed many high profile cases where children have died at the hands of their carers despite the involvement of social workers and other professionals. Governments in the UK have responded to these tragedies by establishing elaborate procedures to try and improve cooperation and communication between the agencies involved (Ferguson, 2011). These changes have included an increased emphasis on assessing and managing risk, with social workers increasingly sat at their desk completing computerised records and other bureaucratic tasks. It has amounted to the 'deskilling' of practice as less and less time is spent with children and families (see, for example, Garrett, 2009b; Broadhurst et al, 2010a, 2010b). Remaining rooted in the office can lead to omitting, or at the very least paying less attention to, a core component of practice, namely, relating to children and families. It is surely hard not to accept that if social workers have suspicions of child abuse, then they need to see and spend time with the children and families involved; they need to see and hear what children and families say.

When it comes to looked-after children, even though they are a disadvantaged group by their very looked-after status, this can be compounded by their experience of public care (Charles and Wilton, 2004), although this should not be overstated (Wade et al, 2011; see also below). Even so, some become isolated from their families, with parents feeling devalued and hopeless. Health and education needs can receive little priority, and those leaving the care system are often poorly prepared and ill equipped for independent living. Such a situation has been linked to the prioritising of child protection and substitute home finding (Utting, 1997) rather than those children who are already accommodated by the local authority. It is also related to the fact that the emotional elements of social work practice are devalued in environments where managerialism and bureaucracy dominate, one result being that direct work with children and young people is a neglected area, especially for those living away from home.

There are two other points to note. First, both child protection and looked-after user groups increasingly have to experience a defensive social work practice, one that is designed to protect their organisation's reputation if things go wrong, rather than one geared to genuinely ascertaining and meeting the needs of such children and families. Second, looked-after children can also be seen as objects in the sense that they become commodities in the marketisation and privatisation of services.

In this chapter I outline some of the challenges and difficulties faced by social workers in relation to child protection and with looked-after children and young people, together with some more positive, critical social work possibilities.

Child protection: from therapy and welfare to surveillance and control

As Nigel Parton (1985) pointed out in the seminal *The politics of child abuse*, during the 1970s child abuse was essentially seen as a medical-social problem that was best dealt with by the medical and social work professions. They were the ones to diagnose, treat and recommend ways of preventing the phenomenon. It was only after a number of child abuse tragedies, notably Maria Colwell, in the 1970s that the role of the police became significant. Further concerns about social work's role in child abuse arose in the late 1980s/into the 1990s following events such as in Rochdale, Cleveland and Orkney, where many children were removed from families. On the one hand, practitioners were criticised for being overzealous in removing children, while on the other, they were seen as too gullible and trusting of parents. Such criticisms led to the increasing influence of the socio-legal model, the emphasis being on investigating, assessing and examining the evidence. It was a move that saw social workers move from working *therapeutically* to *protecting* children, with the law and order agencies of the police and courts taking an increased role, particularly following the Children Act 1989 and the subsequent Home Office et al's (1991) *Working together* document.

The Children Act 1989 was progressive in that every local authority had a duty to safeguard and promote the welfare of children within their area who were 'in need' (Section 17). In addition, if there was any suspicion that a child was or likely to suffer significant harm, they had a duty to make enquiries necessary to decide whether they should take action to safeguard or promote the child's welfare (Section 47). However, the Act and the associated guidance had the effect of social workers moving away from a role that involved therapy and welfare to one of surveillance and control, with organisations keen to ensure they could not be criticised if things went wrong (Howe, 1992). Another result was that the 1989 Act's intention to provide an approach to childcare that was preventative and partnership-oriented, together with a focus on children in need, was largely ignored.

To remedy the situation, *Messages from research* (DH, 1995) argued for a move away from child protection *investigations* to an emphasis on *enquiries* to see if a child was in need and what services could be offered. However, it also met with little success as the preoccupation with child protection continued. The then relatively new breed of managers, as opposed to senior social workers and social work consultants, were arguably even more concerned about organisations being criticised if things went wrong rather than meeting the needs of children and families.

New Labour's introduction of a standardised initial and core assessment framework (DH et al 2000a) was yet another attempt to redress the balance towards prevention and children in need, notwithstanding the increased bureaucracy this entailed for practitioners. However, following further child abuse tragedies such as Victoria Climbié and 'Baby Peter' in the 2000s, the emphasis continues to be on child protection, even though it is often subsumed under child safeguarding (HM Government, 2006). It now seems that all governments have given up in thinking that social workers should, or indeed can, work more preventatively with children and families, particularly following the introduction of CAF (again see Chapter 5).

Child safeguarding refers to more than protection from abuse by parents/carers (Hughes and Owen, 2009). It includes protecting children from mistreatment, preventing impairment of children's health or development, and ensuring that children grow up in circumstances consistent with the provision of safe and effective care. The onus is on agencies and individuals working proactively to safeguard and promote the welfare of children so that the need for action through child protection procedures is reduced. Despite the intention, and especially since 'Baby Peter', social work with children and families continues to be dominated by child protection, with social workers perhaps being given even more official recognition of their role in this area (see Parton, 2011).

Importantly, child protection is not an absolute concept and varies over time, hence being a social construction (see Chapter 2). It currently involves physical, sexual and emotional abuse as well as neglect, and even within these categories, there is contestation. For instance, there can be a thin line between 'normal' sexual exploration and abusive behaviour when children are concerned. Definitions continue to be widened, amounting to 'definitional inflation' (Lonne et al, 2008) with, for example, concerns about domestic abuse/violence and obese children being relatively recent developments.[1] Then again, following events in Orkney in the early 1990s, there is a reluctance to accept that ritual abuse exists (Macleod and Saraga, 1994), which is not to deny that you can have overzealous social workers and other professionals in this area.

From a feminist perspective, it is often mothers who are blamed for 'failing to protect' the children, despite the fact it is their partners who have inflicted the abuse; getting away from such 'mother blaming' is a key aspect of critical practice (Ferguson, 2011). From a Marxist perspective, child abuse is seen largely as a working-class phenomenon because most investigations involve them. Is this about better policing of the poor, or because middle-class parents are more private and are better at covering up their wrong doings (Thorpe, 1995)? At times it is simply that 'respectable' families are dealt with differently. For example, I recall a senior officer in the fire service who had assaulted his teenage daughter causing bruising to her face after an altercation about her challenging behaviour. The next day she told teachers what had happened and child protection procedures were implemented, which led to a case conference. At the conference, largely because of the views of the police, it was decided that no further action was needed. Now while the altercation and resulting assault might well have been a one-off, isolated incident, would the same view be taken of an unemployed, working-class father who had engaged in similar behaviour?

Another relevant point is that certain practices in wealthy families, such as sending young children to boarding schools where they may be met with degrading punishments in the name of character building, could also be socially constructed as child abuse. It is not, because of unequal power relationships in a neoliberal/capitalist society that tends to accuse the poor and to protect the rich and powerful, because the latter largely decide who and what is socially constructed as problematic (Corrigan and Leonard, 1979).

Bear the above comments in mind when considering the initial and core assessments in relation to children and their needs (DH et al, 2000a), the completion of which, along with the associated bureaucracy and timescales, amounts to a 'procedural model' (Sayer, 2008) rather than a professional one. It can involve contact/referral, initial investigation and assessment, strategy discussion with other agencies notably the police, core assessment and child protection case conferences. At any stage, if there is a need for immediate protection, the child can be removed from home. The process involves the following of detailed procedures, completing bureaucracy within specified timescales, and discussions with managers at every step.

Assessment is part of a process of intervention which, at least in its 'old' social democratic, and still is in its critical, form, identifies needs and provides access to appropriate resources. It is, or should be, far less concerned with current preoccupations of rationing and assessing risk (more of which below). The assessment framework looks at the child's developmental needs, parenting capacity and family and environmental factors. While the inclusion of family and environmental factors is welcomed because there is some acknowledgement of wider structural factors, such issues are often neglected in the resultant analysis and outcome of the assessment process (Garrett, 2003). For example, I recall referring to the impact of government policy in relation to public expenditure cuts on a specific child and family (not to mention the effects on many others in a similar situation), but was faced with managerial comments such as "That's very political, we should not be writing and arguing that." The implication was that a more acceptable analysis and outcome for many managers is to find fault and (often unduly) place the blame on parents doing their best in difficult circumstances.

In carrying out the assessment process various themes emerge (Sayer, 2008). First, following the Children Act 1989, there is the notion of partnership with children and families. This presents a challenge for practitioners because of the power imbalance and the very fact that they help to decide whether parenting is 'good enough'. To remedy this, social workers have to be aware of the impact of their interactions with the children and families they work with, along with issues in relation to power and use of authority (Okitikpi, 2011). There is also a need to genuinely listen to children and parents and to work anti-oppressively wherever possible. Importantly, the 'tick box' nature of assessments is problematic and they should not replace professional judgement as to the nature of the problem and what to do about it.

A second theme relates to current emphasis on 'evidence-based practice'. Such an approach may sound all well and good, but such practice is not always applicable to the 'messy' and complicated area of social problems and social work (Smith, 2004). This is particularly so when it comes to the current preoccupation with risk (see below). The emphasis on risk assessment/management is somewhat spurious in that you can get false negatives and false positives, which is the case with medecine(Heller et al, 2004) and even more so with social work. The 'evidence' may point 80 per cent to a particular outcome of abuse, but you could also be dealing with the 20 per cent that is not. The decision to be made, admittedly not always an easy one, should be a professional one based on knowledge and experience.

The third theme is that it should not always be assumed that social work and other interventions will make things better. The likely outcomes of intervention and non-intervention should be carefully evaluated. Sometimes damage limitation is all that can be achieved, especially if you are dealing with older children/young people and their parents who refuse to cooperate.

Defensive practice

Turning more specifically to actual practice in child protection, the impact of managerialism, bureaucratisation and deprofessionalisation cannot be overstated. From the initial contact/referral, through the various stages leading to a possible case conference, the power and influence of managers is paramount. They decide how to proceed, dealing with the what, how and when of things subsequently occurring (although less attention often being paid to the 'why' question). Further, depending on the seriousness of the child protection concerns, the manager may well have to consult and in turn be directed by their own manager. Admittedly in this hierarchical 'procedural game' there may be an element of discretion and autonomy allowed to more experienced social workers, but this should not be overstated.

It is clear to see why the scenario just outlined has arisen. It is because of the overriding priority of being able to defend the organisation's reputation if things 'go wrong', and this is easier to do if the 'rules' have been followed. In addition, this can be linked to the fact that external monitoring and scrutiny of organisations means that decisions are increasingly made on the basis of the organisation's needs rather than those of users. As touched on previously, it can mean organisations devise and follow procedures that meet their own needs rather than those of children and families (Laming, 2003).

Another problem with current child protection practice is that many see social work as being increasingly tied into a system of social control rather than offering help and support. Note how it is now the police that often dominate proceedings, especially in the initial stages of child protection investigations, some even going on to argue that social workers should be trained in police interview and interrogation techniques (see Rogowski, 2010b, 2011c). It must be remembered that the police's overriding goal is to gain evidence for a criminal prosecution, while the social work aim is, or should be, to ensure that the child is protected and the family have the help and support that they need to care adequately for their children.

Preoccupation with risk

Linked with defensive practice is the current preoccupation with risk (also a feature of youth justice practice; see Chapter 6). There are two points here. First, following the 'Baby Peter' tragedy much was rightly made about increased bureaucracy, particularly the Integrated Children's System, having a negative effect on social workers' ability to spend time with children and families, including those subject to child protection plans. As we saw in Chapter 3, the Munro Review (2011) pointed out that earlier child protection/safeguarding reforms led to too much bureaucracy and less of a focus on the needs of children. Instead, centrally imposed targets and bureaucracy should be reduced, with social workers being given more scope to exercise professional judgement. Despite this, some authorities are actually increasing bureaucracy, such as requiring repetitive risk assessments be added to initial and core assessments (Rogowski, 2011c). Surely, by completing the various (and numerous) assessment headings and then doing an analysis, one has actually done the risk assessment? We also come back to doubts about the scientific credence given to such assessments, given the issues in relation to false negatives and false positives.

The second point is a more general one in relation to risk. Beck's (1992) *Risk society* argued that society now demands that risks be identified and controlled by appropriate bodies, even though there is actually limited capacity to do so. Nevertheless, 'risk' has now largely replaced 'need' as the principle around which health and social work/care services are organised. One could even go so far as to argue that unless a child is defined to be at substantial risk of abuse, then little or no help or support will be provided by social workers. In addition, risk assessment in itself constrains social work practice, and in turn service users, by privileging notions of predictability rather than the uncertainty and ambiguity of everyday practice (Peckover et al, 2011). This relates to policy and practice in social work with children and families becoming tragedy-led as resulting enquiries ignore the complexities of policies, procedures, decision-making processes, organisational cultures and contradictory societal expectations (Dixon, 2010). Another, perhaps paramount, consideration is the influence of managerialism whereby an essentially neoliberal social work has been imposed on practitioners, involving a minimal role limited to rationing and risk assessment. A brief one-off encounter with children and families, followed by the completion of paperwork as speedily as possible, is often the 'be all and end all' of 'the social work experience'. The case of three-year-old Ryan Lovell-Hancox, who was killed by two carers in December 2008 in Wolverhampton, shows what can happen when people are forced to rely on charity and friends (Wolverhampton SCB, 2011). Ryan's mother was struggling with his care but was supported by a worker from a voluntary organisation. After approaching children's services for help, she ended up paying friends to look after him while she decorated her home. Perhaps a more pro-active social work approach involving the provision of respite care would have prevented the tragedy.

A Relative Success Story

Despite concerns about the deprofessionalisation inherent in managerialism, research shows that social workers and other professionals have been relatively successful in dealing with child abuse (Pritchard and Williams, 2010). The researchers explored 'child abuse-related deaths' (CARD) and possible CARD rates of children aged from birth to 14 years over the period 1974-2006. It used the latest available World Health Organization mortality data to compare England and Wales outcomes with the other major developed countries (MDCs). The results tell a relative 'success story' for England and Wales, whose violent CARD rates of children have never been lower since records began, and who have made significantly greater progress in reducing violent possible CARD rates than the majority of the other MDCs. Moreover, England and Wales were only one of four MDCs whose CARD deaths, primarily the responsibility of the children protection services (CPS), fell significantly more than 'All causes of death', the primary responsibility of medicine. As the authors state, 'This should help to offset some of the media stereotypes and be a boost for the morale of front line staff of the CPS and the families whom they serve' (Pritchard and Williams, 2010, p 1700). However, as much of the data relates to the pre-managerialist era of the present, it would be useful to compare that more professionally oriented period with the managerial-dominated situation of now. Nevertheless, such findings are welcome given it is usually only the child abuse tragedies that the media highlights.

Overall, however, there are concerns with the 'procedural model' of child protection. In the first place, it is based on a residual welfare state, where legal and bureaucratic processes dominate, along with the assessment of risk, and resources devoted to those children considered at most risk (Stafford et al, 2012). It is also a neoliberal model, one that can be counter-posed to more social democratic family support systems that dominate in continental Western Europe. Here there are more comprehensive welfare states, and voluntary and collaborative practice focuses on the family unit with resources available to more families at an earlier stage. At least four other concerns can be identified.

First, the child protection investigation itself can be damaging, particularly in the case of sexual abuse when intimate medical examinations might be needed or the victim often has to repeat their story. Second, and as noted above, the model provides little opportunity for therapeutic work. Third, after the closure of a child protection issue, although the child may still be 'in need' under the Children Act 1989, ongoing help and support is seldom offered; resource constraints lead to case closure so new cases can be dealt with. And fourth, most child protection referrals come to nothing and yet consume vast resources, so being more precise and restrictive when it comes to the definition of child abuse would enable priorities and resources to be devoted to child *welfare* rather than child *protection* (Thorpe, 1994), which chimes with *Messages from research* (DH, 1995).

There is also the argument that the focus on *protection* has resulted in children being overprotected to the point where their whole childhood is threatened. 'Stranger danger' is the obvious example, with children frightened to interact with adults and vice versa, despite the fact that child abuse is largely perpetrated by parents and close family members or friends. An over-emphasis on 'stranger danger' can result in children not even being allowed to travel to school on their own. They can also be deprived of play, socialisation with peers, exercise and fresh air.

Case study 4.1: Child protection or child in need?

Jason (10 years old) and his sister, Emily (8 years old), live with their parents George and Ann. George is unemployed and has difficulties with alcohol and cannabis use. Financial problems cause stress leading to arguments between the parents, sometimes leading to violence. The house is often dirty, untidy, cluttered and on occasions there is a lack of food. Jason and Emily sometimes turn up at school late and ill clad. Despite all this, they are happy and healthy and have a close bond with their parents. One morning, however, they arrive at school upset and distressed, telling a teacher about 'mummy and daddy arguing and fighting', and contact is made with children's services, asking for help and support for the family.

Issues to consider:

1   Is this a 'child in need' case or one of child protection because of emotional abuse and neglect concerns? The notion of 'good enough parenting' is an important consideration and raises complex issues, especially as Jason and Emily clearly want to remain at home despite the difficulties.

2   Following an initial assessment there are two possibilities:

a   The situation being dealt with as a 'child in need' case (this often depends on the view of the manager). Short-term intervention involving a family worker might be offered, focusing on helping the parents tidy their house, stressing the importance of regular school attendance, together with reinforcing social work advice about agencies dealing with benefits, alcohol/drug and domestic abuse/violence issues. Advice about counselling for the children might also be given. The case is then quickly closed.

b   If the case is dealt with as a child protection one, it could lead to a core assessment, case conference and resulting child protection plan, the latter essentially focusing on what George and Ann had to do before the plan would cease. This could include George having to engage with the alcohol/drugs team and anger management, Ann having to see a domestic abuse worker, and both having to keep on top of home conditions and ensure that the children were adequately clothed and arrived at school on time. Jason and Emily could also be expected to undertake counselling. In the background, implicitly or explicitly, would be the threat of removing the children from their parents if the plan was not complied with. If George and Ann 'cooperate' along the lines suggested, the case would be quickly closed, although if they did/could not, care proceedings could be initiated.

Such ways of working are a form of authoritarian, neoliberal social work.

3   A critical approach is to argue for the case to be dealt with on a 'children in need' basis, although failing that, admittedly one would have go down the child protection route. However, either situation involves a genuine emphasis on building relationships with the family and working in partnership, at their pace, and, as far as possible, on the issues defined by them. Importantly, in both scenarios a more structural view of the family's situation would be taken. Poverty, poor housing and lack of employment opportunities, which can cause parental stress leading to alcohol/drug misuse and domestic abuse, would all be considered. Consciousness raising about such issues as well as ensuring George and Ann were receiving their correct benefit entitlements are ways forward. Issues around lack of meaningful employment opportunities and cuts in benefits as a result of the recession, globalisation and the overall neoliberal project are all relevant. Similarly, the notion of patriarchy and its relation to domestic abuse would be considered. In relation to Jason and Emily, they would be given time and permission to tell their story, and an overzealous child protection response in the form of removing them would be resisted because overall they are happy at home. Finally, in relation to George's alcohol and drug misuse, again an overzealous response would be avoided; many substance users have stable habits and can function well as parents.

The discussion of child protection raises some intricate and complex issues, compounded by other factors such as parents having mental health or learning difficulties (see Green, 2002, and Roberts, 2005, respectively). For example, research at the University of Bristol reveals that parents with learning difficulties are up to 50 times more likely to be involved in child protection and care proceedings (Hunt, 2011), often because they have not been provided with appropriate help and support. The complexity referred to here also applies to social work with looked-after children.

Looked-after children

The state acts as a corporate parent to tens of thousands of children and young people, and in March 2010 this totalled over 68,000 in England and Wales (Wilson et al, 2011). Becoming looked-after (often still referred to as being 'in care') involves voluntary arrangements with parents ('accommodated') or under care orders. The state shares parental responsibility with those who had it prior to admission, so there is a crucial partnership arrangement between the state, parents and the child. Importantly, the Children Act 1989 includes a duty to promote contact between looked-after children and their parents, other significant adults and siblings. Most children spend relatively short periods being looked after before returning home, while for those needing long-term substitute care, permanence is provided by adoption, residence orders or special guardianship (Adoption and Children Act 2002), with kinship and private fostering also having a role to play. Some young people leave the looked-after children's system to live independently.

Placements for looked-after children and young people

Placements for looked-after young people usually vary between foster care and residential care. The former involves emergency to long-term placements, while the latter involves various possibilities, from small children's homes through to secure accommodation. In broad terms, best practice is served by placing younger children with foster carers, while older children usually neither want nor need a family environment, so residential care can be appropriate. In both scenarios, what used to be local authority provision is increasingly being provided by the private and voluntary sector. A concern in relation to such privatised residential care is that it can mean the use of less qualified/trained staff employed on worse terms and conditions than their local authority colleagues; it is not hard to see that this can have repercussions regarding the quality of care provided.

Secure accommodation amounts to locked children's homes, and is used for vulnerable young offenders, young people who are a danger to themselves or others, and those detained under Her Majesty's pleasure, mainly young people who have committed murder.

An important issue, highlighted by government targets and performance indicators, is the number of placement moves both in terms of foster homes and/ or residential care. Such moves lead to difficulties relating to changes of school, maintaining contact with family and friends, getting to know a new area and so on. The frequency of placement moves is partly explained by young people having to be placed outside of their home area if their local authority has had to purchase resources from the private or voluntary sector because of lack of local provision. Then, when vacancies arise 'in-house', they are often brought back regardless of their wishes and feelings, and whether it is in their best interests.

As for kinship care and private fostering, the former relates to children who are no longer able to live with their natural parents being cared for by extended family – it is on the threshold between public and private care arrangements. On occasions such relatives can be approved as foster carers. Private fostering (having nothing to do here with the use of private fostering agencies) usually refers to arrangements made directly between parents and carers outside of the formal 'care' system.

The looked-after children's system

The looked-after children's system again uses a 'procedural' approach, having merged with the *Framework for the assessment of children in need and their families* in 2006 to form the Integrated Children's System (Sayer, 2008). The aim is to provide a seamless information-gathering and planning system from first contact/referral of a child through to rehabilitation home, permanency or independent living. However, such paper/electronic arrangements are geared to the needs of the management and bureaucratic culture that pervades social work rather than the needs of children and young people. Note the various forms that social workers have to complete and update: Essential Information Records parts 1 and 2, Placement Plans parts 1 and 2, Care Plan, Review of Arrangements Forms, and Assessment and Action records. Other forms that social workers must ensure are completed include Personal and Individual Education Plans.

One reason for the increased documentation no doubt relates to the marketisation and privatisation of foster and residential care provision, with the looked-after children's forms providing information that helps in drawing up contractual specifications. Put simply, voluminous details of the difficulties and challenges a young person poses means providers of services can charge more. In addition, it is not surprising, given the proliferation of bureaucracy, that the social work role has been reduced to little more than completing paperwork and undertaking statutory visits aimed at ensuring that there are no signs of abuse. Looked-after children and young people surely expect more from their social workers.

Perhaps the most significant result of the procedural approach is that there is no longer an emphasis on the relationship social workers have with children and young people; instead 'success' is measured through performance indicators and targets. Young people bemoan the bureaucratic process taking over, which often results in social workers finding it difficult to relate to them. Common complaints include social workers not listening and not trying to understand their point of view (Morgan, 2006). They do not want social workers who are focused towards carers or their employers; instead they value qualities of trustworthiness, availability and reliability. I have often been told by young people that they like social workers who are friendly, approachable and "someone who you can have a laugh with". This resonates with research showing that social workers need to focus their attention on children and young people by engaging directly with them and their parents in sustained, thoughtful, sometimes therapeutic, work (Simmonds, 2008). Unfortunately, the movement has been in the opposite direction, and it is now exceptional for social workers to be engaged in such relational work.

Reflective practice

Despite the increased bureaucratisation and proceduralisation of practice with looked-after children and young people, it remains possible to work in more critical ways. An example of this is in the imaginative use of the Assessment and Action Records (see Charles and Wilton, 2004). Such records were devised as a means of assessing whether appropriate action had been taken to ensure good outcomes for specific age groups of looked-after children. However, they can be criticised at various levels, for instance, because of the imposition of white middle-class values that ignore the context within which individual development takes place. Or again, there is an overly directive checklist approach that is not child-friendly, and that is more about data collection and the 'processing' of children. These are important criticisms, but reflective practitioners, working from a critical social work perspective, can alleviate them.

Such practitioners can use the forms as a flexible means of purposeful questioning and exploration of aspects of children's lives, and it can be a task that engages children, their parents, carers and significant others in discussion and debate. Such discourse can lead to joint decisions about what action needs to be done, and by whom, and thereby improve an individual's life chances. Practitioners working on these lines emphasise the professional control and autonomy they possess over the process, manner and methods by which the forms are completed. They use them to seize the chance to spend more time with children as a means of combating the scant time they usually formally have for relationship building. Importantly, the physical completion of the forms does not become the 'be all and end all', with the forms used instead as a means of gathering qualitative rather than quantitative data. Details are collected at the child's pace, and information is set in the cultural and structural context in which they live, identifying resource inequalities in the process. Currently, for example, and subject to the age and understanding of the individual concerned, their particular circumstances could be related to the global crisis of neoliberalism leading to policies and cutbacks that adversely affect the most vulnerable in society. In a different vein, the emphasis is on the interactions themselves as they are just as important as the gathering of information. All this is geared to ensuring that the child is not exploited, being expected to 'give' while receiving nothing in return, pointing to the fact that 'The secret to liberation from the technical bureaucratic straitjacket and into child centred practice lies in relationship building and effective communication with children' (Charles and Wilton, 2004, p 188).

A failing system?

Although the looked-after children's system and its antecedents are often portrayed as failing children and young people (DCSF, 2007), a more balanced view needs to be taken. After all, being looked-after can be a positive experience, especially when one looks at aspects of safety, stability and emotional well-being (Wade et al, 2011). Indeed, Rees and Stein (2011, p 190) comment that 'some recent studies [indicate] being looked after can be associated with better than expected outcomes.' When looking at such issues, various factors need to be borne in mind.

First, most care episodes are relatively short, so the care system should not be blamed for poor outcomes. Second, many of those who leave care have entered the system in their mid-teens having already suffered various deprivations, and begin their care experience from an unusually low starting point. One should therefore be sceptical of simple outcome indicators, and perhaps a broader measure of 'success' should be used such as young people's own evaluation of their well-being and progress (Stein, 2004, 2006; Bullock et al, 2006). Indeed, blunt measures such as exam results, moves and ethnicity can be inappropriate for many looked-after children and young people, and furthermore they can be too general to accommodate diversity (Roy et al, 2009). Third, merely expecting young people, who have already had a deprived upbringing, simply to be future workers contributing to Britain PLC is a limited view of their futures. This is not to say that the looked-after children's system cannot be improved. But one should be wary of expecting miracles, bearing in mind the suffering already experienced by most looked-after children as a result of often coming from families facing poverty, bad housing and other structural pressures.

Given these caveats, there are three particular areas where there have been attempts to improve the situation in relation to looked-after children's education, those leaving care and the recent emphasis on adoption.

There have been long-standing concerns about the poor education achievements of looked-after children (SEU, 2003). This is often due to poor liaison between schools and care services, or schools not understanding looked-after children's difficulties or special needs (DES, 2006a, 2006b). However, under New Labour the response largely amounted to setting new targets and introducing the aforementioned Personal and Individual Education Plans. Regarding the latter I well recall one headteacher saying "They are not worth the paper they are written on," simply seeing such plans as yet another bureaucratic burden. On another occasion, I was the social worker for an 11-year-old boy who had returned home to his single-parent mother after a spell in foster care. He was bright and keen to learn, and needed a computer to help with his homework. My request was initially refused by managers because the need for a computer was not mentioned in the Personal Education Plan. No doubt the real reason was to save money, and it was only with a degree of perseverance and persistence that a computer was eventually provided.

Until the Children (Leaving Care) Act 2000, social services departments had a power rather than a duty to support care leavers. Practice could be patchy and many young people were in effect 'dumped' in bed and breakfast accommodation. Social services departments and their successor children's trusts now have established specialist aftercare teams, and financial and personal support lasts until 21 years of age, or 25 if the young person remains in education or employment. However, as in other areas of social work, the managerial emphasis is on ensuring that documentation is completed within specified timescales, and in the case of care leavers, the key document is the Pathway Plan. It can take the form of an Assessment and Action Record, and is supposed to address needs through various transitions. But despite the 2000 Act there are still concerns about the services care leavers receive with, for example, their health and educational needs not being properly addressed within bureaucratic, target-driven services (Broad, 2005).

New Labour was keen to increase the number of looked-after children and young people who were adopted, and, as we saw in Chapter 3, this sentiment has been echoed by the Coalition government. In the background is criticism of the alleged social work obsession with 'same race' placements, despite the fact that there can be damaging consequences for black children placed with white adopters (Small with Goldstein, 2000). The idea of securing 'permanence' in a stable, loving home sounds all well and good, but there are difficulties in this 'rush for permanence' (Sayer, 2008, p 140). Arguably, behind it lies a 'new paternalism' that involves helping those children and families in need, but doing this by requiring certain behavioural requirements on the part of parents. It amounts to conditional welfare, which has affinities with developments during the Clinton administrations of the 1990s in the US (Prideaux, 2001). Consequently, should birth parents not cooperate with social workers and quickly make behavioural and lifestyle changes, they can 'lose' their children (Garrett, 2002). The emphasis on adoption, therefore, might well be more about getting children out of expensive local authority care rather than meeting their needs. Or again, it could be about meeting white middle-class couples' needs rather than children's. After all, adoption often involves the transfer of children from poor families, often living on welfare benefits, to wealthier families who are willing and able to bear the full cost of caring for them.

Case study 4.2: Avoiding the rush for permanence

Michael and Ryan are mixed race half-brothers aged five and two years old respectively. Michael is of African-Caribbean/white/South Asian ethnicity, while Ryan is African-Caribbean/white/Chinese. Their mother, Sara, had left them 'home alone' overnight. The following day neighbours saw Michael banging on his bedroom window saying his mother had died. The police were called and had to break into the house that was found to be in a chaotic state – there was no heating or food, with dirty clothes and toys scattered everywhere. Michael had tried to tape blankets to Ryan to keep him warm; both were cold and hungry. They had to be taken to hospital where they soon recovered and were accommodated with foster carers while care proceedings were initiated.

Sara and her partner, Ronnie, Ryan's father, presented themselves at the office shortly afterwards. Ronnie lived in a neighbouring authority although he was in regular contact with the family. Sara did not give a clear explanation as to why the boys had been left, but both she and Ronnie wanted to be assessed in the hope of the boys being returned to their joint care.

Issues to consider:

1   Managers, influenced by the emphasis on increasing the number of looked-after children adopted, had already made up their minds that the boys would have to be adopted.
2   The social workers involved were more open-minded, one factor being the difficulties of ensuring the children's 'race'/ethnic/cultural needs were met should adoption be pursued. Perhaps more importantly, they took the view that wherever possible, children should be reunited with their parents/family, notwithstanding the difficult presenting situation.

Ensuing developments

Sara and Ronnie cooperated with the parenting assessment that was positive, and kept to the contact arrangements, so it was proposed that the boys be returned to their care. However, on one occasion Ronnie assaulted Sara in front of the boys at a children's centre. Not surprisingly adoption became the favoured option, but Ronnie persuasively put himself forward as a sole carer supported by his mother, Chloe. Meanwhile, Sara dropped out of the care proceedings and, for the time being, the boys' lives.

Chloe was duly assessed and approved as a relative foster carer and the boys moved to her care, while Ronnie underwent further parenting and psychological assessments, together with anger management, all of which were positive. The eventual care order and final care plan saw the boys remaining with Chloe under a care order, but with Ronnie closely involved in their day-to-day care and not ruling out the possibility of him eventually becoming the sole carer. By now the whole family were living in the neighbouring local authority but were supervised by their 'home' authority.

Michael and Ryan remained settled and thrived in the shared care arrangement involving Chloe and Ronnie. This continued when Ronnie and Sara reconciled and she became pregnant. Because of the previous child protection concerns, the new baby, Lisa, was subject to a child protection plan at birth. She made good progress but Ronnie and Sara eventually separated because he felt she did not 'pull her weight' in terms of caring for the children. He placed Lisa in Chloe's care. He continued to play a key role in both her and the boys' care, although again Sara disappeared from all their lives. Despite the continued progress of all three children, the neighbouring authority, in what amounted to defensive practice, initiated care proceedings in respect of Lisa. This dragged on for some time and involved Ronnie and Chloe having to undergo further assessments that again were positive. As a result, a supervision order was eventually made in respect of Lisa. By now the boys had moved to Ronnie's sole care, supported by Chloe.

Outcome

The boys continued to thrive in Ronnie's care and the care orders in respect of them were discharged. The court noted that Michael and Ryan were making good progress in all areas of their lives, including being in regular contact with Chloe and Lisa.

As far as this family, not least the children, were concerned, and despite the twists and turns along the way, there had certainly been a successful outcome. Furthermore, this had been achieved without recourse to the somewhat draconian, if cheaper, option of having the boys adopted at an earlier stage. It goes to show that working in genuine partnership with children and their families, even if this means swimming against the managerial tide and ignoring short-term targets along the way, can prove to be the best course of action for all concerned. Such outcomes might involve disagreements with some colleagues and managers, but this has always been and remains part of critical social work.

It should also be noted that the rush for permanence does not only relate to adoption. I recall siblings Martin (15 years old) and Dawn (11 years old) who were happy and settled with long-term foster carers following neglect concerns when they were at home. It was envisaged that they would remain in the placement until they left 'care'. However, a new manager arrived and saw the possibility of saving money if the young people were made the subject of special guardianship orders to their foster carers. I was pressured to 'persuade' the foster carers to apply for special guardianship *not* because it would secure a stable, loving home for Martin and Dawn, but simply because it would save some money. Needless to say the managerial pressure was successfully resisted, not least because both the children and their foster carers were happy with the current care arrangements. It is important to note, however, that there are ongoing concerns about managers wanting to 'convert' foster carers into special guardians just to save money (Pemberton, 2011a).

Conclusion

Critical social work in child protection and with looked-after children and young people has always been difficult and demanding, and this is even more so in 'managerialist times'. The need for effectiveness, efficiency and economy, alongside resulting bureaucratisation and proceduralisation, means relational work is grossly undervalued. Nevertheless, despite all the constraints on practitioners, this chapter shows that critical social work remains possible.

Child protection is the most high profile aspect of social work, certainly as far as the media, politicians and general public are concerned. Over recent years emphasis has been placed on the failures of the interprofessional system to communicate and to share vital information about children at risk, and entire new bureaucratic systems have been built up around it (Ferguson, 2011). As we have seen, this is more about defending organisations should things go wrong than meeting the needs of children and families. Too often assessments focus on rationing and risk rather than the help and support parents need to care for their children. Resultant practice focuses on the personal inadequacies of parents/carers rather than wider societal factors underlying problems, which amounts to 'blaming the victim'. The argument presented here is that critical social work pays attention to these wider factors. For instance, it has long been acknowledged that the stress of poverty can lead to child abuse, particularly physical abuse and neglect (Parton, 1985). In addition, parental/carer misuse of such as drugs and alcohol often relates to the stress of living in contemporary society with such issues sometimes having a bearing on child abuse. The critical social worker has to address such matters in genuine partnership with children and families, rather than adopting an overt, authoritarian response.

As for critical social work with looked-after children and young people, again bureaucratic systems have been built up around practice, which are procedural hurdles that practitioners have to overcome. For instance, it is all very well to set targets and forms to be completed in relation to educational attainment, for example, but this means little without the allocation of adequate resources. The critical practitioner needs to be aware of and acknowledge such issues in their day-to-day practice, and in so doing, try to create space for more relationship-based work focusing on the real needs of children and families. As we saw, such practice can lead to important successes, and it can even be carried out while completing the more bureaucratic tasks of social work, namely, filling in Assessment and Action Records, for example. When used as Pathway Plans for older teenagers, for instance, it is essential that they reflect the problems and difficulties facing young people today – employment/training/education, accommodation, finance and so on – together with determined action designed to address them.

Key points

Critical social work in relation to child protection/safeguarding and with looked-after children needs a critical approach to avoid 'blaming the victims', essentially the casualties of neoliberalism, for their problems and difficulties.

'Defensible' rather than defensive practice is a prerequisite of critical social work, not least in child protection and with looked-after children. One should not automatically accept 'best practice' as being what the 'powers that be' want practitioners to believe.

Child abuse is a social construct that varies over time and in response to different understandings of abuse, families and the role of the state. One should be wary of definitional inflation.

Contrary to what politicians and the media propagate, child protection social work is a relative success story.

The looked-after children's system should not automatically be seen as a failing system with a more balanced, nuanced analysis needing to be taken.

Further reading
Cocker, C. and Allen, L. (2008) *Social work with looked-after children*, Exeter: Learning Matters. Although not written from an explicitly critical perspective, this provides a practical, introductory book, highlighting some of the key issues for practice with looked-after children.

Corby, B. (2005) *Child abuse: Towards a knowledge base* (3rd edn), London: Open University Press. A well-informed review of the historical development, definition, extent, causation and consequences of child abuse.

Parton, N. (2005) *Safeguarding childhood: Early intervention and surveillance in late modern society*, Basingstoke: Palgrave Macmillan. A clear commentary on developments in child abuse and child welfare policy, explaining how changes have been informed by the economic, political and cultural context.

Sayer, T. (2008) *Critical practice in working with children*, Basingstoke: Palgrave Macmillan. An introductory text, with chapters on critical practice in child protection and with looked-after children.

Note
[1] I recall an Eastern European travelling family moving into our area which coincided with a spate of minor shoplifting, robbery and burglary offences. The three older teenage boys were involved, but not the three younger children who were all aged under 10, one being a 10-month-old baby. The social worker was under pressure from managers (who were in turn under pressure from the police) to argue that there were child protection concerns

because of inadequate parenting in relation to the teenage boys. Rather than allow the youth justice system to run its course in relation to the offending, it was suggested that a child protection case conference was required with all the children needing to be made subject to child protection plans. Fortunately, such a scenario was successfully resisted.

'Definitional inflation' is also evidenced by arguments for the commercial exploitation of children and young people to be taken seriously because it can lead to significant harm, including mental health issues (see Wild, 2012); this is taken up further in Chapter 5.

5

Children in need and those with mental health issues

Social work with children and young people in need and those with mental health issues is facing considerable challenges. Practice with children in need, in effect preventative social work, is an area that is now increasingly less in evidence. This is particularly so since the introduction of the Common Assessment Framework in 2006 (Rogowski, 2011b, 2011c). Meanwhile, younger children with mental health issues are bearing the brunt of cuts to Child and Adolescent Mental Health Services (CAMHS), with the Royal College of Psychiatrists predicting that there will be a sharp rise in the number of teenagers with severe mental health problems over the next decade (Cooper, 2011b).

Preventative social work with children and families used to be an important aspect of practice during the many the years of social services departments. Such practice entailed getting to know young mothers and fathers, providing advice about local community resources, together with help in establishing support groups for single parents with young children, for example. Families with older children and young people could similarly be helped in terms of dealing with such as behavioural difficulties. An example is a groupwork approach involving parents meeting to discuss issues and concerns, and how they dealt with them. They would not be blamed for their predicament; instead they would be encouraged to support and 'learn' from each other. Such practice would have occurred in a non-threatening, partnership-oriented way. Bringing such parents together encourages the view that there are many 'in the same boat'. This includes living in difficult circumstances because of the stresses and strains of poverty which can impinge on the care of children. It is hard to argue that such individuals are responsible for their situation, which negates the view of much current policy and practice that involves the privatisation of public ills (Pearson, 1973). Sadly, preventative social work as a whole, regardless of critical possibilities, has been on the wane since the 1980s/1990s.

Children and young people being diagnosed with mental health issues may be a contentious subject, but as CAMHS budgets are increasingly squeezed, it is only the more serious cases that receive attention. Specialist clinical care may be spared for such 'urgent' individuals, but 'low level' provision for children under 12 years of age tends to be neglected. The focus is increasingly on adolescents who exhibit more tangible problems, such as suicide or self-harm. While younger children are less likely to exhibit this level of disorder, if their emotional and psychological difficulties are neglected, they are likely to become more serious cases later. The Coalition government's public expenditure cuts have contributed to this situation and run counter to their rhetoric in support of early intervention. Such cuts lead to the tightening of eligibility criteria, waiting times for referrals increasing and staff posts disappearing, with privatisation possibilities clearly on the horizon, as Richard Branson hopes to take over CAMHS in Devon (*Community Care*, 2012a). Relationships between children and family social workers who want to refer cases to CAMHS are strained, as instead of referrals being accepted, various gatekeeping measures have to be overcome. This includes 'consultation sessions' between children and families social workers and their CAMHS colleagues prior to the latter accepting (or often refusing) a referral. The reason for such sessions is often stated as CAMHS staff 'offering advice' on how children and young people's mental health issues might be addressed without referral to CAMHS. The obvious charge is that it is a gatekeeping ploy to ration resources.

Not surprisingly, this chapter is divided into two halves. First, I look at social work with children in need, including what seems to be the demise of preventative social work (Rogowski, 2011b, 2011c). Admittedly, New Labour advocated early intervention strategies such as Sure Start and the Children's Fund, but social work was barely involved. Although the Coalition government has a similar emphasis on early intervention, this is being undermined by the severe public expenditure cuts.

Second I turn to children and young people with mental health issues. Social work in this area has often occupied a marginalised position, even though issues of children's emotional and psychological needs have been seen as key in theoretical terms (Walker, 2011). Children in care, asylum and refugee children, those who have been the victims of abuse, young offenders and those with learning difficulties are just some of the groups that need social work intervention. Social work therefore has a particularly important contribution to make in CAMHS, although again, resource constraints mean that there are significant challenges.

Children in need and preventative social work

The Children and Young Persons Act 1963 enshrined prevention as part of social work by placing a duty on local authorities to promote the welfare of children by diminishing the need for them to be received into care, including financial payments. This duty continues under Section 17 of the Children Act 1989, which introduced the concept of children 'in need'. Under the Act they are defined as children who are aged under 18 in need of local authority services to achieve or maintain a reasonable standard of health or development. This is a somewhat vague definition, in practice enabling local authority services, influenced by media and political pressure, to focus social work intervention in high profile user areas. Hence the emphasis is on child protection rather than children in need and prevention. Some may consider working with the latter group and their families as a more a mundane aspect of social work, but I totally disagree. It is a practice that has benefited large numbers of children and families, and is one which should not be lost.

The Seebohm Report (1968) envisaged social services departments having a key preventative role in relation to deprivation, including a commitment to community development. In the 1970s and 1980s some departments were organised along the lines of generic social work and 'patch' teams so as to facilitate getting to know and understand the needs and strengths of the local area. Community social work epitomised such developments, although repeated child abuse tragedies increasingly led to a retreat towards specialism. As we saw in Chapter 4, it was a move away from a concern with child welfare and prevention to one preoccupied with child abuse. Another factor was that in the later Thatcher years, prevention was not a priority simply because it could not be easily measured quantitatively. In the 1990s there was concern about the disproportionate deployment of resources on child protection investigations, most of which came to nothing. Again, as we saw in Chapter 4, *Messages from research* (DH, 1995) recognised this, as did New Labour's standardised initial and core assessment framework. Both were attempts to redress the balance towards prevention, family support and children in need, notwithstanding the increased bureaucracy placed on practitioners by the assessment changes. However, as we will see, preventative social work with children and families remains a neglected area.

New Labour: new prevention?

To the extent that New Labour exhibited a more firm commitment to preventative strategies there are four areas I want to comment on – Sure Start, the Children's Fund, Connexions and Parenting Initiatives, including family support. Importantly, social work's involvement in these developments was often limited.

Sure Start was New Labour's flagship policy to provide support to the most deprived young children and their families. The idea behind it was that providing a stimulating first few years can have an impact on a child's whole life, reducing crime and mental illness in adolescence and adulthood (DfEE, 2001). It initially operated in the most deprived areas, although became more universally available following the growth of children's centres under the Children Act 2004. Childcare facilities were provided, together with a range of other services for parents, such as advice about education and employment. Most of the staff and users were women, although this gender imbalance was addressed by offering schemes to fathers. However, a key criticism of Sure Start was that services were not meeting the needs of the most disadvantaged families (NAO, 2006), despite the appointment of outreach workers to promote the services on offer.

The Children's Fund was established in 2001 and made government money available to local collaborative services aimed at meeting the needs of children aged 5-13. This included addressing the risks of social exclusion and enabling such children to develop as healthy, responsible and engaged citizens (Morris et al, 2009). The schemes focused on the most deprived areas and/or identified problem groups such as young people at risk of anti-social behaviour. However, the various support, outreach and other staff involved were often engaged in the surveillance and control of the young people concerned rather than the meeting of needs as identified by them.

Connexions was established to assist young people aged 14-19 in the transition from school to work, and incorporated the functions of the previous careers service. Personal advisers were supposed to offer advice and support to this age group, although in practice services were and are targeted at NEET young people, those not in education, employment or training. Most of the functions of Connexions were absorbed into Children's Trusts from 2008 onwards and now face the brunt of austerity measures.

There was a plethora of Parenting Initiatives under New Labour, ranging from the national helpline, through to parenting classes and a national 'academy' to train workers (the National Academy for Parenting Practitioners) to support parents, and family support itself. The latter covers a range of interventions aimed at improving parenting in disadvantaged families. It often operates from family centres, although increasingly it deals with families in crisis, often where there are child protection issues, rather than wider preventative issues.

New Labour saw 'better parenting' as the solution for various social problems ranging from falling standards in schools to childhood obesity (Broadhurst, 2009). However, we come back to the point that the support offered focused intervention narrowly on individual lifestyle and behavioural change. It was about breaking the so-called 'cycle of deprivation' by tackling a perceived poverty of ambition or attainment rather than the multifaceted socioeconomic causes of disadvantage.

One example of New Labour's concern with parenting was the establishment of Family Intervention Projects (FIPs) run by Action for Children, which were seen as an answer to anti-social behaviour caused by 'neighbours from hell' and their troublesome children (Garrett, 2009b). The outreach services and residential components of the projects arose following the rediscovery of 'problem families', the opposite of 'hardworking families'. They were often perceived as from a time gone by, unable or unwilling to show a commitment to be self-activating and responsibilised neoliberal citizens. Much of the research into the projects was positive although there were a number of concerns. First, the research played down or ignored the fact that many of the families had characteristics of poverty and physical and mental ill health. Second, there was the question of the morality of, in effect, forcing vulnerable families into projects under the threat of eviction, losing benefits and having their children taken into care. Third, notions of control of, and intrusion into, the lives of the families, resulting in the infantilisation of the adults, was apparent. Finally, one could argue the residential component of the projects was a form of pre-emptive or preventative detention (Garrett, 2009b). They are perhaps an example of neoliberal punitiveness in relation to people facing problems and difficulties, another being residential provision for teenage parents.

Many of the concerns in relation to FIPs relate to the various parenting initiatives as a whole. This includes the focus being on those considered to be 'inadequate' parents with the threat of compulsion if they did not cooperate. Another relates to the labelling of such families that was likely to achieve the opposite of the desired objective.

I have already referred to the lack of social work involvement in most of New Labour's preventative initiatives, which is an unfortunate comment on their attitude to the profession. But it is worth noting that social work values of empathy, being non-judgemental, working at the user's pace and so on could have actually led to more success for the projects. A particular example is in engaging 'hard-to-reach' families. It is of little use an outreach worker turning up at a family's house with a Sure Start leaflet, staying a few minutes before leaving and never to be seen again. Some families, often because of past experiences, distrust authority figures, and need to get to know and trust whom they are dealing with. This involves relationship building and takes time. It is what social work is or should be about, and as such, social work should have been given a far more important role in New Labour's 'new prevention' strategy.

In delivering preventative support to families, there is ample evidence about what parents want (see, for example, Ghate and Hazel, 2002; Quinton, 2004). For instance, parents need more information about parenting and child rearing and what services are available. Second, they need to feel they are in control by being listened to and respected; after all, they are experts in their own lives. Third, parents want practical services to meet their own self-defined needs, not those decided by others. Finally, they continue to emphasise the importance of formal support from the statutory sector, despite what advocates of the 'Big Society' might argue. In particular, high-need families, those living in the poorest environments, are positive in their comments about this sector, perhaps because they are least able to engage in the reciprocal give and take of informal support relationships.

I must also mention the concept 'negative support' (Ghate and Hazel, 2002, p 257). This refers to the fact that support is not always seen in a positive light, with a fine dividing line between help and interference, including losing control of one's life and even one's children. Confidentiality and control often loom large in parents' willingness to accept the formal support provided by agencies. Perhaps this is no wonder given that much current social work practice concentrates on information sharing and partnership working, as well as 'telling parents what to do' or face the consequences.

Much of New Labour's preventative ethos was, therefore, at odds with what families wanted. This is because the focus was largely concerned with the responsibilisation and remoralisation (and adulteration in relation to young offenders; see Chapter 6) of the poor (Broadhurst et al, 2009). New Labour went further than previous Conservative governments in structuring welfare interventions through concerns with the responsibilities of individuals and moral standards. Great store was set on transferring responsibilities from the state to children, young people and families, requiring such individuals to avail themselves of the opportunities available in order to secure their own well-being. This caused difficulties because it legitimated a more coercive approach to welfare, as well as detracting from the structural antecedents of disadvantage and need (Deacon, 2002).

Linked to responsibilisation is the concept of remoralisation, the belief that most economic and social problems are a consequence of a decline in moral standards. Such ideas have been expressed in relation to illegitimacy, single parenthood, teenage pregnancy and welfare dependency (although conversely, of course, it is all well and good to be dependent on the market). In order to address these issues, the argument is that remoralisation is needed, particularly because of the supposed 'parenting deficit' and the need to improve parenting.

Remoralisation comes together with responsibilisation in relation to issues that affect the children of economically poor parents, as the concepts are increasingly used to frame access to a range of universal and selective welfare benefits and services, including, for instance, education, social housing and social security. In relation to safeguarding, the concern with the well-being of children becomes contingent on the behaviour and actions of children themselves or that of their parents; again an example of this are the FIPs. In addition, one does not often hear about concerns for the well-being of young offenders (see Chapter 6) or the children of asylum seekers (see Chapter 7).

Coalition government: same prevention?

The Coalition government emphasises seeing children and young people as future workers, consumers and law-abiding citizens, rather than having a broader concept of what well-being entails. Such a view includes the continued focus on early intervention in an effort to prevent the social ills of tomorrow. Recall the continued importance given to dealing with 'problem families', including the need for them to change their behaviour and lifestyles so that they can engage in the employment 'opportunities' on offer.

Taking one example, following the riots of August 2011 in London, Manchester and other cities in England, David Cameron announced plans to transform the lives of England's 120,000 most troubled families by 2015. The campaign initially hinged on the idea of 'family champions' helping families back to work, although this changed to 'trouble shooters' working with such families (BBC, 2011b), a mix of volunteers and professionals employed by local authorities. The target was a broader range of families than FIPs, although it began working alongside such FIPs in Hull, Westminster and Blackpool, which were among the first authorities to pilot the government's community budget arrangements for families with complex needs. These budgets do not provide areas with extra cash, but give councils new freedoms to pool budgets to coordinate joined-up services for families.

A key criticism, however, is that the most troubled families are those where the parents have mental health, alcohol and drug problems, as well as learning needs and chaotic lifestyles in general. These families have serious difficulties and it is hard to see work in itself as the solution to their problems. Surely if the Coalition government was serious about wanting long-term change to such individual lives, it would ensure that, for example, there was properly funded mental health, domestic violence/abuse, drug/alcohol services as well as help and support for those with learning needs. Even if one accepts that there are 'opportunities' in terms of employment and training, how, for example, are young people going to access these given that Connexions and careers services in general are being dismantled as the Coalition's public expenditure cuts bite home?

CAFs: the demise of preventative social work?

Turning more specifically to social work in relation to children 'in need' and preventative practice, we have already seen that it has been severely curtailed as, despite the wider children safeguarding agenda, the preoccupation with child protection continues and appears to have been bolstered by the introduction of the Common Assessment Framework (CAF).

CAFs aim to ensure that teachers, health visitors, children's centre staff and others use the framework to improve multidisciplinary working and provide preventative help to children with 'additional needs' and their parents. A key problem, however, is that the assessment aspect of the tool predominates (much as is the case with the assessments that social workers have to do) rather than the provision of any additional services. Many teachers and health visitors, for example, see it simply as an administrative/bureaucratic burden to be avoided at all costs. To be blunt, when such professionals contact a social worker about a child and their family, they do not want to be told to 'fill in a CAF form'. Two examples spring to mind.

On one occasion a teacher was concerned about Jason, a 12-year-old pupil with irregular school attendance whose mother had alcohol and mental health issues. The teacher felt that social work help and support might be appropriate, but was told that a CAF was 'all that is needed'. As no other agencies were involved with Jason, the teacher felt that the school should not have to deal with all the social issues affecting their pupil.

On another occasion a health visitor was concerned about a mother and her three young children. Her partner had left suddenly, and she was eight months pregnant and had no support from friends and relatives because she was new to the area. The health visitor thought that respite foster care might be needed when she went in to hospital to give birth. Again she was told to 'do a CAF', her retort being that the professionals involved were already working together and a CAF would be superfluous.

In both cases a social worker faced with such queries has two options: either to simply accept the managerial decision or, more critically, to sympathetically listen to the referrer and perhaps suggest that they take up the issue with their senior colleagues and consider putting in a complaint on behalf of the family they were dealing with. Of course, they could also encourage the family to complain in their own right. Essentially I am arguing for social workers to be wary about their role in encouraging the CAF process, because there is a real danger of hastening the demise of a social work identity. It is worth re-emphasising that CAFs are often about what traditional, preventative social work was and is about, and a time when actual services were provided (Rogowski, 2010b, 2011b, 2011c).

There are further problems with CAFs (see Pithouse and Broadhurst, 2009). First, as alluded to, they can be seen as a low cost technical fix to deliver early intervention without additional funding to the agencies expected to deal with the increased demand. Second, there is a risk that children in need will be filtered out as children with 'additional needs', thereby becoming the subject for a CAF, so that social work is devoted to child protection. Third, at the other end of the spectrum, CAFs can have a net-widening effect with children and families coming to official notice and listed on a database when a more informal, low key response was all that was needed. And fourth, CAFs do nothing to challenge the broader structural inequalities that plague poor families.

Social work with children in need: preventative possibilities

So, given that children in need might be reclassified as CAF cases, that is, those children with 'additional needs' not requiring social work involvement, what scope is there for working more preventatively? Given the continued focus on child protection, the short answer is that the prospects are rather bleak. This is because of the pressure of having to close cases as quickly as possible if there are no child protection concerns. If there are some identified areas where 'additional' help and support is required, more often than not the CAF system is the preferred managerial route. For the critical practitioner some scope remains by keeping the case open pending the transfer to a CAF via a 'child in need' plan. During this, usually brief, period, there might be some opportunity for some critical practice which might entail advocating in terms of appropriate help from children's centres, and housing and welfare benefits issues.

Case study 5.1: Preventative social work

Anna and her partner Natasha are in their early twenties and originate from Latvia, having come to the UK in their teenage years 'for a better life'. Anna was divorced after an abusive marriage and has a three-year-old daughter, Lucy. Both Anna and Natasha had been heroin users but are now on a methadone programme and cooperating with the local drugs team. The family have just moved into in a sparsely furnished housing association flat. Lucy is a happy, healthy little girl who appeared to be thriving.

The drugs worker referred Lucy to social workers because neither Anna nor Natasha had mentioned that they had a daughter. During a home visit the drugs worker was surprised to see Lucy. Other concerns related to their financial situation, the lack of furniture and the need for a nursery place for Lucy.

Issues to consider:

1   One approach would be to carry out a quick initial assessment noting that the care of Lucy was 'good enough' (Anna had not told the drugs worker about her daughter as she was afraid that social workers would remove her because of the drug use) and 'signpost' the family to Citizens' Advice, a local voluntary agency and children's centre regarding benefits, furniture and nursery issues respectively. The case would then be quickly closed.

2   A more critical proactive/preventative approach would build on the above, especially as far as benefits, furniture and nursery issues were concerned. This would entail the case being kept open even though, at the behest of managers, the social worker would have to write a 'child in need' plan with a view to 'cascading' the case to a CAF as speedily as possible. Meanwhile, Anna and Natasha would be reassured about the social work role, contact would be made with the job centre and children's centre, and, if necessary, Anna and Natasha would be accompanied by the social worker to meetings and interviews. Depending on progress made with the job centre, a charity could also be contacted as a last resort, not forgetting that Section 17 money could be accessed. The emphasis would be on empowerment and advocacy in this process, with a view to ensuring that the family were receiving their full entitlements. The CAF process would be fully explained, including that it was not always a mere monitoring exercise. Finally, there may be some scope for discussing and raising the plight of Eastern European immigrants and the fact that they are often scapegoated for being the cause of unemployment and other social problems in the UK, without acknowledging the impact of neoliberalisation.

Children and young people with mental health issues

Statistics indicate that a significant number of children and young people suffer with mental health issues (Maughan et al, 2004; UNICEF, 2007; Bradshaw, 2011). Some studies indicate that around 1 in 10 children suffer from a diagnosable mental health *issue*, the latter being a generic term. Mental health *problems* refer to common difficulties of brief duration not requiring formal intervention, while *disorders* refer to abnormalities of behaviour, emotion or social relationships that are more prolonged and require intervention. Mental *illness* is a clinically recognised set of symptoms or behaviour that causes distress and interferes with personal functions (see Walker, 2011, p 49). Within these categorisations, there are a broad range of labels that can be applied: behavioural and conduct disorders such as attention deficit hyperactivity disorder (ADHD); attachment disorders; emotional disorders such as depression, self-harming, anxiety and eating disorders; psychosis such as schizophrenia; psychopathy, usually to do with dangerous personality disorders; and autism spectrum disorders such as Asperger's syndrome. A key question is whether these increases are real, or whether they merely reflect modern social constructions around childhood, adolescence and 'normality'. Then there is the contradiction that, despite the current financial and economic crisis, we live in an affluent period with greater opportunities, but children seem less happy than in the aftermath of the Second World War (Layard, 2005).

What are the characteristics of those children who are more likely to be diagnosed as having a mental disorder? Findings from the first nationally representative survey of the mental health of children and adolescents (Meltzer et al, 2000) indicate that mental disorders are more prevalent in boys than girls. Thus, in 5- to 10-year-olds, 10 per cent of boys and 6 per cent of girls were diagnosed with a disorder, while in 11- to 15-year-olds, the figure was 13 per cent of boys and 10 per cent of girls. Such disorders are more likely in children with lone parents and reconstituted families, and those who had parents that were poor, unemployed, in social housing and without educational qualifications. Disorders were also linked to irregular school attendance, special educational needs, having a parent with a mental health issue and family discord. In short, the survey painted 'a picture of children with disrupted lives in families with a multitude of personal and structural problems' (Sayer, 2008, p 188). No doubt a similar statistical profile could be applied to young people identified as offenders or who become looked-after. Perhaps the same young people go through different systems depending on who initially identifies them as a problem. As we will see, the reference to multiple personal and structural problems is something that a critical social work practice with children who have mental health issues has to continually bear in mind.

Children and mental health issues: a social construction?

When considering mental health issues among the young, a number of points need to be borne in mind. First, there have been changes in the way deviant behaviour is defined. Over the postwar period there has been a range of new diagnoses, for example, ADHD, and while such behaviour existed 60 years ago, it was not medically labelled as such, with sufferers instead seen as 'odd', 'different' or 'naughty'. Related to this is the 'up and coming' diagnosis of oppositional defiance disorder (ODD), with some of the 'symptoms' of this condition being a child or young person not doing as they are told, arguing, having temper tantrums, sulking and only reluctantly accepting punishments/sanctions (Pruit, 2000). The obvious retort is that such 'symptoms' are precisely what normal childhood and adolescent behaviour is all about. There is also evidence that children as young as five are being prescribed anti-psychotic drugs for mental health issues, with all the debilitating side effects this can lead to (Channel 4, 2011).

A second factor to consider is that professional and public awareness of the disorders has increased, and so have the services offered, notably with the introduction of CAMHS. This has meant that more young people have been drawn into the 'psychiatric' net, as they are presented for diagnosis and treatment.

A third factor is that in the current more authoritarian, neoliberal state, there is an increased emphasis on compliance and conformity (Wacquant, 2009). This means that there is less tolerance of any form of deviant behaviour and consequently more willingness to use authoritarian methods to deal with it. Such arguments usually centre on the move from a 'social' to a 'penal' state as a result of welfare retrenchment, but these arguments can equally be applied to other areas of social control, in our case, those young people who exhibit 'different' behaviour.

There are a couple of other issues to consider. First, one has to note the relationship between 'race'/ethnicity of young people and mental health issues. There is evidence that African-Caribbean young people are far more likely to be defined as experiencing serious mental health difficulties, such as schizophrenia, than other ethnic groups (Tolmac and Hodes, 2004; Walker, 2004). This is probably because of poorer levels of social support and higher levels of exposure to stressful situations. Other possible explanations include black young people being less likely to seek early help as a result of distrust of a mental health system which is seen as white-dominated, or mistrust of the mental health system because of institutional racism arising from white staff not fully understanding that some behaviours could be attributed to cultural differences rather than disturbance.

The second issue is that looked-after children in England seem to be over-represented in those diagnosed with mental health problems, with 37 per cent having a clinical conduct disorder compared to 5 per cent nationally (Sayer, 2008). More worryingly, 42 per cent of looked-after 5- to 10-year-old children are diagnosed with mental illness compared with 8 per cent nationally. Child mental health issues may have contributed to family breakdown and hence having to be accommodated, but equally, aspects of family functioning can give rise to the mental health difficulties of the child.

Children and mental health issues: some contributory factors

To the extent that there might be a genuine increase in childhood mental health issues, the increased pressure to compete and achieve, in education, for example, can lead to anxiety-linked disorders. Frequent school tests in England can and do lead to worry and anxiety for many children and young people. There are also many other aspects of modern childhood that promote, or even lead to, behaviour that can be labelled as mental illness.

First, there are the practicalities of many children's lives, an obvious concern being diet and the link with junk food and behaviour problems (this is taken up below in relation to ADHD). This can lead to being overweight and obesity which can promote bullying, in turn leading to feelings of unhappiness. Then there is the concern with lack of exercise of young people because of their sedentary lifestyle associated with excessive computer and technology use more generally. Exercise in itself, by releasing the hormone serotonin to the brain, can promote well-being, but sadly, we come back to many parents', usually unfounded, concern with 'stranger danger'. This can result in restrictions placed on children playing out with their friends, and is ironic given that rather than safeguarding their children by doing this, parents may actually be doing them harm.

A second area relates to relationships that young people currently have, relationships being the main way we feel valued and wanted. Parents are the obvious ones to provide emotional support to their children, but they often have to work long hours, and as a result can be too tired and stressed to spend meaningful time with them. This is an example of how the neoliberal world works against the formation and maintenance of long-term trusting relationships between parents and children. Grandparents might be a countervailing possibility, but increasingly they do not live nearby and are not in a position to provide this. Teachers used to provide some support, but are usually no longer in a position to establish a personal relationship with individual children. This is because of the pressures arising from the increased bureaucracy and performance targets of their job (a comment that equally applies to social workers, of course). Peer relationships have always been important to the young, but if this is all they have, it is not surprising that they can be influenced by 'a bad crowd' and all the negative effects such as drug and alcohol misuse and, in some circumstances, resulting mental health issues.

Third, there is the role of the media, and in turn, big business, in promoting what a successful child or young person is or should be. This can create stress for those unable or unwilling to conform, or who lack the resources to do so. For instance, eating disorders such as anorexia and bulimia can result from sufferers trying to live up to the media hype of slim being beautiful and being the only way to be. This can include having to wear expensive designer clothes and other fashion accessories, such pressures on young people amounting to commercial exploitation as well as leading to mental health issues such as anxiety and depression.

Linked to much of the foregoing is a UNICEF report indicating that UK children are trapped in a cycle of 'compulsive consumption' as parents shower them with gifts to make up for their long working hours (Nairn, 2011). Parents seem to be locked into a system of consumption because of 'brand bullying' that they find hard to resist. The researchers questioned hundreds of children in Britain, Spain and Sweden to discover what made them happy. Interestingly, compulsive consumption was almost completely absent in both Spain and Sweden. Children told researchers that their happiness relied on spending time with family and friends and having plenty to do outdoors, which is at odds with the world of consumption that afflicts Britain. The report goes on to blame British parents for using television and computer games as 'babysitters', which deprives them of the outdoors, exercise and fresh air. It is also worth noting that many of the issues raised here can be linked to the fact that Britain has been at the forefront of neoliberalisation.

Resilience

Resilience is an important theoretical concept that acknowledges the influence of both social and environmental factors and individual differences, and identifies what helps individuals cope and what increases the risk they will not (see, for example, Sayer, 2008; Walker, 2011). Secure early attachments improve resilience, while there is a correlation between poor mental health and other health issues, such as poor physical health and learning difficulties, as well as special educational needs. Parental factors such as those who themselves have mental health problems, or where the family are disrupted, detract from resilience. Perhaps most tellingly there is a link between socioeconomic disadvantage, poverty and deprivation, and poor childhood mental health.

ADHD: social construction and medication issues

One of the more controversial aspects of children's mental health relates to the contested diagnosis of ADHD and the resultant use of medication, notably Ritalin, to treat it. Many see it as being over-diagnosed and that medication is overused to control children's natural boisterous and sometimes 'naughty' behaviour (Walker, 2011). Its diagnosis has multiplied in recent years and there are concerns about the side effects of drug treatment. The use of drugs results from it being seen as a genetic condition needing medication to rectify imbalances in parts of the brain that control attention, impulses and concentration. However, others see such medication as a 'chemical cosh', and argue that ADHD is a convenient diagnosis to justify enforcing conformity in children.

Clearly there are some vested interests when it comes to the diagnosis of ADHD, including pharmaceutical companies who benefit financially, schools who have more settled pupils and parents who can avoid the blame of being accused of poor parenting because of their child's 'naughty' behaviour. However, perhaps a more appropriate view of the condition is to see it as a response to food additives in the modern diet, together with the pressures of living in the neoliberal world where notions of conformity and achievement are ever more prevalent. Regardless of the causes, there is the moral issue of whether it is right to medicate high numbers of children, especially if the condition is socially constructed rather than a biological condition. Those children who exhibit symptoms such as lack of concentration and hyperactivity might be better dealt with by having their diets changed, in particular avoiding sugary foods and food additives. Then again, cognitive behaviour therapy might be more appropriate in order to manage such behaviours.

CAMHS and social work

There is a long history of social work involvement in childhood mental health issues going back to the child guidance services in the 1920s. These were largely dominated by a psycho-analytical approach to individuals, although this neglected social and environmental factors. Such a situation continued after the formation of social services departments when child guidance clinics, later renamed child and family consultation services, were often seen as somewhat costly luxuries when compared with the 'real' social work taking place in the community or in child protection. Long waiting lists developed in the 1980s and 1990s, with only the most serious cases being dealt with, leading to the neglect of work aimed at dealing with emerging difficulties and stopping them becoming entrenched.

New Labour initially began by wanting to improve the provision of care and treatment for children and young people by building up locally based CAMHS

(DH, 1999). Thereafter, however, the emphasis was on interagency communication, shared data bases, collaborative working and Children's Trusts, and, most significantly, by 2006 there was a failure to increase capacity in CAMHS (Walker, 2011). New multidisciplinary primary mental health worker posts are currently being created to improve capacity, and these are proving attractive to some social workers, notwithstanding such developments can again contribute to the demise of the social work identity. In any case, as stated earlier in this chapter, during an age of austerity inflicted by the current Coalition government, it might be best not to be over-optimistic in terms of future service developments.

CAMHS have a four-tier framework for services. These range from tier 1 services provided by practitioners who are not mental health specialists such as school nurses, GPs, teachers, health visitors and social workers who provide advice with less severe problems, through to tier 4 services staffed by specialists for those with the most serious difficulties, often being provided in day and in-patient units. Despite this structure, or even because of it, perhaps the main weakness in the services is that they are neither completely specialist nor are they fully integrated into other children's services. Another concern is that notwithstanding the emphasis on collaboration and multidisciplinary working, in CAMHS it is the medical model of diagnosis and treatment that predominates, with child psychiatrists being the dominant voice. In the not too distant past it was not unheard of the social work role, along with that of other practitioners, as largely amounting to being the 'handmaiden' of the psychiatrist. These days some strongly argue that adopting a psycho-social model of social work in CAMHS settings can provide a professionally satisfying and effective antidote to care management or repetitive assessment work (Walker, 2011). Social work certainly has an important role in the current emphasis on well-being (Jordan, 2007), and such a holistic model helps get away from child mental health being a pathological labelling process or simply believing that the parents only require support to cope with their child's moods and behaviour, rather than helping the child themselves. The model does not have to be seen as narrow Freudianism, which it might have been in the past. Instead, the psycho-social approach concentrates on the present, attempts to help individuals achieve equilibrium between their inner emotional states and the pressures they face in the outside world, and uses the user's relationship with the social worker (Stepney and Ford, 2000). The importance of such a perspective is that it does not focus solely on the child but on the family and broader environment. Some argue that it can even be used in more community work/ community-oriented practice by improving parenting skills and preventing the emergence of mental health problems and improving the emotional well-being of children and young people (Walker, 2004). However, this fails to deal with criticisms relating to the model that include it being antipathetic to black and working-class users. It also fails to adequately address issues that relate to critical social work, namely, the wider structural factors that impinge on children and young people's mental health.

Case study 5.2:¹ A holistic approach to childhood mental health

The family – Mark (father), Norma (mother), daughter Shannon (15 years) and son Noel (4 years) – face a number of difficulties. Mark is unemployed and there are housing and financial problems. His relationship with Norma is volatile and features domestic violence/abuse. Shannon is often depressed and refuses to go to school, while Noel exhibits attachment difficulties such as always crying, being clingy, making constant demands and often shouting/tugging at his mother.

There are at least three possible approaches to this case:

1   A social worker completing an initial assessment indicating there are no child protection concerns after warnings are given about domestic abuse. Mark and Norma are told to see their health visitor about Noel and to contact their GP regarding Shannon's depression, but are warned about what could happen if she continued to miss school, including being fined or taken to court. More positively they might be told to see their local housing officer and contact the Department for Work and Pensions about housing and benefits respectably. After contacting the health visitor about completing a CAF, the case is quickly closed.

2   A social worker completing an initial assessment indicates that the family had never received consistent or coherent support, but a reactive service based on superficial risk assessments and anxieties generated by health and school staff. This time, a 'child in need' plan is drawn up using a systems approach to discuss the options with all the family members present. This sets the scene for ongoing work that might include individual work with some of the family members and/or combinations of them. There could also be more meaningful liaison with the other agencies referred to in (1) above but also CAMHS. The advantage of this approach is that it works in partnership with the family, seeks to avoid blame and scapegoating, while maximising opportunities for change.

3   A more overtly critical social work approach would build on (2). As well as working as far as possible on the problems and difficulties as defined by the family, this could involve using empowerment and advocacy strategies in terms of such as housing, benefits and other issues, if necessary accompanying Mark and Norma to agencies/organisations/community groups responsible for/dealing with their concerns. Contact with local councillors or the family's MP might be necessary. There might be a need to assist in arranging a school transfer for Shannon. Discussions could also take place about the injustices faced by many people and the fact that current societal arrangements could be far more just and equitable. Having hopefully ensured CAMHS involvement, the issues of concern and ways of dealing with them would be encouraged along the lines outlined.

As for CAMHS social workers more specifically, they should ensure that they are for more readily available for the children and young people being seen by frontline social workers. In so doing, and as indicated, they could well work with the family on the lines suggested in (3).

Conclusion

Despite the contrasting situations as far as overall policy and practice is concerned, social work with children in need and those with mental health issues both provide some opportunities for critical practice.

Preventative social work with children in need is certainly less evident than it was, with two factors needing to be emphasised. First, the preventative work that does take place generally occurs outside social work and, as we saw, focuses on the responsibilisation and remoralisation of children and families through parents who are increasingly expected, even coerced, to become involved in the various parenting initiatives and other targeted early intervention projects. Many of these initiatives and projects may have started out with 'welfarist' intentions, but all too easily this can lead to more punitive interventions, so it is vital that the dangers of untended consequences are always borne in mind. The second factor to emphasise relates to CAFs, the way that preventative work is increasingly provided. Social workers may become involved in this process but often only to the extent of filtering out children 'in need' so that they become children with 'additional needs'. As a result, it is largely in the, usually brief, period between being 'in need' prior to being redefined as having 'additional needs' that some scope for critical practice possibilities remain.

When it comes to children and young people with mental health issues, some persuasively argue that social work can no longer stay on the margins of such practice (Walker, 2011). Instead, the profession needs to take the opportunities available to actively engage with the CAMHS agenda, notwithstanding the challenges in current straitened financial times. As Walker (2011, p 220) notes, social welfare services are 'subjected to the gyrations of speculative global financial markets [which] invariably corrodes the quality and depth of services designed to reach children and families.' This means services are reduced to the minimum, focus on crisis intervention and are designed to conform with inflexible eligibility criteria that limits access. Even so, social work can make a positive contribution in understanding mental health issues, particularly if it stays true to its critical tradition. An important aspect of this is the part social construction plays in discussions of childhood, adolescence and notions of 'normality'. This, however, is not to deny that there is undoubtedly ever more anxiousness and insecurity arising from the current neoliberal world, which in turn affects children. It is not surprising that childhood mental health and well-being is an increasing concern. In working with such issues, an important point for critical social work is that while not ignoring the intra or inter-psychic processes, one has to be continually alert to the influence of wider socioeconomic factors affecting children and families.

Key points

Preventative social work with children in need is increasingly under threat, especially since the introduction of the Common Assessment Framework (CAF). Critical practitioners need to make imaginative use of the limited spaces that remain.

The current emphasis on early intervention needs to be examined critically, rather than embraced, so as to ensure anti-oppressive practice dominates and wherever possible focuses on issues as defined by children and families.

Critical social work has a key role in CAMHS, not least in ensuring that holistic responses take place, ones that act as a counter-balance to the current dominant medical/individualistic model. The latter can all too easily lead to the medicalisation of economic, social and political issues.

The happiness and well-being of children and young people in the UK is an increasing concern, and critical social work has a key role to play in addressing the issue.

Further reading

Pithouse, A. and Broadhurst, K. (2009) 'The Common Assessment Framework: Effective innovation for children and young people with "additional needs" or simply more technical hype?', in K. Broadhurst, C. Grover and J. Jamieson (eds) *Critical perspectives in safeguarding children*, Chichester: Wiley-Blackwell. A critical account of the introduction and progress of the Common Assessment Framework.

Sayer, T. (2008) *Critical practice in working with children*, Basingstoke: Palgrave Macmillan. An introductory text, with chapters on critical practice with children and young people in need and those with mental health issues.

UNICEF (United Nations Children's Fund) (2007) *Child poverty in perspective: An overview of child well-being in rich countries*, Report Card 7, Florence: UNICEF Innocenti Research Centre. Although perhaps children's mental health and emotional well-being is under-represented, this is a damning report on the well-being of children and young people in the UK.

Walker, S. (2011) *The social worker's guide to child and adolescent mental health*, London: Jessica Kingsley Publishers. A comprehensive guide to social work's involvement in child and adolescent mental health.

Note

[1] This is adapted from Walker (2011).

6

Young offenders and youth justice

> ... the Bulger case came to signify something more than an isolated tragic event. It set in motion fears about juvenile crime in particular and young people in general. Demons had invaded the innocents. (Muncie, 1999, p 7)

> Young offenders today are more likely to be criminalised and subject to a greater level of intervention than before the 1998 reforms. If dealt with pre-court their warning is more likely to be accompanied by an intervention. They are more likely to be prosecuted. If convicted they are less likely to receive a discharge or fine. If subject to a community sentence it is more likely to be onerous. And last but not least ... the number of children and young people sentenced to custody is 35% higher than a few years before the 1998 Act. (Morgan and Newburn, 2007, pp 1046-7)

Youth crime is never far away from the media headlines as politicians try to 'out tough' each other in their response to the problem. It seems that the politics of young offending fuels the rhetoric of governments and political parties as they compete to be in tune with the alleged punitiveness of the general public. With the demise of the social democratic consensus, and despite the social work-led progress of the 1980s, there has been an increasingly authoritarian response – to condemn more and understand less, as former Prime Minister John Major said in the 1990s. This has resulted in 'populist punitiveness' (Bottoms, 1995) or 'penal populism' (Pratt, 2007), which sees varying degrees of punishment and control as key for addressing the problem. The culmination was New Labour's flagship Crime and Disorder Act 1998 and thereafter increasing concern with anti-social behaviour and a 'Respect' agenda. The 'get tough' approach was initially carried out by Youth Offending Teams (YOTs), now the Youth Offending Service (YOS), in which the role of social work has been diminished. Such developments have parallelled the embracement of neoliberalism by both Conservative and Labour governments, now thriving under the current Coalition government. Although there has been a welcome decline in the use of custody since the beginning of 2009, it is premature to see this as evidence of a more tolerant attitude towards young offenders (Bateman, 2011); instead, it probably has more to do with curtailing public expenditure during the current financial and economic crisis. In fact, evidence of a continued hard line towards young people in conflict with the law was David Cameron's enthusiasm for the draconian punishments dealt out to young people following the riots in England during August 2011. Most obviously, this neglects the structural factors that deny a large number of young people a stake in society.

Over the last 30 years the response to juvenile delinquency, or young offending/ youth crime as it is now referred to, has changed from a concern with the welfare of the young person to one of punishment (see Gelsthorpe and Morris, 1994). This, in turn, has coincided with the processes of economic deregulation and welfare retrenchment that have been filled by neoliberal penality and the advance of punitiveness (Wacquant, 2009). This has involved the transmogrification from the 'social state' to the 'penal state', driven by an underpinning dialectical relationship with, the 'invisible hand' of deregulated labour markets conjoined with the 'iron fist' of a diversifying, expanding and increasingly intrusive penal apparatus. More specifically in relation to young offending, instead of a focus on the deprivation and disadvantage that leads to youth crime, such behaviour is now seen as a matter of opportunity and rational choice, with young people being responsible for their actions. Such a perspective sees punishment as a valid response to such criminal behaviour, both as an expression of society's disapproval and as an individual deterrent. But what do young offenders think of these changes, and what do they think the way forward should entail? This is what my research study attempted to answer (see below), which points to the need for a policy and practice that engages with the issues and concerns of young offenders as well as their parents and carers.

This chapter begins by outlining the move to punitiveness, one coinciding with the development of the 'exclusive society' (Young, 1999), and culminating in the Crime and Disorder Act 1998. This is followed by a wider discussion of New Labour and its approaches to youth justice, one that neglected the socioeconomic factors that lead to much youth crime, instead focusing on the offence itself. Despite the *Every Child Matters* reform agenda, it involved actuarialist and managerialist approaches, together with that of adulteration, and a concern with evidence-based practice and 'what works'. More positively, restorative justice maintains its relevance. I consider such developments prior to briefly referring to my research before summarising the 'findings', the latter pointing to the need for fundamental change to current social policy and social work practice if youth crime is to be seriously addressed. Such possible changes are discussed, particularly in relation to practice, along with ways forward involving reconnecting with the past and a fundamental policy of putting children first (Haines, 2009), something which, despite *Every Child Matters*, does not apply to young offenders.

The rise in penal populism

It must be initially emphasised that social work's success with young offenders in the 1980s (see Chapter 3) was based on professional knowledge about the effectiveness of different types of intervention, including the potential to have negative short and long-term consequences. However, this was ignored in the early 1990s as 'populist punitiveness', now more commonly referred to as 'penal populism', took hold. This refers to the current situation where politicians manipulate public concerns about law and order to justify more punitive legislation. Such legislation and policy changes can be traced back to the urban disturbances of 1991 in areas of Oxford, Cardiff and Tyneside that featured young men in large-scale violent confrontations with the police. This allowed long-standing concerns about young offenders to be distorted, exaggerated and presented in the media. There was talk of individuals terrorising communities and of the police and courts being powerless to deal with them, and eventually 'persistent young offenders' became the moral panic of the day (Hagell and Newburn, 1994).

As referred to at the outset of this chapter, the Bulger case, the murder of a two-year-old boy by two ten-year-olds, in February 1993, was also significant. Much of the media was concerned with how something must be wrong with society in general, and with youth crime and youth justice in particular. Simultaneously, the Conservative government was low in the opinion polls and the police and media were preoccupied with issues such as car crime in the form of 'ram raiders' and 'joy/grief riders', and with young people who breached bail, the so-called 'bail bandits'. The Conservatives hoped a tough law and order approach would help their electoral chances, with the Criminal Justice Act 1993 and Criminal Justice and Public Order Act 1994 introducing increasingly punitive sanctions. There were, for example, reductions in the levels of cautioning, together with increased maximum custodial sentences.

New Labour largely followed on the Conservative Party's coat tails. Although Tony Blair emphasised being tough on crime as well as its causes, it was being tough on crime, particularly youth crime, that dominated subsequent New Labour government policies. Essentially the 1990s saw both parties denying 'the social basis of youth crime [emphasising] punitive approaches in relation to young offenders' (Littlechild, 1997, p 73), importantly this being at odds with the UN and European Conventions on the Rights of the Child. New Labour's landslide general election victory in 1997 saw the punitive approach to young offending continuing. Cautioning was again criticised because young people were supposedly offending with impunity, and an interventionist approach was advocated to stop tomorrow's career criminals. Such ideas were quickly framed into legislation, which became the Crime and Disorder Act 1998. Among its key provisions were reprimands and final warnings replacing cautions, and children under the age of 10 could be made the subject of local curfews. Parents of convicted young people could also be made the subject of parenting orders which could include having to attend parenting classes. The renewed focus on custody continued, together with an array of other orders, for instance, referral orders, reparation orders, drug treatment and testing orders and action plan orders (Goldson, 1999, 2000). This 'get tough' approach to youth crime, now continued under the Coalition government, is carried out by YOS, and although initially comprising of teams of, for example, the police, probation, education, health and social workers, the emerging 'profession' of youth offending practitioner/

worker/officer has emerged. The emphasis is on swift administration of justice, punishment, confronting young offenders with their behaviour and reinforcing the responsibilities of parents. The overall effect of current youth justice policy and practice is correctional early intervention, deterrence and punishment (Pitts, 2000, 2001). Furthermore, young offenders, and young people in general, continue to be vilified; recall Blair's enthusiasm for focusing on anti-social behaviour and for the 'Respect' agenda. Despite Coalition attempts to rebrand anti-social behaviour orders, they are granted for 'sub-criminal activities' which have lower standards of proof than criminal cases and can, when breached, lead to custodial sentences (Squires, 2006, 2008). Such orders are unnecessarily criminalising many young people, with all the negative consequences this entails.

As indicated, New Labour's response to young offending coincided with the move from an inclusive to an exclusive society (Young, 1999). During the social democratic era the concern was to deal with deviant behaviour or 'otherness', in our case, young offending, by making the individuals concerned more like 'us' by means of reform, rehabilitation or 'cure'. This has changed with issues of moral blame and recrimination now dominating the political and public discourse, leading to policies that increasingly exclude young people by punitive and thereby exclusionary sanctions. The demonisation of young offenders and young people in general is evidenced by politicians' and the media's frequent references to 'hoodies', 'yobs' and a 'yob culture'. There is less concern with their needs or rights, but rather the focus is on their deeds and risks; young people who offend are increasingly not cast as vulnerable subjects of risks to their welfare but as dangerous or anti-social bearers of risks to the welfare of 'the community' (Goldson and Muncie, 2006).

Case study 6.1:[1] Young offenders: tackling the real issues

Andy is 15 years old and in a private remand centre a long way from his home. He has a short history of petty offences and resulting interventions. Many of his problems relate to difficulties at secondary school where he was bullied and this resulted in his truanting.

His first offence was criminal damage committed when he was 13 years old and he received a police reprimand. Shortly after he carried out a similar offence while truanting and was given a final warning and referred to YOS. He became involved in an offending behaviour programme but failed to complete it. He was then involved in anti-social behaviour of underage drinking and throwing stones at houses during the school holidays. He received a warning letter from the anti-social behaviour unit.

On returning to school Andy committed a shoplifting offence and was prosecuted and given a referral order by the youth court. During the youth offender panel he talked about his problems with school and bullying, and complained about the lack of youth facilities, also saying he lacked the fashionable clothing that many of his peers took for granted. The panel agreed a programme for Andy consisting of a letter of apology to the shop, parentally supervised after-school only visits to the shopping centre, 15 hours' community service and a requirement to attend school. However, he soon breached the programme and was angry about its punitive and restrictive elements.

Andy's truanting and offending slowly increased, the latter including shoplifting from a sports shop and being found in possession of a knife at school. He said he stole trainers so he could 'fit in' with his peers, and had the knife to protect himself after being threatened by other boys. He was suspended from school, and arrested for carrying an offensive weapon; he was prosecuted and remanded in custody as a result.

He was seen in custody by YOS bail support staff, but they assessed him as unsuitable for a bail support programme because of his previous non-compliance. They noted Andy was lonely and isolated in custody, was not receiving any visits and said he was being bullied and felt frightened. He had to be given special supervision by remand centre staff.

A critical social work approach could have prevented Andy's situation and involves a number of issues:

1   Andy would not have been referred to an offending behaviour programme without a more holistic evaluation of his behaviour.
2   The social worker would have advocated for the youth offender panel to have dealt with the school problems more effectively, as well as those relating to poverty, deprivation and social exclusion.
3   The social worker would have listened to Andy's story, acted constructively to improve his situation and focused more on the bullying issues at school, along with the poverty/deprivation/social exclusion issues at home and his local community.

The interventions that took place focused on Andy's offending and did not address the underlying issues. The youth justice system saw him first and foremost as a problem, an offender, responding accordingly with punitive sanctions. Consequently, Andy, an average 15-year-old, sits alone, sad and frightened, in custody awaiting his fate. The overall predicament experienced by young people such as Andy needs to be taken up with the managerial hierarchy.

New Labour, young offenders and youth justice

As well as confirming the move to penal populism, New Labour's period in office saw a paradigm shift in thinking about welfare and the welfare state. Rather than the 'old' Labour focus on equality, the emphasis was on social inclusion; arguably the Coalition government does not even do this. Three interrelated aspects can be discerned in this social exclusion agenda (Lister, 2000; see also Pierson, 2010). First, a rejection of the discourse of promoting equality per se for that of equality of opportunity and in turn an emphasis on education, training and paid work rather than redistribution. Second, there is the use of the language of social exclusion and inclusion rather than poverty, with the emphasis on paid work and education being the mechanisms for inclusion. Third, there is an emphasis on social obligations and responsibilities rather than rights, leading to the questioning of the so-called 'entitlement culture' in relation to welfare benefits, something that the Coalition government is particularly intent on continuing.

The Social Exclusion Unit was established in 1997, with a remit of better understanding the causes and consequences of, among other things, youth crime. One result was the publication of *Bridging the gap* (SEU, 1999). This report rightly referred to the difficulties faced by many young people including educational underachievement and disaffection, family disadvantage and poverty, but in effect, such difficulties were blamed on the young people themselves (Colley and Hodkinson, 2001). They were portrayed as deficient, delinquent, or a combination of the two, as were their dysfunctional families and communities. The deep-rooted, structural factors such as class, 'race' and gender that profoundly affect young people's life chances were ignored. The expectation was that young offenders, not their social and economic circumstances, must change. Under a right-wing Coalition government implementing savage public expenditure cuts, leading to reduced welfare benefits and increasing youth unemployment, the situation continues.

In pursuing its interventionist, supposedly 'nipping crime in the bud' approach, and its punitive youth justice policy, New Labour discredited the 'old' youth justice system as excusing young offenders' behaviour because of their social circumstances. It aimed to establish a discontinuity with the past by refusing to tolerate such behaviour and those, social workers in particular, who 'made excuses' for it (Home Office, 1997). Consequently, 'the heavy baggage of those who operated the "old" system did not need to be unpacked and examined, it was simply left behind' (Haines, 2009, p 296).

The Youth Justice Board was established in September 1998 and although the Coalition government initially intended to abolish it, they did a U-turn and it was reprieved in November 2011. Much like New Labour, the reason can be seen as needing to ensure that the YOS continued to operate as the government wanted. In any case, it has, and continues to adopt, an actuarialist and managerialist approach, involving the setting of objectives, the development of administrative/ professional tools and performance measurement, all imposed on essentially local criminal justice agencies in an ongoing, ever-changing manner. Another notion to consider is adulteration, the ways in which over recent years children have been increasingly treated in a manner similar to that of adults (Muncie, 2008). As alluded to in Chapter 3, such changes can be contrasted with the *Every Child Matters* agenda that aimed to support and promote the quality of children and families' lives (DES, 2004), all of which was incorporated into the Children Act 2004. Laudable aims they well might have been, but when it comes to young offenders, questions are raised about protecting or safeguarding children from, and within, an ever tougher, more punitive, youth justice system (Jamieson, 2009). At any rate, the *Every Child Matters* reforms, along with wider youth justice changes, which also included an emphasis on evidence-based practice and on 'what works', at best only tenuously made a positive impact on young people's lives, whether they had committed an offence or not.

Actuarialism and managerialism

The presence and representation of youth crime are typically characterised by public fears about threat and danger, and there has been a long-standing concern with the methods used to deal with the problem (R. Smith, 2006). Recent developments in policy and practice suggest that there has been a significant shift in the ways these concerns are conceptualised, leading to the actuarialist approach. This is an approach to crime control and its management that disregards the possible causes of, and the meaning or motives behind, offending, replacing these with an emphasis on minimising *risk* and eliminating threats to social order. It is derived from broader social, political and ideological movements associated with 'modernisation' and the 'risk society' (Beck, 1992; see Chapter 4 in relation to risk and child protection). The change is from a positive concern with trying to improve things in relation to social problems, to a peculiarly negative concern with merely stopping things getting worse. Alongside the notion of risk there are two other factors to note: first, there is the attempt to perfect *scientific* means of quantifying the potential for the commission of offences; and second, there is the application of *managerial* techniques to control the threat to the community (Hudson, 2003). In pursuing this process, objectives of reform and rehabilitation become subsumed under mechanical functions such as the measurement and classification of risk and the efficient deployment of resources to minimise the threat of harm. A result is that information sharing and the 'flagging up' of early concerns about children's well-being and/or risk factors have become central to government strategy and policy formation (DES, 2004).

Young offending is therefore reframed, by intervention being based on a calculative approach to assessing future risks and taking action to minimise this (Smith, 2008). What were previously prioritised as welfare needs are only seen as of interest in terms of the possibility of future offending.

Such an approach to youth crime, along with anti-social behaviour, can be seen in aspects of New Labour's approach to preventing offending. This was based on assumptions about the possibility of quantifying and targeting 'risk' factors. For instance, dispersal orders, whereby the police have the power to disperse two or more young people from supposed anti-social behaviour areas, are based on risk estimates and predictions of future behaviour, and do not require substantive evidence of wrong doing.

Another example of this actuarial and managerial approach is indicated in the ASSET and ONSET tools. The former highlights the use of formalised and routinised instruments of assessment, used for decision making for all young people identified as offenders, at whatever stage they are in the youth justice system. The ONSET tool was subsequently developed for the pre-offending stage. Such tools aim to identify those at risk of offending and the subsequent need for risk control should they do so (Hudson, 2003).

There are at least two problems with these approaches. First, actuarialism might achieve symbolic ends in that it creates a sense of reliability and certainty in assessing and intervening with troublesome young people. However, the sense of certainty is illusory in that the procedural and epistemological limitations have to be acknowledged, simply because the indicators of risk are based on subjective and contested judgements. Second, the tools emphasise the negative aspects of children and young people's lives at the expense of protective or more positive factors (Smith, 2007). Perhaps the best that can be said is that many of the 'new' prevention programmes resemble nothing more than well-established best practice in youth work. But at worst, individualised risk-oriented interventions have criminogenic tendencies in that young people in breach of them become liable to subsequent punitive, even custodial, sanctions.

There are also moral and political inadequacies with actuarial and managerial practices. It is surely not sufficient to follow a policy based on it is 'better to be safe than sorry', not least because there are serious children's rights and child welfare concerns. This is because the targeting of individuals and communities leads to an undue focus on young people from working–class and minority ethnic backgrounds. Equally, the preoccupation with 'risk' rather than 'need' is problematic, a key reason being that it can confirm young people's perceptions of themselves as 'offenders' and consolidate their deviant identities (Becker, 1963). Overall, a major concern is that actuarial approaches are based on speculative and unsupportable assumptions about risk, about how it can be measured and the feasibility of risk control (R. Smith, 2006).

Adulteration

The most obvious example of adulteration was the abolition of *doli incapax*, the presumption in England and Wales, that a child under 10 years old cannot be legally responsible for their actions. Others include the possibility of imprisoning children from the age of 12, and the application of the 'grave crime' provisions to children (Muncie, 2008). These latter provisions apply to certain serious offences, and enable the Crown Court to impose longer terms of detention up to a maximum that would be available for an adult. Adulteration can be linked to responsibilisation and remoralisation (see Chapter 5) because it is premised on young offenders, like adult offenders, being fully responsible for their actions.

Responsibilisation developed alongside a critique of state dependency that served to legitimate the withdrawal of the state from universal measures of welfare support including the contraction of conventional child welfare services. Instead, responsibilisation includes encouraging and forcing individuals to take full responsibility for their actions. In the case of youth crime, it is seen as a consequence of the individual deficits of children and their parents rather than being related to the social problems and inequalities that do actually underlie most young offending (Jamieson, 2009).

As for remoralisation, the argument that in order to prevent the break-up of the moral fabric and cohesion of society, values incorporating the work ethic, 'normal' orderly/hardworking families and respect have to be emphasised (Muncie, 2006). This coincides with the expansion of surveillance, correctional and ultimately punitive interventions. What is neglected, however, is the fact that the state and the 'law-abiding' community also have responsibilities, including the responsibility to ensure social justice for all members of society.

Adulteration, responsibilisation and remoralisation brings us back to the current dominant view that child offending is a product of free will and volition, so all such offenders should be made fully accountable for their actions. This is notwithstanding the somewhat obvious fact that this view of the moral culpability of children is problematic because it divorces their behaviour from their material and emotional circumstances that are often severely deprived (Broadhurst et al, 2009). As suggested earlier, such notions are difficult to reconcile with the potentially more holistic and inclusionary aspects of *Every Child Matters*. Indeed, when governments pursue an authoritarian youth justice policy and practice of incarcerating children, and yet have a supposed commitment to safeguarding and promoting the well-being of children, such claims sound somewhat hollow. This is particularly so given that governments also 'comprehensively recognise' the personal and financial costs of incarcerating children (Goldson, 2006, p 149).

Evidence-based practice?

New Labour's agenda of 'modernisation' for public services, and the welfare state in particular, included an emphasis on policy and practice being based on evidence of 'what works'. This is nowhere more apparent than in their approach to youth justice and young offenders, notwithstanding the difficulties associated with such a proposition (D. Smith, 2006).

The problem is that the policy and practice formation processes are not as rational as some might have us believe: resource constraints, political ideology and considerations of electoral popularity all enter the decision-making process. As stated earlier, a prime example relates to the fact that evidence pertaining to the knowledge, skills and experience of social workers in youth justice prior to the 1998 reforms was totally ignored. The successes relating to the diversion of young people from the criminal justice system and from custody (Blagg and Smith, 1989) were abandoned, even though it is difficult to see that it was based on any kind of evidence. Instead, early intervention was the new goal, meaning that 'net widening' was actually promoted rather than something to be avoided (Cohen, 1985). New Labour's 'no more excuses' agenda and 1998 reforms were, therefore, more about the ideological need to be seen to be tough on crime, the preoccupation being on surveillance and control, which led to excessive intervention in the lives of young people and their families (Smith, 2001). On the face of it, it seems impossible to see this major change as based on a rational, empirical, evidence-based model. At best, to the extent that New Labour used evidence to shape policy, it was, like the Coalition government, very selective (Goldson, 2000).

Even if policy makers want to use evidence from research, in a field like youth justice they need to be reminded that they should wary of expecting universal truths. Instead, 'what they ought to expect are empirically informed ideas about what looks promising, what, if properly implemented (and what "properly" means should be specified as far as possible), will work, for what people and what purposes, and in what contexts' (D. Smith, 2006, p 88).

Restorative justice

Mention needs to be made of restorative justice because it stresses the virtues of a direct encounter between victim and offender as opposed to the abstract and alienating procedures of formal judicial systems (Smith, 1995; Masters and Smith, 1998). In the UK it originated in the diversionary and alternative to incarceration schemes of the 1980s including mediation and reparation, which were social work-led processes. Admittedly, nowadays, the police often play a more dominant role, but the emphasis needs to remain on problem solving, promoting empathy, expressing care, and reintegration of the offender rather than exclusion. It has much in common with the feminist-based ethics of care (see Chapter 9), the concern being with young offenders coming to understand the harm done by their behaviour and its consequences for themselves and others, this in turn an important element in their social and moral development. Put another way, it is about a holistic and reintegrative practice rather than one that excludes, and it is one that attempts to salvage more meaningful and humane practices from a youth justice system based on punishment and retribution (Whyte, 2009).

Young offenders' views and experiences

Having looked at New Labour and its approach to youth justice (and again, it must be emphasised that this is largely being continued by the Coalition government), what do young offenders think of the interventionist and punitive approach to young offending? My study (see, for example, Rogowski, 2000/01, 2006) aimed to compare young people's views and experiences of offending and the youth justice system with some of the policy and practice issues outlined above. It was a qualitative study adopting a cross-paradigm approach (Firestone, 1990), drawing on ethnographic (Hammersley and Atkinson, 1995), feminist (for example, Reinharz, 1992) and critical perspectives (Harvey, 1990). I was interested in the meaning the young people ascribed to events, moving the experiences of women nearer to centre stage, and relating observable social phenomena to the wider social context. I completed a series of semi-structured interviews with 20, mainly 'heavy end', property offenders, aged 14-17, drawn from two local authorities in North West

England. They comprised 13 young men and 7 young women including one each of black (African-Caribbean), South Asian (Bangladeshi) and mixed race (white/African-Caribbean) young men and one mixed race (white/African-Caribbean) young woman. I also conducted three focus group discussions with some of these young people and their friends. In addition to focusing on their experiences of offending and the youth justice system, other key aspects of their lives were covered, such as family/carers, recreation, school and employment/training.

In brief, the young people saw offending as related to boredom and material gain, and the move from welfare/treatment to punitiveness was almost unanimously condemned. In particular the increased emphasis on custody and early intervention was seen as an ineffective, even a counter-productive, way of dealing with the issue. They referred to the need for schools to be made more interesting and relevant, for recreational facilities to be improved, and for genuine and meaningful employment and training opportunities to be made available. In addition, they felt parents and carers needed more help, support and resources (not simply to be told where they were at fault by having to attend parenting classes), adding that social workers were in a good position to provide this. Interestingly, they thought the changes advocated should be financed by progressive, redistributive taxation. I recall one young woman simply saying, "Just think of all these millionaires, they don't even bother about tax do they? They could pay more ... they've got the money to do it. I don't know why we don't take a bit more off 'em." Such comments clearly highlight concerns with inequality and social justice, and despite an element of critical pessimism, many of the young people thought a more fair and just society would lead to less crime. Finally, rather than seeing the youth justice system as impartial, administering fairness and justice to all, the young people saw it as "focusing on people like us", those from deprived areas, and as sexist and racist in its operations.

Overall, the young people's views were certainly out of tune with New Labour's and the current Coalition government's thinking, and they have implications both in terms of radical/critical social policy and social work practice. Considerations of a radical/social policy are dealt with in the concluding chapter of this book; suffice to say here that it involves engaging with the age-old project of modernity and ensuring equality and social justice for all. It is to a radical/critical social work practice in relation to young offenders that I now turn.

Towards a radical/critical social work practice with young offenders

The influence of neoliberalism on social work has been well documented, both in this book and elsewhere (see, for example, Harris, 2003; Ferguson, 2008; Rogowski, 2010b, 2011a, 2011b). The emphasis is on completing bureaucracy speedily so as to meet targets that actually mean little or nothing to practitioners or, more importantly, those with whom they work. The influence of such managerialism in work with young offenders is particularly apparent in the ASSET and ONSET forms which, although aimed at assisting decision making in practice, are often management tools to improve information gathering (Smith, 2007; Whyte. 2009). Echoing the introduction to this book, such prescriptive form-filling within a managerial ethos has led to the 'zombification of youth justice' (Pitts, 2001).

Then again, as noted, the emergence of YOS practitioners has meant the influence of social work has diminished, along with the emphasis on the young person's wider social and economic environment. In many youth justice texts (see, for example, Smith, 2007; Stephenson et al, 2007), social work is barely mentioned, indicating that whereas social work *was* pivotal to dealing with young offending, this is no longer the case. The obvious manifestation of this is services for young people in trouble being separated from mainstream children and families social work services (Goldson, 2007). However, although what remains of social work is tied to a system primarily concerned with assessing and managing risk, and controlling the behaviour of young people who represent a threat to the community (Smith, 2008), some spaces can still be found for radical/critical practice.

Radical/critical practice may often have to amount to 'quiet challenges' and resistance to actuarial and managerial-oriented discourses and practice (White, 2009). For instance, one can mystify or conceal knowledge of users in order to acquire resources, amounting to the manipulation of knowledge and information on their behalf. Or again, one could delay or exaggerate paperwork or assessment plans so that managers are manipulated into taking a particular course of action. Ignoring, bending or reinterpreting rules and procedures also have a role to play. Despite such 'quiet challenges', the relevance of more overt radical/critical social work practice remains.

'Old' radical/critical practice of the 1980s might have involved, for instance, group and community-oriented strategies aimed at politicisation and consciousness raising in relation to injustices in society, particularly those pertaining to young offenders (Rogowski, 2003/04). Largely as a result of the 1998 reforms this might no longer be possible. However, politicisation and consciousness-raising strategies can still be used, albeit on an individual basis. Work with a young offender could focus on their motivation for offending rather than simply issues of control and surveillance. Mirroring the views of the young people I met, one could also stress issues of boredom and material gain being addressed by ensuring adequate, publically funded, recreational, educational and employment/training opportunities were available to all young people. Then again discussions could turn to the need for equality (in terms of opportunities *and* outcome) and social justice, and resulting redistributive taxation policies pending fundamental societal change, Utopian as it seems. In the meantime, problems and difficulties as defined by young offenders, and their parents/carers, have to be addressed and this could involve putting them in touch with groups and organisations that deal with their particular circumstances. Social workers' links with, and pressure on, the managerial hierarchy, along with councillors and MPs, for example, still retains its relevance.

There is also potential for engaging in radical/critical practice by working with colleagues who work in organisations and agencies that work alongside, but outside of, YOS. There are now a myriad of projects that focus on an array of issues that affect young offenders – drugs, crime prevention, homelessness, education, employment, community and neighbourhood regeneration and so on. Admittedly, current austerity measures will have a negative impact on such projects but some will probably emerge relatively unscathed. Arguably, practitioners, including social workers, working within such settings have more scope to use their initiative and hence engage in the type of radical/critical practice advocated here. In addition, even YOS social workers can be involved, perhaps at a distance, for example, in terms of suggesting methods and ways of working. This could include advocating the social action approach that draws on self-directed group work (see, for example, Mullender and Ward, 1991; Dearling and Skinner, 2002). It means talking and listening to young people on their own ground, which entails discussion of what the problems are, why they exist and how things can be changed. Such an approach leads to serious consideration about the real cause of social ills including youth crime, particularly injustice and inequality. At a practical level it might involve contacting the local council about the need for improved youth recreational facilities. Contact with local councillors and MPs might also be required. The social action approach goes hand-in-hand with more traditional social work that emphasises relationship-based work involving values of warmth, empathy and respect for people (Ruch et al, 2010).

Case study 6.2: Punitiveness or understanding for young offenders?

Jason is a 16-year-old of mixed race/dual heritage (white/African-Caribbean), and has experienced a difficult teenage period. Like many others, he found the transition to secondary school difficult and was soon truanting with friends. When at school he could be difficult and challenging for teachers, and when not there he started drinking alcohol, smoking cannabis and committing offences – shoplifting, criminal damage, burglary and carrying an offensive weapon (a penknife) being examples. Anti-social behaviour included 'hanging around' the local shopping precinct 'causing a nuisance', although he complained of being harassed and racially abused by the police.

His family and home life had been difficult for many years. He lived with his mother and five younger siblings, some of whom had different fathers. Home was a house on a run-down estate with few youth and other facilities. His mother was a single parent who could not work because of her childcare responsibilities and she was living on benefits. He rarely saw his father and whenever he did, his father 'promised the earth' but then would 'disappear' for months at a time. His mother did her best to keep 'keep him on the straight and narrow', but she had her own problems in terms of depression, financial and housing difficulties, and coping with the care of the younger children.

There are at least two possible approaches to Jason's predicament:

1   Accept the 'no more excuses agenda' and increasingly deal with Jason's offending in a 'no-nonsense', ever more punitive way by recommending increasingly draconian youth court orders. The ASSET forms, along with all the other actuarial and managerial tools and processes, would reflect this authoritarian stance by emphasising individual or parental culpability at each stage of Jason's and his mother's journey through the youth justice system.

2   Adopt a more holistic view of Jason and his situation, seeing his offending, family background and overall social and environmental situation in terms of wider structural factors, including those of class and 'race'. Importantly his complaints about harassment and racist abuse would be taken seriously. These considerations would be emphasised in the ASSET form and again in the other actuarial and managerial tools and processes. Such an emphasis is not to condone his behaviour but to try and explain and make sense of it, particularly from his and his mother's point of view. In addition, in discussions with them, politicisation and consciousness-raising strategies about the social and economic injustices in society and how they could be remedied could take place. Linking Jason and his mother with local youth/parent groups and having discussions with youth workers and others about, for example, the potentially empowering self-directed groupwork and social action approach, would be considered. For instance, and echoing earlier comments, the need for decent recreational and other facilities might be among issues that need to be addressed. Such strategies aim to get away from much of the current 'blame the victim(s)' approaches of most YOS work.

Putting children and young people first and reconnecting with the past

Critical social work with young offenders begins with what we know about young people, the social and economic conditions that shape their behaviour and the effectiveness of interventions (Haines, 2009). The actuarialist and managerialist present, therefore, has to be reconnected to the professionally based past. This has to go hand in hand with a principled youth justice that draws on developments in other jurisdictions in the UK, as well as those international treaties and conventions that provide the children's human rights framework. It all amounts to a progressive policy and practice based on *genuine* research evidence and practice experience (Goldson and Muncie, 2006), rather than successive governments' stress on so-called evidence-based policy.

While there has been 'a pernicious encroachment of increasing punitive responses to young people who offend across all UK jurisdictions' (Jamieson, 2009, p 202), this is not always the case. The Welsh Assembly has purposively decided to locate youth justice services under the portfolio of health and social services rather than crime and community safety in order to promote a child-centred ethos. In Northern Ireland, the Youth Justice Service's emphasis on preventing offending has prioritised a concern for the child's welfare (UK Children's Commissioners, 2008). But it is in Scotland that the most child-centred approach has developed. Following the 1964 Kilbrandon Report, the Social Work (Scotland) Act 1968 introduced the Children's Hearing System to provide a unified response to children who offend and those who need care and protection. It is premised on the 'best interests' of the child, seeking to offer holistic support and supervision that does not stigmatise children and young people (McAra, 2006). Indeed, Scotland's long-standing commitment to welfarism is in stark contrast to developments in England and Wales and many other Western jurisdictions.

International texts concerning the special treatment that should be given to children, including young offenders, have developed over the last 100 years. For instance, the 1924 Geneva Declaration of the Rights of the Child stated that particular attention should be extended to children. Then again, the 1985 UN Minimum Rules for the Administration for Juvenile Justice – the Beijing Rules – state that the fundamental aim of the juvenile justice system should be the promotion of the well-being of the juvenile. The 1989 UN Convention on the Rights of the Child reinforced this, with Article 2 providing for non-discrimination and Article 3 providing that the best interests of the child should be the primary consideration in all actions, courts and law. Such international instruments provide clear guidance in two crucial areas.

First, any reaction to young offending should always be in proportion to the circumstances of both the offender and the offence. This includes restrictions on personal liberty being limited to the possible minimum, and the well-being of the young person should be the guiding factor in their particular case. Second, in relation to custody, the placement of young offenders in custody should be the disposition of last resort and for the minimum necessary period.

It is hard to argue that the 1998 reforms are in keeping with such international exhortations. Although New Labour was in favour of notions of 'evidence-based policy' on the one hand, this was in tension with a 'consolidating politics of "toughness" on the other', fracturing and distorting 'the broader corpus of policy in relation to children and young people' (Goldson and Muncie, 2006, p 207). This is clearly evidenced by the inconsistency in the 'no more excuses' and *Every Child Matters* agendas, with this certainly *not* amounting to a principled youth justice, one that involves six key points (Goldson and Muncie, 2006).

In the first place, policy should deal with the social and economic conditions that lead to youth crime, not least poverty and inequality; it is surely undeniable that the latter are key to understanding the problems both experienced and perpetuated by many children and young people (Dorling, 2010; Wilkinson and Pickett, 2010). Second, and linked, the provision of holistic services to meet the needs and promote the well-being of all children and young people must be a priority, including curtailing the youth justice system and redirecting resources to 'children first' or 'in need' services. Third, children and young people should be diverted away from the youth justice system, the opposite of what is currently occurring. Diversion is consistent with the human rights framework and the more progressive international youth justice systems, but it is also an effective strategy in terms of crime prevention. Fourth, in the minority of cases where justice is needed, it should be child-appropriate rather than simply largely replicating the adult system. Fifth, interventions that are ineffective or violate international human rights obligations, especially incarceration, should be abolished. And sixth, youth crime and youth justice must be depoliticised with a more tolerant response to the phenomenon being required. Rather than demonising children and young people, politicians would be better off engaging in more sophisticated, measured and dignified responses.

In a similar vein is 'normalisation', whereby in thinking about work with young offenders one starts by thinking about linking the interventions for young people in trouble with the range of provisions or activities that exist for all young people (Haines, 2009). Such a normalised and inclusive practice is characterised by three elements. First, *justice*, not only in a formal legal sense, but in accordance with the principles of natural justice. Second, the *participation* of young people in the full range of social and educational provision for youth. And third, *engagement*, giving expression to the right of young people to make their own choices and decisions, and to be fully involved in all matters concerning them. It involves a critical practice based on the accumulated professional knowledge of the effectiveness of approaches and methods of working with young offenders, one that aims to protect and promote the best interests of the child. Sadly, all this might seem a far cry from the situation we now have.

Conclusion

As Cook (2006) points out, if society cannot guarantee the equal worth of all citizens, mutual and self-respect, and the meeting of everyone's basic needs, it cannot expect all citizens to have an equal stake in abiding by the law. It also cannot dispense justice fairly and augment confidence in the law; criminal and social justice is, therefore, inseparable. However, we live in a society in which young people do not have a sense of inclusion, of well-being and of social justice. It is a society that has become less tolerant and less just towards its youth. This is what critical social workers have to bear in mind in their work with young offenders, and importantly it involves a rejection of the popular punitiveness or penal populism of the present, instead working more constructively with young offenders. Smith (2007) offers a few pointers in this regard. For instance, a 'problem-solving' approach should be adopted. This can be linked to restorative justice, but also incorporates the principle that any problem associated with an offence should be addressed. Two other examples are voluntarism and minimum intervention, the former requiring the consent of the young person, for example, in making amends in relation to restorative justice, the latter referring to pursuing the least intrusive and coercive means of intervention achievable. Crucially such examples highlight 'giving hope' and 'having trust' in young people (Stephen, 2009).

Giving hope to young people means tackling the structural inequalities that lead to deprivation and disaffection. Even if we had a government seriously committed to addressing this, the current financial and economic crisis makes this much harder. Youth unemployment is a particular concern, and the Coalition government's regurgitation of youth training schemes of the past is surely not an adequate response. Other issues relate to education and the increased academic orientation rather than traditional skilled manual trades. It is not hard to see that if young people live in a society that does not value manual skills, while simultaneously eulogising academic qualifications, the outcome could lead to disenchantment with school, truancy and youth crime.

Young people also need to be listened to, which ensures that they are recognised and not merely demonised or 'written off'. This listening involves having trust in young people and must be extended to fostering a dialogue about their marginalisation, this helping to explain their involvement in offending. This has to go hand in hand with a wider dialogue with young people about the impact of society's often discriminatory discourse about, and actions on, them.

Justice for children and young people might be becoming more elusive in a neoliberal world intent on criminalising measures to control those who do not 'play by the rules'. Nevertheless, critical social work, despite its reduced role in the YOS, has a responsibility to confront such issues and ensure that the UK does not become an even bleaker place to be for a young person in conflict with the law.

Key points

The youth justice system has changed from a focus on the welfare of the young offender to one concerned with punitiveness and control.

Parallelling this move, there has been a reduction in the influence of social work, a prime reason why critical social work is needed, to ensure that wherever possible, youth justice aligns itself with emancipatory and social justice ideals.

When working with young offenders and their parents/carers, it is paramount that their concerns are seriously considered and, wherever possible, acted upon. Such an approach includes addressing issues of class, 'race' and gender, as well as other aspects of diversity.

Critical practice is based on the professional knowledge of effective approaches, placed in the context of international conventions on the treatment of young people. It means promoting and protecting the best interests of the child.

Further reading

Goldson, B. and Muncie, J. (eds) (2006) *Youth crime and justice: Critical issues*, London: Sage Publications. An authoritative overview of youth crime and youth justice, covering theory, policy and practice.

Muncie, J. (2009) *Youth and crime* (3rd edn), London: Sage Publications. This is the most comprehensive and accessible account of youth justice, covering criminological and sociological theory, as well as policy and practice.

Pickford, J. and Dugmore, P. (2012) *Youth justice and social work* (2nd edn), London: Learning Matters/Sage Publications. An introductory text that highlights the continuing, if reduced, role of social work in youth justice.

Smith, R. (2007 & forthcoming Aug 2013) *Youth justice: Ideas, policy and practice*, Cullompton: Willan. A critical account of the youth justice system, outlining some progressive practice possibilities.

Note
[1] This is adapted from Haines (2009).

7

Asylum-seeking and refugee children and families

'Rather than living over here in poverty, surely it would be better to go home.' (Comment by a social worker to a family with young children who had recently entered the UK from abroad)

Critical social workers do not want the type of neoliberal social work which is highlighted in the above quote. Instead, they endeavour to make a positive difference to the lives of the asylum-seeking and refugee children and families they work with. This is necessary simply because, as the Children's Society reports, many young asylum seekers are often left homeless and hungry because immigration control is prioritised over the best interests of children (Mahadevan, 2012).

Recent years have seen increasing media and political attention given to the issue of people seeking asylum in the UK, and social workers are faced with the challenge of providing services that are responsive to the needs of an ever more culturally plural service user group. This chapter is concerned with critical practice with children and families who are seeking refuge or who have refugee status in the UK because of major threats to their welfare, and possibly their lives, in their countries of origin (Hill and Hopkins, 2009).

At the outset, there are a few definitional points to make. When such children and families arrive they are classified as *asylum seekers*, people who have applied to be recognised formally as *refugees* in the UK. The majority of children come with a parent or responsible adult, although some come unaccompanied and have immediate care needs in addition to those in relation to asylum. If and when asylum seekers are granted leave to stay, they become 'refugees', although nowadays this is usually a label that they and others do not wish to emphasise. The terms 'asylum seeker' and 'refugee' need to be distinguished from the term *economic migrant*, the first two associated with protection and safeguarding issues, while economic migrants are associated with moving in order to work.

Another factor to consider is that children and young people who are seeking asylum or who are refugees and are apart from their families, can be separated for different reasons. Some are sent abroad by their parents in order to save their lives, while others are left behind in the UK when parents return home or resettle elsewhere. A particularly vulnerable sub-group of refugee children are those who have entered the country as a result of 'trafficking'; they are those who are in the UK against their wishes and possibly those of their parents too (Bokhari, 2008).[1]

Social workers face substantial practical and ethical challenges working with asylum-seeking and refugee children and families. The tension that exists between traditional anti-oppressive values and the role social workers increasingly play as gatekeepers to services is particularly evident (Hayes and Humphries, 2004a). The profession has always had a role in policing the boundaries of welfare, but under New Labour there was a decisive shift towards this increasingly narrow and negative practice, particularly in relation to immigration controls (Humphries, 2004). This can be contrasted with, for instance, the Kindertransport of children fleeing Nazi Europe before and during the Second World War, how these movements were welcomed and fostered, and what a contribution the children subsequently made to British society. Today, however, social work has increasingly had to emphasise its control functions rather than those of care, a prime example being the Nationality, Immigration and Asylum Act 2002 that committed social services to being inquisitors of immigration status and reporters to the Home Office. Immigration controls aim to restrict the number and 'types' of individuals entering the UK or becoming citizens, and even when in the country, children and families can often find themselves without 'recourse to public funds' with all the resulting hardship that this can cause. It is not surprising that such controls can bring practitioners into conflict with their more humanitarian impulses towards immigrant populations, ones that are more consistent with safeguarding children and young people (Hill and Hopkins, 2009). As we will see, it was only towards the end of the New Labour governments that there were some more positive developments, although the Coalition government is now broadly continuing with an anti-asylum seeking and immigration policy and practice.

This chapter looks at ways of dealing with the complex situations of people subject to immigration control, and seeks to develop critical social work interventions appropriate to the differing needs of asylum-seeking and refugee children and families. I begin by examining the historical and contextual impact of immigration control on welfare (Hayes, 2004; Hayes and Humphries, 2004a), including current legislation and policies for immigration, asylum and citizenship. This is followed by a discussion of social work with asylum-seeking and refugee children and families, including the dilemmas of care and control as well as safeguarding issues more generally; accompanied, unaccompanied and trafficked children, along with age assessments, private fostering and returning children to countries of origin, are all discussed.

The impact of immigration control on welfare

This section draws on the helpful work of Debra Hayes (2004) who makes the point that the geographical movement of people has been, and is, part of human history and experience, with controlling it only taking place relatively recently. As far as the UK is concerned, it is only over the last hundred years or so that this controlling element has increasingly come to the fore. For example, the Aliens Act 1905 was preoccupied with Jewish refugees fleeing pogroms in Eastern Europe, and the post-Second World War period featured concerns about, and attacks on, Commonwealth black immigration. Today the focus is on asylum seekers.

Although the current concern with asylum seekers has been taken up by Far Right political parties, New Labour and the Coalition government seem to be aware of the support to be gained by encouraging a popular nationalism based on fears of immigration. For instance, parts of the Nationality, Immigration and Asylum Act 2002 concerned the withdrawal of even subsistence level support for asylum seekers, together with the setting up of accommodation centres where health and education needs were also dealt with. However, it is surely questionable whether asylum seekers should be set apart from normal society and be denied the opportunity to engage and participate in communities while their claims are being processed. The 2002 Act is only one of a long line of increasingly restrictive immigration controls that have 'succeeded in completely separating and excluding those subject to control and have further strengthened the ideology which constructs that group as costly, dangerous and damaging to the national interest' (Hayes, 2004, p15).

In looking at the ideology underpinning the existence and delivery of welfare, those constructed as *outside* of nation have also been placed *outside* of welfare (Hayes, 2004). Those who are constructed *outside* is not just a question of blood or geography; rather it is a political question steeped in racism and Britain's imperialist past, and linked to the concern with improving 'the nation' and its stock (Cohen, 2001, 2002). Thus, for example, the Irish were outside of the Poor Law because they did not 'belong' to any parish. Subsequent welfare reforms aimed to improve the ability of the nation to compete with emerging rivals in global markets and global conflicts. The Liberal welfare reforms of 1906-14, for example, in relation to pensions and national insurance, contained residency and citizenship requirements. It is no coincidence that the first immigration controls also emerged in the form of the Aliens Act 1905.

Even the postwar welfare state, created in a period of hope and optimism, did not mean that black immigrants benefited from the golden age of welfare. They often had problems in accessing services to council housing, health, education and social security (see Hayes, 2004, pp 18-19). For example, the 1944 Education Act excluded education grants to those 'not ordinarily resident', and in 1967 differential fees were introduced for overseas students (Cohen, 2002). In the 1980s the practice of requesting passports by the Department of Health and Social Security fell mostly on to black claimants, and significantly this involved workers in the welfare state in the internal policing of immigration. Increasingly during this period separate state agencies were encouraged to play a part in the enforcement of immigration controls, something that was to impact on social work.

The shift to asylum

The 1990s saw attention shift to asylum seekers as migration for long-term settlement all but ended in the UK. Similar to the construction of economic migrants being 'organised travellers' wanting to gain from the British labour market and welfare state, asylum seekers were constructed as a 'poor, burdensome and costly addition *we* can ill afford' (Hayes, 2004, p 21). This has allowed an inferior system of welfare to be legitimised, underlining the link between control of immigration and access to welfare. The Asylum and Immigration Appeals Act 1993 and the Asylum and Immigration Act 1996 began to restrict the social rights of asylum seekers by, for example, withdrawing benefits for in-country asylum applicants (Sales, 2002). The Immigration and Asylum Act 1999 formalised the category of 'asylum seeker' and removed entitlement to a range of non-contributory family and disability benefits from those subject to immigration control. The Act extended the use of vouchers to this group, introduced a system of compulsory dispersal, and created the National Asylum Support Service (NASS), now part of the UK Border Agency, which works with local authorities and voluntary organisations concerning arrangements for asylum seekers. Importantly, many asylum seekers do not accept the NASS dispersal package, instead living with fellow nationals and getting by on undocumented work. This is not surprising given that under NASS, subsistence is given by money or vouchers to a value less than basic income support, meaning asylum seekers have to live well below the 'normal' subsistence level. And an obvious problem with vouchers is that it stigmatises this group of people and can reinforce racist tensions within the host community. Meanwhile, NASS increasingly relies on private sector landlords where there are concerns about poor standards, malpractice and profiteering. Essentially the 1999 Act 'constitutes a qualitative leap in the link between welfare and immigration status. It accomplishes this by reducing [the] assistance to asylum seekers to a form of Poor Law' (Cohen, 2001, p 24). Another key problem is that separating a group of people from mainstream services has profound effects on their daily living, and it does not do anything to reduce a climate of hostility towards them. Then there is the fact that the essentially separate welfare system for asylum seekers inevitably causes problems at the interface between that system and other public services such as health and education. Another concern is that an undue burden falls on voluntary agencies, including Citizens' Advice, who become overwhelmed by the volume of people needing support, and as a result have to pick up the pieces (CAB, 2002).

Immigration, asylum and citizenship policy: international, European and UK strategies

Despite the differing and reduced welfare services provided for asylum seekers and others subject to immigration control in the UK, it should be noted that legislation and policy often draws on more benign international and European legislation and policy. As Hill and Hopkins (2009) point out, immigration, asylum and citizenship policy has multiple scales of legislation and policy, and despite the devolved context of the UK, the three main ones relate to the international, European and UK spheres.

The starting point is the Convention Relating to the Rights of Refugees (UNHCR, 1951). This states that the term 'refugee' applies to anyone who has a 'well-founded fear of being persecuted for reason of race, religion, nationality, membership of a particular social group or political opinion', is outside their country of nationality and is unable or, because of fear, unwilling to avail themselves of the protection of that country. It also applies to those who do not have a nationality and who are outside the country of former habitual residence as a result of persecution and are unable or, again because of fear, are unwilling to return. As mentioned, a refugee is a person whose asylum application has been successful and who is allowed to stay in another country, having proved they would face persecution back at home.

Another important international document is the UN Convention on the Rights of the Child (UN, 1989). This sets out a wide range of children's rights including an overarching principle of non-discrimination, along with rights to protection, participation, provision of services and promotion of development (but see below, in relation to Article 22).

Turning to European policy, in 1950 the European Convention on Human Rights and subsequent five protocols outlined a range of articles to guide efforts to maximise the well-being and welfare of asylum-seeking and refugee children. These included no one being the subject of torture or degrading treatment or punishment, the right to respect private and family life, people not being denied access to education and so on.

Later, the European Union (EU) was keen to promote the free movement of labour as part of the internal market to improve prosperity, but simultaneously there was an emphasis on controlling inward migration. In 1999 member states established a Common European Asylum System, laying down minimum standards for the reception of asylum seekers including the reception of families, schooling and education of minors, the reception of unaccompanied minors and the right to family reunification.

The Council of Europe is a more informal association of countries with less power than the EU, exerting influence by guidance and persuasion. It has devised standards for safeguarding the interests of asylum-seeking and refugee children. For instance, it advocated for guardians for all unaccompanied asylum-seeking children, and it has a Convention designed to protect children and adults from trafficking and its consequences.

As stated earlier, at the heart of UK policy is a desire to control both the numbers and 'types' of people adding to the population through inward migration. However, asylum seeker and refugee entitlements to enter or stay are largely determined by asylum policy which originates in international law. Domestic law has been passed to incorporate the relevant international conventions and sets out national procedures and enforcement mechanisms (Hill and Hopkins, 2009). Two basic principles are that refugees should not be returned to persecution, and the government must provide an asylum applicant with a procedure to make a claim to stay.

Although domestic law incorporates many of the international conventions, this is not always the case. The most obvious example was the government's specific reservation on Article 22 of the UN Convention on the Rights of the Child, which states ' ... a child ... whether unaccompanied or accompanied by his or her parents or by any other person, [should] receive appropriate protection and humanitarian assistance in the enjoyment of applicable rights' (UN, 1989, Article 22 [1]). This reservation allowed the UK to act outside the letter and the spirit of the Convention by retaining the right to pass laws concerning asylum and immigration without having to take account of the rights of any child affected. This was confirmed in the Nationality, Immigration and Asylum Act 2002 whereby a family receiving support from NASS is not entitled to support from a local authority by way of destitution (Grady, 2004). In essence, the children of destitute asylum seekers are not entitled to the support of the state through Section 17 of the Children Act 1989 as a 'child in need', although if NASS withdraws support (for example, if the family has been a nuisance or their asylum application has failed) a local authority could assist. The rational for this stance is that NASS provides that support elsewhere, but a problem is that their role is one of housing and financial support rather than welfare more broadly. Such a situation highlights government priorities, with successive ones seeming to take the view that any measure aimed at immigration control is unaffected by the UN Convention.

More positively perhaps, and after various concerns voiced by the UN in relation to the UK's approach to asylum and immigration, in 2005 New Labour announced a five-year plan entitled *Controlling our borders: Making migration work for Britain* (HM Government, 2005), which led to the development of the New Asylum Model to expedite asylum cases, and the Immigration, Asylum and Nationality Act 2006. Since 2006 the Home Office has begun a reform programme for immigration and asylum policy, and subsequently published *Better outcomes: The way forward* (Home Office, 2008). Following this, the reservation on Article 22 was withdrawn in November 2008, and under Section 55 of the Borders, Citizenship and Immigration Act 2009 the Border Agency has to have regard to safeguarding and promoting the welfare of children in the UK (Bokhari, 2012). However, despite what seems to be progress, many see the reform programme as remaining premised on the assumption that most children are not genuine asylum seekers, instead being seen as abusers of the system (Crawley, 2010).

Social work with asylum-seeking and refugee children and families: care or control?

The developments in relation to immigration, asylum-seeking and refugee children and families since the 1990s have heightened the tensions between care and control, which have always been endemic to social work. The policies pursued during this period have pushed social workers into becoming 'gatekeepers to subsistence', and 'forced [them] to operate in an environment of ever greater scrutiny of immigration status' (Sales and Hek, 2004, p 60).

State intervention in the lives of children and families through social work, and indeed in the lives of all user groups, has always served a dual purpose. Social workers express society's altruism (care) as well as enforcing society's norms (control) (Banks, 2001). Put differently, on the one hand, they work with those who are destitute or needy, those deemed 'deserving' of help, and on the other, they intervene to control the behaviour of the 'deviant' or attempt to reform the 'undeserving poor'. There are obvious problems in balancing these caring and controlling aspects, although over recent decades it is the latter aspect that has increasingly dominated (Humphries, 2002). In relation to asylum seekers and refugees, the split between care and control is clearly evident in the way that successive governments and the media have emphasised the so-called division between 'genuine' refugees and 'bogus' asylum seekers. Social workers, who regularly have to define need and decide eligibility, are not always immune from this discourse. Asylum seekers often arrive in the UK without means of support and have to negotiate with social workers from a situation of disadvantage, which is compounded by the problem of communication arising from language difficulties. Such pressures can lead to a strengthening of the control rather than the caring aspects of the relationship.

Asylum teams

The exclusion of 'undesirable aliens' from welfare and preventing immigrants from 'recourse to public funds' has been part of the welfare state since its inception (Cohen et al, 2002; Cohen, 2003). The legislation and policy changes of the 1990s moved welfare to the centre of the asylum debate as entitlement to support was reduced and benefits more tightly related to immigration status (Sales, 2002). Governments also encouraged greater cooperation between service providers, including social services and the Home Office, in detecting illegal immigration. Ostensibly this took place because of an increased flow of asylum seekers and delays in processing cases, which increased the cost of supporting them.

Because of the number of asylum seekers and refugees in their areas, some London boroughs established specialised asylum teams, mainly in social services departments, but involving departments such as housing. They became responsible for providing subsistence and for making decisions about who was eligible, and because of growing demands during a time of budget restraint, this became their core work rather than a broader social work role. With the establishment of NASS, responsibility was largely devolved to the existing London asylum teams.

As for actual practice in such asylum teams, research indicates that the emphasis is on the very narrow role of gatekeeping and assessing eligibility (Sales and Hek, 2004). Many practitioners express a concern about eroding asylum seekers' rights, arguing instead that they should have basic citizenship rights and not be treated as second-class citizens. They are concerned about what amounts to the separation of the 'deserving' and 'undeserving', resulting in a focus on control rather than care. The concern relates to the initial screening of users to ensure eligibility based on proof of a connection with the borough and 'destitution', followed by an assessment of their entitlement to support and of other needs. Users could then be referred to other services, both statutory and voluntary, for support with longer-term issues. However, after this process it was rare to see users again, with the social work experience thereby limited to a brief, one-off encounter. Not surprisingly, there are serious problems with this approach.

Some practitioners described their role as more akin to 'inquisitors', 'immigration officers' and 'police officers' rather than social workers. This means their role could be seen as hostile, especially for people who had experienced torture and persecution. It is not surprising that users and members of the local community can often see social workers as state interrogators from whom information has to be concealed, rather than people who can be trusted and relied on. This is linked to individual social workers often feeling a tension between ways of working that emphasise qualities such as warmth and empathy, and others such as detachment, in order to establish entitlement to support. The dilemmas involved in the care and control aspects of social work are clearly evident here, with practitioners having to attempt to 'get around' the system in order to work more humanely, and in effect, work in more deviant ways (Carey and Foster, 2011). This can entail providing more than the strict entitlement policy and procedures might suggest, often involving individuals working in their own time. Similarly it includes attempts to evade the problems inherent in establishing eligibility, by spending more time with users, listening to them and heeding their views whenever possible. It can be counter-posed to a more orthodox, managerial practice which has an overriding concern with 'sticking to the rules' and completing bureaucracy quickly. Bending rules and procedures therefore becomes a more important priority for more critical workers.

Asylum teams, especially following their close relationship with NASS, have highlighted the tensions and dilemmas in what is, after all, an intentionally deterrent service. Constructive, indeed critical, social work with asylum seekers and refugees depends on building up relationships of trust, and it is hard to argue against the view that immigration scrutiny works against this.

Accompanied asylum-seeking children and young people

Whereas recent governments have emphasised policies and practice to protect and safeguard children and young people, this has not applied to them all (see Sales, 2002; Grady, 2004). Asylum-seeking and refugee children have been marginal within policies and practice concerned with children in need, and even in relation to child protection (Munro, 2002).

As indicated, over recent decades asylum and immigration policy in the UK has developed a discourse of exclusion for those not seen as genuine citizens. Asylum seekers and their children are excluded from mainstream welfare services essentially because of the role of NASS. Such a position is justified with reference to the need to contain and deter 'bogus' asylum seekers from making inordinate demands on the welfare state. Again we come to the concerns in relation to the government's initial reservation on Article 22 and the UN's concerns about this.

If we look at social work provision to children and families, poverty and other structural issues are often the key markers in identifying the typical 'consumer'. Such users then go on to access many more services through that initial social work contact, for instance day care, financial assistance, parenting support and so on. For asylum-seeking children and families there is no access to such a breadth of services (Grady, 2004). Indeed, they may not come into contact with welfare professionals at all, or if they do, it may well be at a crisis point in relation to child protection, when the situation may not be easily resolvable. What has happened to successive governments' mantra of 'early intervention'? When it comes to asylum-seeking children and families it does not seem to apply, leaving us with another question: bearing in mind the issues discussed here, how do we provide critical practice with this user group?

In addition to 'deviant' social work (Carey and Foster, 2011), the assessment framework for children in need (DH, 2000a) provides some possibilities. Despite earlier misgivings (see, for example, Chapter 3), aspects of the framework are compatible with critical practice in relation to asylum-seeking children and families. Importantly the framework aimed to shift policy and practice from protection towards one where prevention and welfare were more generally to the fore. There is a debate as to whether it achieved this (see Rogowski, 2011c), but in any case, the proposed shift is clearly at odds with what asylum-seeking children and families face in relation to their involvement with NASS. Further, the assessment framework assists in highlighting the relationship between particular factors and for children to be defined 'in need', and this has the potential to assist in practice. As an example, let us consider the 'family, community and environmental factors' of the assessment.

Social isolation and the mental and physical health needs of parents or carers can have a considerable bearing on whether a child is in need. In particular, social isolation, combined with concerns about personal safety as a result of living in a hostile neighbourhood, has an impact on parents' mental health and well-being, and hence parental capacity (DH, 2000a, p 14). However, the role of NASS in dispersal to inadequate housing and the lack of welfare-oriented services leads precisely to the sense of isolation and feelings of abandonment by the state that are felt by many asylum seekers and their families (Sales, 2002). In addition, dispersal and relocation outside of established communities is likely to produce feelings of helplessness and of continued oppression. It is not hard to see that the situation asylum seekers and their families often find themselves in after arriving in the UK compounds, rather than alleviates, the traumatic nature of their experiences. At the very least it is ironic that governments, through the work of NASS, create such circumstances for these service users, circumstances that we actually seek to limit and reduce for those who normally come to the attention of welfare services.

Case study 7.1: Asylum seekers: addressing their issues

A Libyan family including a husband and wife and two daughters, Howazen (6 years) and Maria (4 years), arrived in the UK after being threatened, harassed and persecuted by Colonel Gaddafi's security forces and supporters. The father suffers with severe arthritis, and since living in the UK the mother has had severe depression, anxiety and is afraid to go outside the family home. Howazen has difficulty sleeping and often has nightmares. Both girls enjoy school, although their parents are not always able to ensure regular and punctual attendance because of their own health needs.

NASS placed the family in a run-down private property in a northern town away from London where they had some family and friends. Their home was in a predominantly white British area and on occasions the family were the subject of racist abuse, which upset the girls in particular. In many ways the family coped despite their social isolation, although the mother's mental health issues were exacerbated by this.

Other than providing minimal financial assistance and accommodation, NASS were largely unconcerned with the other issues referred to. The parents approached social workers on several occasions about their predicament.

1   One way of responding, and sadly the most usual one, is that unless there are serious child protection concerns the family are 'fobbed off' by being told to 'go back to NASS, who will try and help'. Sadly, of course, it is not always the case that any help ensues.

2   A more critical approach would be to ensure that a thorough assessment of the girls' and family's situation is made. This would highlight the problems and difficulties faced by the family – social isolation and racial harassment, the father's physical health, and the mother's and Howazen's mental health issues – all of which impinge on parental capacity and in turn whether the needs of the girls are always adequately addressed. There might be a role in terms of advocating for the family and ensuring that: the health service was properly addressing the family's health needs; the school and education services were doing all they could in terms of support and help regarding the girls' attendance and punctuality; the police and local neighbourhood safety/anti-social behaviour unit were proactively involved regarding the family's harassment; and that NASS and the private landlord were fulfilling their responsibilities in relation to the family's housing. There might be a need for financial assistance from children's services, notwithstanding the role of NASS in this regard.

Essentially the critical social work proposed here uses the assessment framework to draw attention to the plight of Howazen and Maria and their parents, and to construct arguments that show the need for services that can resolve the issues.

The assessment framework can therefore be used as a potential tool, not only to identify areas of concern but also as an aid to using practice skills so as to effectively address the concerns. The quandary for the critical practitioner is in trying to use the framework to access services and enable asylum-seeking families to use welfare services given the current policy and managerial-controlled climate. Nevertheless, as well as highlighting need, the framework can draw attention to the inadequacies of NASS in meeting the most basic welfare needs of asylum seekers, and to the contradictions inherent in current legislation. As well as using assessments in this way, much can be gained from consideration of previous developments in social work, including engaging with contentious issues around the oppressive nature of the state, particularly issues of 'race' and culture, and the impact on the provision of welfare services and especially those provided to children (Grady, 2004).

The impact of difference on the experiences of children and their families, and its impact on their treatment by welfare and 'caring' professions, have caused concern for decades. Social work has responded to this by embracing issues of discrimination, and challenging the racism and disadvantage experienced by many in society (Dominelli, 1997, 2002b, 2009a; Dalrymple and Burke, 2006). Social work has had some success in these matters, despite often being accused of 'political correctness' when attempting to challenge more 'common-sense' views; witness, for example, the controversy surrounding social work's call for 'same race' placements for children in foster and adoptive care (see Chapters 3 and 4). Issues of 'race' and culture, then, continue to challenge social work at both the policy and practice levels. These ongoing issues are the direct result of previous migration, particularly of the former Commonwealth citizens in the middle of the last century (Dominelli, 1997), with similar discourses framing the experiences of asylum seekers at the beginning of the 21st century, as were used to understand migrants in the 1950s and 1960s. Policy and practice, again in the form of the assessment framework, reflect the realisation that 'race' and cultural specificity are important aspects of delivering services. Assessments should be racially and culturally appropriate and take account of children's experiences at the global and personal level (DH, 2000a), such as in the area of private fostering (see below). The goal is to avoid placements that do not match children's 'race' and cultural needs as well as the possibility of 'agencies' arranging placements for financial reward rather than being based on need (Holman, 2002; Bostock, 2003).

Unaccompanied asylum-seeking children and young people

Issues of 'race' and culture are of particular concern when it comes to unaccompanied asylum-seeking children. If they come to official attention on immediate arrival, they are referred to children's services or NASS (Wells and Hoikkala, 2004). The latter may disperse them on an ad hoc basis around the UK. If they come to official attention after entering the UK, they are referred to children's services.

Children's services' social workers make an assessment under Section 17 of the Children Act 1989 and this may or may not lead to the child or young person being accommodated under Section 20 of the same Act. In practice, those assessed under Section 17 receive less support than those felt to be in need of accommodation.

Under Section 17, usually unaccompanied 16- and 17-year-olds can be placed in 'supported accommodation' with private landlords who 'signpost' them to services. The landlord receives financial support from children's services, and the young person is given a weekly allowance. A problem is that the accommodation is often inappropriate and the landlord provides only minimal support. On reaching 18 years of age, if their immigration status is unresolved, they can be transferred to adult services or receive financial support and possible dispersal by NASS. If at any stage prior to this their asylum application is unsuccessful, subject to the right of appeal, they could be returned to their country of origin.

Under Section 20, children and young people, usually under 16 years of age, can be accommodated in foster or children's homes, or other approved accommodation. They are subject to a care plan and given regular and ongoing support. Again, on reaching 18 years of age, they could receive financial support from NASS or aftercare services that are ongoing until they reach 21 years of age, or 25 if they are in full-time education. And again, if their asylum application is unsuccessful at any stage, subject to the right of appeal, they could be returned to their country of origin.

Case study 7.2:[2] Unaccompanied asylum-seeking children: Section 20 accommodation?

An is a young girl (15 years) from China. She was placed with 'foster carers' because she was a female and passed on to a Chinese female trafficker who kept her locked up with other girls. She was then passed on to various men who treated her badly by imprisoning and sexually abusing her, before being flown to the UK by one of them. He told her to tell people she was 19 years old and that if she did not, she would have to 'suffer the consequences', possibly being taken back to China and to the life she had led previously.

On arriving at Heathrow, An hid in the toilets and was eventually found by security personnel. She was anxious and afraid. Although she had a passport claiming she was 19 years old, she said she was 15. Despite this, the UK Border Agency treated her as an adult and sent her to the north of England where she was placed in NASS accommodation. Later she had to move and was placed in accommodation with other adult females. Support staff from voluntary agencies who were involved with her made referrals to the police and children's services regarding their concerns about her age and welfare.

Subsequently, there were reports about a man staying with An in the accommodation. A private landlord investigated, visited and found a Chinese man hiding in the toilet, but he said he was her brother. The voluntary agencies, however, thought he was the trafficker. Not long afterwards, An disappeared and she is now officially reported as a missing person.

> The point here is that if An had been provided with accommodation under Section 20 of the Children Act 1989, then her issues and concerns, along with her welfare, would have been far more likely to have been addressed and thereby led to a more successful outcome. Financial constraints mean that Section 20 is only used as a last resort.

Looking more specifically at the details of practice, it should be emphasised that unaccompanied asylum-seeking children and young people are not all locked into inevitable cycles of depression and psycho-social symptoms of trauma following events in their country of origin (Wells and Hoikkala, 2004). By any criteria they do not *all* require mental health interventions. Instead, more consideration should be given to acculturation research into the impact on individuals from different cultural backgrounds resettling in different cultures (Berry, 1988), this helping social workers understand the well-being of unaccompanied and separated asylum-seeking children and young people.

Psychological and social problems such as anxiety, depression, alienation, marginality and identity confusion, may materialise during acculturation. These stress indicators are linked with the orientation the young person has towards maintenance of his or her cultural identity and which characteristics are considered to be of value, or will maintain relationships with the larger society. These formative questions concerning acculturative stress can be mediated by adopting one of four acculturative attitudes: assimilation, integration, marginalisation and separation. *Assimilation* occurs when migrants choose to identify with the host culture and sever ties with their traditional culture. *Integration* is a strong identification with the host and traditional culture. *Marginalisation* is a lack of involvement in the host and traditional culture. *Separation* is an exclusive interaction within one's traditional culture, with no interaction with members of the host society. There are a number of comments to make in relation to each of these attitudes.

First, factors such as housing conditions, finances, political, social and cultural isolation can have a negative effect on mental health (Berry, 1988), and to relieve this stress, young people alienated in a community without formal and informal support may assimilate or merge effectively with the host culture. Second, an integration-oriented policy is the optimum resettlement outcome, and reflects the ease or difficulty with which young people maintain networks with their ethnic group and join with the dominant group in the host society. Third, at the heart of marginalisation are the deterministic roles of the young person and the attitudinal position of the host, the latter in particular affecting settlement and well-being. The point to note is that it is easy for unaccompanied minors to become marginalised, alienated and excluded in the UK simply because of the attitude of the host in terms of government policy and resulting practice. Such young people might have to be dispersed around the country and have to survive mainly by themselves, notwithstanding the need for personalised arrangements to assist in the asylum process and to provide ongoing support (Kidane, 2001). Finally, in relation to separation it is important to note that some host countries might want to maintain divisions between asylum seekers and the larger society, as a covert policy of 'divide and rule' or 'keeping people in their place' (Berry, 1988).

As suggested, integration is the optimum acculturation strategy, meaning that support provision needs to maintain a relevant balance between 'dominant' and 'cultural' services. It might be stating the obvious, but foster homes with carers from similar ethnic backgrounds and living in a community with others from a similar ethnic background are likely to be the ideal placement. The carers need guidance and support from social workers and the child/young person requires education, health and leisure services as well as regular support from a social worker. Such care arrangements can help ensure that marginalisation is avoided.

Trafficking

There is no hard data as to the number of children trafficked into the UK, essentially because it is a hidden and complex crime. This lack of data is a significant obstacle to understanding the scope of the problem and in planning an effective response in terms of services to trafficked children. Having said this, there is no doubt that children come from a wide variety of countries to be exploited in a wide variety of ways, including sexual exploitation, domestic servitude/forced labour, benefit fraud and forced crime such as pick-pocketing and theft (Pearce, 2012). After the UK government ratified the Council of Europe Convention on Action against Trafficking in Human Beings in 2005, a National Referral Mechanism was implemented in 2009 for adults and children trafficked into and within the UK. The Convention aims to prevent and combat trafficking and to protect and assist victims and witnesses, with the framework identifying victims with a view to ensuring they receive appropriate help and support (for a discussion, see Ishola, 2012, pp 43-5).

The trafficking of children is largely carried out by criminal gangs, although children are also trafficked by small groups of adults, families and single individuals (CEOP, 2010) (see the example of An above). From a child's perspective, who actually takes the lead in the trafficking is hardly relevant, as the experience of physical and psychological trauma, separation, loss and abuse remains the same. This means that the important element running through the entire response to child victims is the voice of the child (Ishola, 2012). They need to be asked what makes them 'feel safe', and the specific views and experiences of such child victims needs to be incorporated into all aspects of the assessment, care and support process.

As shown above, the safeguarding and protection provisions of the Children Act 1989 have not always applied to trafficked children. One particular concern relates to identifying those who arrive in the UK through routes other than ports of entry. Children who rely on adults with no parental responsibility or family connection (often loosely termed 'agents'), who may have arranged for these children to be smuggled through the UK borders and trafficked for the purpose of exploitation, are especially vulnerable. They are not usually known to statutory agencies which increases the risk of harm to them, and delays the safeguarding process when and if they do become known. The asylum process itself adds to the already complex process of need identification and referral to relevant support services.

When it comes to social work practice with trafficked children, this varies across the UK (see Pearce, 2012). The reality for many such children is that they will be placed in inappropriate bed and breakfast-type accommodation, and to all intents and purposes, left to their own devices. On the other hand, there are some examples of good practice. For instance, the London Borough of Hounslow has an unaccompanied minors team where staff have received training in safeguarding children who have been trafficked. Children under 16 years of age are automatically placed with foster carers, while older ones are placed in semi-independent accommodation where support staff are always available. Another borough, Hillingdon, has introduced good practice guidelines for working with trafficked children, including residential guidance, and this has been successful in reducing the number of trafficked children who go missing. Finally, in Hertfordshire, social workers and the police have worked closely together, with the latter able to contact trained, specialist social workers if there is any suspicion of trafficking. However, it should be noted that the specialist teams/models and resultant good practice outlined here are the exception, as they are not available in most of the UK.

Age assessments

Age assessments of asylum-seeking children are on the rise. As referred to earlier, one factor is the populist, including politicians', belief that many adults are simply abusing the asylum system by claiming to be children in order to benefit from the advantages that it confers (Home Office, 2002). More prosaically, the rise has taken place for two main reasons (see Crawley and Kelly, 2012). First, the Border Agency needs to be clear about whether an applicant is over or under 18 because this determines which asylum process and asylum support arrangements are appropriate. The second reason is the local authority's statutory duty to assess the situation of children in need and it has to decide the applicant's age in order to do this. It is worth emphasising that normally in relation to child protection and safeguarding it is important for the child to feel believed, but this seems to be less the case when it comes to statements made about their age. It is certainly a fraught area for practitioners, having the potential to deflect attention away from the fact that one is faced with an individual who is in need of support.

There are a number of problems with this emphasis on age being directly linked to eligibility for services. Many unaccompanied children genuinely do not know their age or date of birth, as not all countries and cultures attach the same importance to chronological age, with birth records being afforded less importance. In many countries birthdays are not marked or celebrated, which reflects the social and cultural context from which children originate, or conditions of poverty and/or conflict that make such celebrations impossible or inappropriate (Crawley and Kelly, 2012). When asked how old they are, many children calculate or guess their age by recalling events that have happened in their lives or information that has been given to them by others prior to their departure. Children may also have grown up in economic and political contexts where being a child does not confer any particular rights or privileges, where they are forced to grow up quickly because there is no advantage to be gained from being childlike or being dependent for any longer than absolutely necessary.

What becomes clear is that the current age assessment process is complex and problematic. Best practice is to assess age as part of an overall assessment of a child in need rather than a discrete process (IND and ADSS, 2004). It should also comply with the case law findings of *R(B) v Merton London Borough Council* in 2003. In brief, the assessment of age should be holistic and include physical appearance and demeanour, the interactions of the person during assessment, social history and family composition, developmental composition, education, independence and self-care skills, health and medical assessment, and information from documentation and other sources (Crawley and Kelly, 2012).

Private fostering

Some communities have traditionally sent their children abroad to be cared for by distant relatives or friends in order to improve their own and their families' prospects. This amounts to a private fostering arrangement and can be a positive experience, although it can potentially place these children in vulnerable situations (Bokhari, 2012; Shaw and de Sousa, 2012). One has only to recall that Victoria Climbié was privately fostered.

Under Section 67 of the Children Act 1989 local authorities have a duty to safeguard privately fostered children in their area, and it is the fostering adult's responsibility to notify the local authority for arrangements lasting more than 28 days, although most of these children come to official attention by accident or from reporting by neighbours. When a private fostering arrangement comes to the attention of the local authority, it is required to assess the suitability of the carer and their accommodation, and to ensure the well-being of the child. Once a private fostering arrangement is confirmed, appropriate support and services can be sought.

Returning children to countries of origin

The prospect of being returned to their country of origin can be one of the biggest causes of anxiety for asylum-seeking, refugee and trafficked children (Finch, 2012). Although they do not generally face this possibility until they reach 18 years of age, the threat of removal and return is ever present from their point of arrival in the UK. Unaccompanied children can only be returned to their country of origin if the Secretary of State is satisfied that adequate reception arrangements are in place for them there. However, there are exceptions; for instance, where a child has previously claimed asylum in another EU country, they can be returned there. In addition, the Home Office has been developing a policy for returning children prior to their 18th birthday to some countries of origin, notably Afghanistan.

However, within the UK and EU there are concerns about the increasing numbers of vulnerable children arriving in Europe to seek asylum (European Commission, 2010). It is acknowledged that there are four reasons for this. First, they want to escape from wars, conflicts, poverty, natural disasters, and discrimination and persecution. Second, they are seeking a better life, including access to education, welfare and healthcare. Third, they want to join family members. And fourth, they are victims of trafficking and are destined for exploitation.

The likelihood is that over the coming years there will be further efforts to ensure the return of vulnerable children and young people to their countries of origin, and social workers need to be wary of their role in this area.

Conclusion

This chapter is premised on the fact that all children and young people's views and experiences, along with those of their families, are central to child protection and safeguarding without discrimination. All but Far Right political parties would surely agree with this sentiment, but as Grady (2004) points out, there are two challenges for social work with children and families who are seeking asylum. The first is to recognise the constraints of current policy and guidance that generally constructs asylum seekers as not worthy of welfare simply because of their status. There has belatedly been some official recognition of what amounts to an anomaly, hence the withdrawal of the reservation of Article 22 and changes to the Border Agency, which means it has to have regard to child protection and safeguarding. The second challenge is to acknowledge the potentially oppressive effects of asylum systems in isolating families and encouraging the very factors that government policy seeks to reduce for the population as a whole. Just as concerning is the fact that 'social work as a profession has become complicit in this [situation] and has been largely accepting of systems specifically designed to offer less to particular groups of people as a result of their immigration status' (Hayes and Humphries, 2004b, p 217).

Social work needs to improve service delivery to those subject to immigration control, and a good start is to have an understanding of the historical and ideological issues that lead to the racist nature of immigration control and the current construction of the 'bogus' asylum seeker. Equally, the profession needs to awaken and consider its response to this user group, including challenging the state's attempt to subjugate the profession in this (and other) areas (Masocha and Simpson, 2011). Bearing in mind earlier comments about social work's care and control functions, those who want, and seek to maintain, a commitment to the poor and oppressed might feel somewhat disillusioned and marginalised as control functions appear to be dominate. Such gloomy views might be reinforced by the fact that attitudes towards 'asylum seekers and others subject to immigration control hold up a mirror, reflecting back to us the place we have reached as a profession' (Hayes and Humphries, 2004b, p 218). But for the critical social worker there has always been an element of feeling like this; it is a result of having to battle against and challenge dominant ideological and 'common-sense' views, and it is precisely why critical social work thinking and practice is needed. As Daniel (2012, p 8) puts it, 'If we can provide these children and young people with the kind of support, encouragement and empathetic care that they need, we will maximise the chances of them being able to settle, flourish and make their own contribution to the rich diversity of the UK.' After all, there are many examples of the potential of refugees who started as asylum seekers. Fabrice Muamba, the Bolton Wanderers midfielder, came from DR Congo as a child and represented England in his age group before a heart attack unfortunately cut short his career. Then there is the champion distance runner and double Olympic gold medal winner, Mo Farah, who came to the UK as a child refugee from Somalia. Both remind us of humankind's possibilities wherever they come from, and critical social work has a key role in ensuring that all asylum-seeking and refugee children and young people have the opportunity to live their lives to their full potential.

Key points

Social work with asylum-seeking and refugee children and families is embroiled in assessing and providing a different level of service to those who are UK citizens. Critical social work provides a theory and practice for resistance to this, as well as more positive possibilities.

Critical social work rejects turning our backs on those who arrive in the UK having experienced terrible abuse only to encounter more of the same. Instead, it speaks out against the violation of human rights and stays true to principles of human dignity and worth, social justice and service to humanity.

Critical social work, particularly in the form of anti-oppressive perspectives, is vital to practice, reminding practitioners of the universal needs of children, young people and families.

Further reading

Fell, P. and Hayes, D. (2007) *What are they doing here? A critical guide to asylum and immigration*, Birmingham: Venture Press. The treatment of asylum-seeking and refugee children and families poses challenges for social work. This book shows how critical analysis and practice can help resist movements to control rather than care.

Humphries, B. (2004) 'An unacceptable role for social work: Implementing immigration policy', *British Journal of Social Work*, vol 34, no 1, pp 93-107. This article highlights social work's involvement in internal immigration controls and hence its complicity in degrading and inhuman social policies, arguing for more progressive practice.

Kelly, E. and Bokhari, F. (eds) (2012) *Safeguarding children from abroad: Refugee, asylum seeking and trafficked children in the UK*, London: Jessica Kingsley Publishers. An up-to-date account of the challenges facing social work in safeguarding children from abroad, together with some positive ways forward.

Kohli, R. and Mitchell, F. (eds) (2007) *Working with unaccompanied asylum seeking children*, Basingstoke: Palgrave Macmillan. A useful practice guide for working with unaccompanied asylum-seeking children.

Notes

[1] Some argue that the term 'separated children' should be used for the diverse group of children under consideration (see Kelly and Bokhari, 2012a, pp 9-12, for a discussion), but here I use more specific terms such as unaccompanied asylum-seeking children, trafficked children and so on.

[2] This is adapted from Pearce (2012).

8

Disabled children and families

> Support and services for disabled children [and families] has 'a history steeped in vacillating attitudes: extreme cruelty alternating with protection, neglect alternating with enlightened provision, exploitation alternating with respect'. (Oswain, 1998, p 29, cited in Connors and Stalker, 2003)

The above comments retain their relevance because although we might be living in a more benign, enlightened age, when it comes to disabled children and families, perhaps this should not be overstated. Even social workers who work with such children and families can have negative attitudes, to the extent that if families decide to have such children at home rather than being placed in a residential placement, then it was their 'choice' and they would simply have to manage as best they could (see Connors and Stalker, 2003, p 75). Such a view in itself leads to the need for a more critical approach.

There are approximately 770,000 disabled children in the UK, representing 1 child in 20, many of whom live in poverty and receive only minimum support from local authorities (Contact a Family, 2012). This lack of support is related to the fact that social work with disabled children and families does not always receive the priority it should. Some see it as a Cinderella service, with little funding and/or 'kudos' attached to it (Oliver and Sapey, 2006). Child protection and social work with children and families more generally are the 'flagship' service user groups, perhaps being reflected in the way this book has been approached; disabled children and families are the focus of the penultimate chapter rather than the first. All the same, such arguments should not detract from the view that practice with this user group is an essential area of social work, particularly because of the challenges it currently faces.

As I began this chapter, Contact a Family published a revealing survey of the plight of families with disabled children (Pemberton, 2011b). Over 1,000 families with disabled children were contacted, and nearly 75 per cent had experienced anxiety, depression or family breakdown. Almost 50 per cent had asked their GP for medication or counselling, while 65 per cent said they felt isolated frequently or all of the time. One in five said feelings of isolation had even destroyed their family or marriage. Significantly, over half, 56 per cent, said that their feelings of isolation were due to lack of support from social services and the education system, while 57 per cent believed it was because they could not work as much as they wanted to, and 54 per cent blamed lack of time and money. Half of the families said they had experienced discrimination or stigma due to their child's disability.

Overall the research revealed that isolation was having a devastating impact on the well-being of many families with disabled children, and that councils needed to provide more preventative services. In the current jargon this means more 'early intervention', including support groups and short breaks. Participants were also concerned that their situation was going to get worse because of the Coalition government's welfare reforms and the current financial/economic crisis, both likely to result in further stress, isolation and poor mental health. Taken as a whole, it means that it will be that much harder for disabled children to lead rewarding, happy lives by being able to participate fully in society.

Adding weight to the above findings, the Disability Alliance (2011) points out that the overall package of welfare reforms and ensuing cuts risk increasing poverty and despair for the majority of disabled children and their families. Then we have yet another challenge, this time relating to personalisation and the ways this is and will affect services for disabled children and families – although 'sold' as giving parents more power over their children's care, it is, in reality, often more about cost cutting, reducing public expenditure and the 'burden' on the taxpayer.

This chapter is divided into three sections, with the first two drawing on the work of Clawson (2011). First, there is a discussion of disability as a social construct, including models of disability, notably the individual and social models, both of which play a role in social work policy and practice as well as in wider societal views of disability. Second, I turn to legal and policy issues relating to disabled children and their families. The third section looks at some key practice issues including safeguarding disabled children and personalisation.

Disability as a social construct

Making sense of the society and world we live in raises some complex and contentious questions, which is particularly so when it comes to disability. As Clawson (2011, p 568) succinctly puts it, 'where do we get out understanding of disability from and how is it perpetuated?' We come back to the idea of social construction in that the way of understanding the world does not come from objective reality, but rather from other people in society (see Chapter 2).

Disability is a social construct in that it is constructed by the way society is shaped rather than being an inherent physical state (Oliver, 1990, 1996; Oliver and Sapey, 2006). This leads to the view that disability is not about the individual's impairment per se, but about social oppression and discrimination. Society can be seen to disable people through the barriers it places to their obtaining full citizenship rights in terms of full access to education, employment, housing, a social life, physical environment and so on. The use of language plays a key role in these social processes and has a direct impact on disabled people.

Language is important because if impairment or disability is defined in negative terms, it can reinforce disparaging attitudes towards disabled people (Barnes et al, 2005). It is also important in thinking about ways to address the discrimination and oppression of disabled people. The term 'handicapped' has historical associations of being 'cap in hand' and begging, which, following labelling theory, can construct people's identity and define their place in the world; the labelled person can expect a certain response from others and behave in such a way to get that response. Language does not simply reflect a true meaning that already exists, but it actually moulds meaning and has implications for the way disabled people perceive themselves and are perceived by others in social work practice and policy (Clawson, 2011).

Definitions play an influential role in both the construction of disability and in the way in which disabled people are perceived by wider society and professionals. It is important to look at how disability is defined and who defines it, because attitudes and behaviour towards disabled people, professional practice and the ways institutions are run are based on those definitions (French, 1994). A difficulty, however, is that there is no simple way to define disability because it can be viewed from different perspectives, with a range of models having been put forward by different individuals and groups, including policy makers, doctors, charities and disabled people themselves. Historically the models that have dominated are those proposed by the most powerful groups in society such as the government and the medical profession. Since the 1960s disabled people have been campaigning for the right to determine their own needs and how these should be met by social welfare and medical practice. An example of this was the Disabled People's Movement that made a distinction between 'impairment' and 'disability' (UPIAS, 1976). Impairment refers to lacking all or part of a limb, or having a defective limb, organ or mechanism of the body. A disability is the disadvantage or restriction of activity caused by a contemporary social organisation that takes little or no account of people who have physical impairments, thus excluding them from the mainstream of social activities.

Models of disability help in understanding the context in which disability is viewed by different groups and individuals in society, with the individual and social models being predominant. In simple terms the former, also sometimes referred to as the medical or deficit model (Smith, 2008), has its basis as 'curing' the individual or viewing the disability as a personal tragedy, while the latter seeks to break down barriers in society so that disabled people can play a full part in society. Instead of seeing disabled people as passive or 'needy', as problems to be managed, they should be accepted as free-standing individuals with their own, often conventional, hopes and dreams.

Individual model of disability

The individual model sees the difficulties that disabled people face arising as a direct consequence of their impairment. Take, for example, a person who is deaf, has cerebral palsy and uses a wheelchair. The difficulties they might face on public transport, accessing public buildings or in communicating would be seen as a result of their impairments, rather than as a result of transport and buildings being inaccessible for wheelchair users or British Sign Language not being used by many people. The individual model sees health and welfare services having to help the individual overcome the tragedy caused by physical, sensory or intellectual impairment, with them needing to 'fit in' with mainstream society by rehabilitation and/or services being provided to help them cope with their disability.

Many argue that social work is based on the individual model because social policies in respect of disability are influenced, often unknowingly, by the core ideology of individualism (Oliver, 1990). This model is seen as being ingrained in society, focusing on body abnormality and functional incapacity such as whether someone can wash, dress and so on. These 'incapacities' are then used to classify the person as invalid, with the resulting 'victim' seen as in need of care and dependent on help from the welfare state to live in society, or out of it if living in an institution. Disabled people point out that the model makes them dependent, having to rely on professionals to provide therapeutic and social help and support (Barnes et al, 2005).

Going further, if disabled people view themselves in the same way that wider society views them, it can oppress them internally because they behave and think in ways that are expected of them. An example is a disabled person living in a residential home who does not feed or dress himself, even though he is physically able to do so, simply because he has always been used to someone doing this for him.

Children are particularly vulnerable to being socialised into accepting disability as an individual problem by their parents, who are largely influenced by professionals (French, 1994).

Case study 8.1:[1] Challenging the individual model of disability

Michael is 10 years old and lives at home with a younger brother and his single-parent mother. He has been diagnosed with autism, having some communication impairment and a learning disability. To those who know him well he can communicate his needs, but he becomes very frustrated and angry with people who do not know or understand him.

Until he was nine years old Michael attended a local mainstream primary school. However, the school increasingly felt they could not meet his needs so he was moved to a special school, some 10 miles away from his home. He was very unhappy about this and wanted to stay with his brother and friends. This unhappiness was manifested in many ways by his behaviour and attitude, including towards his mother, who found him very challenging at times.

One reason for what happened in this case is that Michael's mother believed he was not capable of attending mainstream school because this was what she was told by teachers, educational psychologists and the like. Hence, she agreed with the move, but a problem could be that Michael in turn would come to believe and internalise what his teachers and mother told him, setting a pattern for his belief system throughout his life. The experience of having to change schools could limit his horizons and hence his future possibilities.

An alternative to simply making Michael move schools would be to question what his primary school and the education psychology service proposed, which is where a more critical social work approach comes in. As Michael's social worker, discussions could take place with Michael's mother and the school so as to challenge the views of teachers and others. Teachers, for instance, do not usually understand the history and politics of disability, and so do not question what is often deemed to be 'normal' practice, for instance, the necessity at times of removing challenging children from their schools. An important point, however, is that tackling discrimination and prejudice needs to begin in school, as school is where children are educated together and learn about each other.

In pursuing the foregoing, the school could be asked to consider whether any other forms of educational, emotional or behavioural support could have been put in place for Michael in order to enable him to stay at the school. After all, an important argument is that moving him to a special school contributes to him being excluded from his own community and peer group.

Although the individual model is sometimes referred to as the medical model, the two are not synonymous. As Clawson (2011) points out, the medical model can be seen as one component that goes to make up the individual model, one that actually covers a number of individualistic perspectives. For instance, another component is the philanthropic model which involves charities portraying disabled people as sad, courageous and in need of care and protection; such images may make lots of money for the organisations concerned, but also cause harm by reinforcing stereotypes (Oliver, 1990).

Nevertheless, the medical model approximates to the individual model in that the latter's solution to disability lies in medical 'cure' and rehabilitation, and involves the expert defining the disabled person's needs and how to meet them. It needs to be emphasised that it is the balance of power and control that is questioned, not the fact that *all* medical intervention is wrong (French, 1994).

Social model of disability

It is largely disabled people who advocate for the social model of disability, notably the academic Mike Oliver (for example, 1990, 1996). This model includes a number of sociological perspectives on disability that emphasise the social factors that disable people. As such it moves away from focusing on the individual's physical limitations to looking at the way physical and social environments create barriers to disabled people becoming full members of society, thereby having all the benefits that arise from this. Rather than definitions of disability being made up of the views of non-disabled people, there has long been a call for disabled people themselves to define the issue.

Connors and Stalker (2003) argue that the social model is particularly applicable when it comes to disabled children. Their study involved guided interviews with disabled children and interviews with their parents and siblings, with a number of themes emerging/being covered in relation to the children's daily lives. These included the 'ordinariness' of children's lives, their perception of impairment and their understandings of difference. Others included friendships, the 'ordinariness' of sibling relationships, the agency of disabled children, their overall positive outlook and communication within families. The children were aware of their impairment, and there was much evidence of disability in their accounts, along with barriers to becoming full members of society. Importantly, some of the older siblings had an awareness of disability and the social restrictions encountered by their brothers and sisters; some had also developed a strong sense of social justice and an understanding of discrimination faced by disabled people as a whole.

The social model sees the solution to disability as lying within the restructuring of society and the removal of social, physical, environmental and institutional barriers. This would actually benefit everyone as no one would be excluded. In the case of Michael above, instead of the local authority's education department agreeing that his needs could only be met in a special school, in the social model of disability, all mainstream schools would be fully equipped and staffed to meet all the needs of all children; there would be no barriers to prevent children being educated together. Furthermore, assumptions would not be made about what people can and cannot do, and welfare services would not be uniform, with social workers having to work with people from their own perceptions of the reality of their lives (Oliver and Sapey, 2006).

The social model is progressive and has affinities with the goals of critical social work, although this is not to say it is without criticism. Some argue that it does not include the views of all disabled people; disabled people are not one homogeneous group and people have very different experiences, beliefs and views (Crow, 1996). If the model is imposed in ways that deny the experience of individuals, it could be seen as oppressive. Although it works well on a large scale in terms of tackling discrimination and oppression, this is less the case on a personal level because it does not represent all disabled people. A final point is that it tends to focus on disability and plays down the impact of impairment on the individual such as pain, fatigue and chronic illness. Shakespeare (2006) argues that what is needed is a new understanding that neither reduces disability to an individual medical model nor neglects body limitation and difference.

Finally, it is worth re-emphasising that disabled people are individuals with different views, needs and wants. People may be born with an impairment or may acquire disability through, for example, illness or injury during their life. Such acquired disability may involve having a physical disability, sensory impairment or cognitive impairment, and it should also be remembered that some people have an impairment that is not obvious to others, and some may have one or a combination of impairments. Individuals, therefore, have their own identity that may or may not include an understanding or agreement about being 'disabled'. A good example of this is that many deaf people who use British Sign Language to communicate do not consider themselves disabled; rather, they view themselves as a linguistic minority. It is therefore important that social workers understand the individual's own perception of identity and how the impairment has an impact on the person, as it is particularly important in assessing their needs.

In brief, following an assessment of need, local authorities should provide services to those with physical, learning or sensory disabilities who meet the eligibility criteria. Support can be provided to children and adults with such disabilities to ensure they develop skills to become as independent as possible. This encompasses a range of services including aids and equipment to help with daily living, supported accommodation, residential services, short breaks, day care/service opportunities/education, housing adaptations, occupational therapy, support to parents, carers and siblings and so on.

Legal and policy issues

Turning to legal and policy issues relating to disabled children and their families, there are two separate, although related, matters to consider – Acts of Parliament and policy/practice guidance (see Clawson, 2011). The main statues are the Children Act 1989, the Carers and Disabled Children Act 2000, the Children Act 2004 and the Children and Young Persons Act 2008. The main policy and practice guidance is to be found in the *Framework for the assessment of children in need and their families* (DH, 2000a), *Every Child Matters* (DES, 2004), the *National service framework for children, young people and maternity services* (DH and DES, 2004, the Early Support programme (2004), *Safeguarding disabled children: Practice guidance* (DCSF, 2009) and *Working together to safeguard children* (HM Government 2010). Such legislative and policy developments are designed to address the needs of all children, including the needs of disabled children, and represent a welcome commitment to bringing disabled children into the main arena of childcare policy. Here I consider the statutes and policy guidance in a little more detail, beginning with the former.

Legislation

The Children Act 1989 set out the underlying principle that disabled children should be seen as children first, bringing them into mainstream legislation for the first time. Disabled children were deemed to be children in need because of their disability, and were therefore entitled to an assessment of need. As Connors and Stalker (2003) note, several key principles in relation to disabled children are embodied in the Act: the promotion of their welfare; normalisation/inclusion; participation of the child; partnership with parents; interagency collaboration; and cultural sensitivity. The safeguarding provisions of the Act also applied to disabled children, and there were also specific provisions for disabled children. These latter provisions included requiring the local authority to ensure that accommodation for looked-after children was not unsuitable; maintaining a register of disabled children in their area so as to enable them to plan services; and providing services to minimise the effect of disability. Services included short breaks/respite care, holiday play schemes, care at home such as help with personal care, befrienders and aids and adaptations.

The Carers and Disabled Children Act 2000 built on the Carers and Recognition Act 1995. The 1995 Act allowed assessment of carers' needs, but this was of the carer's ability to provide and sustain the care provided, and local authorities did not have to offer services to support carers. The 2000 Act gave local authorities the power to provide certain services to carers. Local authorities were also allowed to make direct payments to carers, to people with parental responsibility for disabled children, and to 16- and 17-year-old disabled young people, for services to meet their assessed needs. This could include, for example, payments to purchase personal care support at home, or for a befriender to accompany a child to recreational activities. In relation to Michael in the case study, for example, it might involve paying for someone to take him to a youth club where he wants to go with his friends but does not want his mother to take him. Perhaps a good outcome would be Michael and his mother identifying a friend of the family who they know well, then employing them to do this by using direct payments.

The Children Act 2004 changed the way services were delivered by local authorities so that they became integrated around the child and the family, although in the process it led to the demise of social services departments. Listening to and involving children are at the core of the way services are to be delivered, the challenge being to involve disabled children in this process.

Finally, the Children and Young Persons Act 2008 reformed the statutory framework for the care system, which was aimed at improving outcomes for children looked after by the local authority and for care leavers. An important provision is Section 25 of the Act that imposes a duty on local authorities to provide short breaks to assist parent/carers to continue caring for a disabled child or to do so more effectively. Significantly, such breaks are not only meant for those struggling to cope with the care of their disabled child, but should be available to all families with disabled children.

Policy

The *Framework for the assessment of children in need and their families* (DH, 2000a) has already been discussed (see Chapters 3, 4 and 7). It is important to note here that there is a need to safeguard disabled children from harm, as the indicators of abuse of a disabled child may be difficult to separate out from the effects of their impairments, particularly if they have multiple impairments (Westcott, 1998). I return to safeguarding disabled children below.

Every Child Matters (DES, 2004) has been referred to earlier (see Chapter 3 in particular). This Green Paper was produced following the death of Victoria Climbié and given force under the Children Act 2004 (see above).

The *National service framework for children, young people and maternity services* (DH and DES, 2004) is a 10-year programme setting out the standards for the planning, commissioning and delivery of services. It aims to ensure that integrated health and social care will play a key role in helping children fulfil the outcomes in *Every Child Matters*, thereby ensuring that they fulfil their potential. The Framework has 11 standards, with 5 specifically applying to children and young people with specific needs arising from health and impairment. As an example, Standard 8 states that children and young people who are disabled or who have complex health needs should receive coordinated, high quality child and family-centred services, based on assessed needs, which promote social inclusion and wherever possible enable them to live ordinary lives. The expectation is that there is a need for an integrated diagnosis and assessment process, for early intervention and support to parents and for multi-agency planning.

The Early Support programme was set up in 2004 to achieve better co-ordinated, family-focused services for young disabled children and families, complimenting *Every Child Matters* and the *National service framework*. The programme focuses on children aged under three, and brings together the different services available to disabled children, emphasising multidisciplinary working. Through the programme a key worker is appointed to work with the child and family and to act as a liaison point between the family and all professionals involved.

Finally, in relation to policy we come to *Safeguarding disabled children: Practice guidance* (DCSF, 2009) and *Working together to safeguard children* (HM Government, 2010). Again, safeguarding disabled children is discussed in more detail below, but a couple of points can be made about these publications here. First, the 2009 guidance made it absolutely clear that disabled children have the same human rights as their non-disabled peers. It documents why disabled children are both more vulnerable to being abused and less likely to be protected from harm than non-disabled children. Second, *Working together* updated the 2006 document, providing a national framework within which agencies and professionals at local level could draw up and agree on their own ways of working together to safeguard and promote the welfare of children. It provides specific advice on working with disabled children, again paying attention to recognising why disabled children are more vulnerable than their non-disabled peers, and listening to, and finding ways of, communicating with them.

Although I have only provided a brief outline of the key legal and policy issues here, it should have become clear that working with disabled children and families is a complex and varied area. Arguably a legal and policy framework has been developed from which disabled children can benefit. For instance, much is made about the need for 'high quality', 'coordinated' and 'integrated' care, the need for 'multidisciplinary working' and so forth. However, in these times of austerity, in reality does such language merely amount to fine words, mixed with well-intentioned aspirations? Then again, the introduction of direct payments implies a shift in thinking about how services are, or can be, provided, which is seen as being for the better. Some see care packages as being put together in more positive, creative ways, sometimes using people who are familiar to the child (Clawson, 2011, p 576). However, from a critical perspective, direct payments and the current emphasis on personalisation are merely the logical extension of how public services are to be delivered when neoliberal notions of individualisation, marketisation, privatisation and consumerism are to the fore, together with the need to curtail public expenditure. These are some of the matters to which I return in the next section.

Practice issues

When considering practice with disabled children and families it is important to emphasise that because of the particular issues confronting this service user group, they should be given the same priority and importance as other children and families. This might be stating the obvious, but the point needs to be made because in the not too distant past, practice in this area was, and to some extent remains, a neglected area.

Resonating with some of the points made by the charity Contact a Family in the introduction to this chapter, there are four points I want to make regarding the challenges confronting disabled children and families. The first is that many disabled children live in poverty. Second, the educational attainment of disabled children is unacceptably lower than that of non-disabled children. Third, families with disabled children report high levels of unmet needs, isolation and stress. Last, only a minority of disabled children and families are supported by social workers and social care more generally (Mitchell and Sloper, 2002). For example, in one study, the 25 families who took part 'had little formal or prolonged involvement' with social workers (Connors and Stalker, 2003, p 74). There was also a feeling that social workers and their agencies 'were slow to act, not very helpful and usually not to be relied upon for any sustained support' (Connors and Stalker, 2003, p 75). On the whole, it is probably fair to say that families with disabled children often feel unsupported or have to 'fight' for any services that may be available, with such a situation likely to worsen over the coming years as austerity measures continue to bite.

Over recent times disabled children and their parents/carers have made their views known about what they consider a 'good' service (Mitchell and Sloper, 2002; DH, 2002; Connors and Stalker, 2003). Admittedly, ascertaining their views and the participation of disabled children could be improved because it is not embedded or sustained across all local authorities (Franklin and Sloper, 2006). Even so, they do like to make choices, be involved in decisions, and want professionals to take notice of them and listen to what they say (Connors and Stalker, 2003). Again it is important to emphasise the need for effective communication with them.

'Official' views of a 'good' service focus on the need to have a key worker who knows the child well and who can provide a link between all those involved, having a holistic assessment and all essential information in one central place, agencies and professionals working together, accessible information, and integrated appointments so as to prevent numerous trips the hospital, for example. This is all well and good, although arguably it amounts to stating the somewhat obvious.

More substantial 'demands' include having community-based services local to home and having access to short breaks.

It is worth dwelling on short breaks a little because it is a need that disabled children and families often say is unmet. The meaning of 'short breaks' not only refers to 'respite' or overnight stays outside of the child's home, but also includes breaks provided by a befriender or 'sitting service', where the worker either takes the child out or looks after them at home. Other examples include a place at a play scheme, out-of-school club or nursery, through to overnight care in a residential unit, with foster carers, or at the home of a person employed through direct payments/with such a person at the child's own home. All such breaks need to promote the welfare of the child and provide positive experiences, examples being social activities that provide opportunities to make new friends and to try new things. Many parents/carers point out that short breaks help them to continue in a caring role, and many older children/young people enjoy time away from the family doing different things.

New Labour did recognise the importance of short breaks with the publication of *Aiming high for disabled children: Better support for families* (DES, 2007) which focused on three main areas. First, there was an emphasis on access and empowerment whereby disabled children would become engaged in shaping local services, and increased transparency about what services were available and entitlements to them. The second area referred to the need for flexible, responsive services and timely support. Finally, quality and capacity was improved by the injection of £280 million to increase the provision of short breaks. However, because of the current Coalition government's austerity measures, what will be the effects on short breaks, along with the emphasis on community-based services?

Case study 8.2: A holistic approach to disabled children

Michael and his family live on a deprived estate in a privately rented house that has damp in the bedrooms and two of the radiators do not work. His mother does not work because of her childcare responsibilities, so the family has to manage on welfare benefits. As a result, at times they struggle financially. Michael's mother has also asked about regular short breaks whereby he would receive good quality care and have the opportunity to do some interesting things, thereby adding to his quality of life. This would also enable her and his brother to have some time with each other, both knowing that Michael was happy.

One approach is for the social worker to 'signpost' his mother. In other words, tell her to contact the landlord about the house and Citizens' Advice about benefits. The social worker adds that, "I'll look into" the possibility of short breaks.

A more critical social work approach involves a more proactive stance. This involves the social worker making enquiries on behalf/with Michael's mother about the housing and benefits issues. If necessary, a more overt advocacy role could be adopted, involving letters of complaint and perhaps culminating in contacting the local MP. Discussions could take place with her about increased government attempts to 'persuade' single parents to go to work, and whether this leads to better parenting/parent–child relationships, especially bearing in mind the stress that can arise from having to juggle work and childcare responsibilities. Discussions with her concerning, and putting her in touch with, parent/ community groups facing similar challenges would also take place. Finally, in relation to short breaks, the social worker would spend time with Michael, getting to know him and ascertaining his views about leaving home for short spells. It is likely that he would want to enjoy the new friendships and opportunities such breaks would bring. The overall aim would then be to ensure that breaks were arranged that suited Michael and the whole family.

Having briefly looked at practice issues in general, there are two particularly important areas to consider. These are safeguarding and child protection in relation to disabled children, along with the current emphasis on personalisation, and it is to these that I now turn.

Safeguarding and protecting disabled children

Disabled children are both more vulnerable to abuse and less likely to be protected from harm than non-disabled children (see, for example, Cooke and Standen, 2002; Miller, 2003). For example, Miller (2003) points out that, although there has been little research in this area in the UK, in the US one study showed that they were 3.4 more times to be abused or neglected than non-disabled children. Breaking this down further, they were 3.8 times more likely to be neglected, 3.8 times more likely to be physically abused, 3.1 times more likely to be sexually abused and 3.9 times more likely to be emotionally abused. One problem is that signs and symptoms of abuse can sometimes be masked by the child's disability, with, for example, behaviours or injuries merely attributed to their disability rather than a more serious questioning stance being adopted by the professionals involved.

Historically the focus of child protection services has been on non-disabled children, with policies and procedures being developed with only them in mind. Over the last decade or so the situation has changed – witness the policy and practice guidance referred to above, not least the *Safeguarding disabled children: Practice guidance* (DCSF, 2009) and *Working together to safeguard children* (HM Government, 2010). Nevertheless, it can be easy for social workers to collude with parents/carers and in so doing failing to act on evidence that could be of concern, or accepting standards of care that would not be accepted for non-disabled children. There are many reasons for this, including, as mentioned, seeing behaviour and symptoms as a result of the child's impairment rather than as an indicator of abuse. Another is that there may be a reliance on carers to speak for the child or to explain behaviour and symptoms together with a ready acceptance of explanations given. Then again, the emphasis might be on support for the carers rather than the child's welfare. A final possibility is that there may be a lack of appropriate foster or residential placements if a child needs alternative care, which is especially so in these current times when financial considerations are such dominant factors in decision making.

Where safeguarding concerns become apparent there has been much discussion about who is best placed to investigate (Cook, 2000). Social workers working with disabled children have the knowledge and skills to communicate with disabled children and understand issues linked to their impairment and its impact. However, they might not have much experience of child protection. The situation is the reverse for those social workers working in child protection. The most obvious way this could be addressed is by more co-working and skill sharing between disabled children and child protection social workers and their respective teams.

In relation to safeguarding disabled children, a particularly useful question to bear in mind when assessing a disabled child is: which option(s) under consideration would I choose if the child were not disabled (DH, 2000b)? Reiterating some other points, issues to consider are the child's preferred method of communication, being open minded with the picture presented and not making assumptions about what may or may not have occurred.

Case study 8.3: Safeguarding disabled children

Michael is now 12 years old and has short breaks at a residential unit which he enjoys, and where he has friends, which also enables his mother to have a break. On one occasion he arrives at the unit by taxi after school, and a member of staff notices a bruise on the side of his neck. She asks him how he got it but he shrugs his shoulders and says he does not know.

Almost a week later the member of staff tells Michael's social worker about the bruise, adding that she thinks it must have been caused by the seat belt in the taxi.

The social worker might well be concerned about why the staff member had waited a week before revealing the incident, not least because the bruise would no longer be visible. There would also be a query about whether a seat belt could have caused the injury and whether any other explanations were possible.

The social worker would consult with colleagues, including a manager whose views would probably dictate the next course of action. In any case it should include talking to Michael about what had happened, whether he had any worries and anxieties and so on. Discussions would also take place with his mother, his school and perhaps also his brother.

The key point is that an open mind would be kept about what had occurred, and the staff member's views would not be assumed to be the 'truth'. One has to be wary of over-reacting in situations such as this, but at the same time, the incident would be taken as seriously as it is with non-disabled children.

Safeguarding disabled children is further complicated by the recent emphasis on direct payments. This change has opened up a new area of working with disabled children in their own homes, the point being that some abusers of children are attracted to jobs that involve the care of children. The provision of direct payments has therefore brought attention to further safeguarding issues, and created new dilemmas for social workers and parents.

The Protection of Children Act 1999 allows people who are considering employing someone to care for their child to request a criminal background check from the Criminal Records Bureau (CRB). Although local authorities have a duty to check when employing people to work with children, the legislation does not apply to people employed by direct payments. Good practice, however, would suggest that it is best to have had a CRB check carried out, and payments should only be made if a child is safe. The question arises as to the measures taken by the local authority to ensure this happens. This is a task for the social worker in carrying out the assessment, with a number of factors needing to be considered in deciding whether a person is safe to work with children. Examples of these include whether the person has already had a CRB check, whether they already work with children, and whether they are personally known to the family. Carers can also be advised of the need to check a person's references by speaking directly to the referees. In general, a balance has to be struck between the right of carers to make a choice as to whom they employ, and the right of the child to be safe.

Personalisation

Personalisation echoes many of the themes of the NHS and Community Care Act 1990 which aimed to develop new arrangements for the assessment and care management of older people, to ensure that individuals received tailored packages of care instead of more standardised services. Although this arguably led to the virtual demise of social work with older people (Postle, 2001), New Labour, via the Social Care Institute for Excellence (SCIE), pushed forward changes in relation to personalisation, which are ongoing.

Personalisation was a central feature of New Labour's agenda for public sector reform and envisaged individuals having maximum choice and control over the services they received (HM Government, 2007a, 2007b). This was supposed to be achieved by direct payments (see above in relation to Michael), individual and personal budgets, and co-production, the latter concerned with ways of creating support systems that valued partnership between all parties.

SCIE argued that personalisation originated from social work values such as respect for the individual and self-determination, and had its roots in the service user movement and the social model of disability, with notions of participation, control, choice and empowerment being to the fore. The individual (in our case the parents/carers of disabled children or older disabled young people) was seen as best placed to know what they needed and how those needs could best be met. The aim was to make people self-responsible so they made their own decisions about what they required. But should the burden of sorting out the credentials, references and even CRB checks really be placed on the parents/carers and young disabled people who are often already isolated and living stressful lives?

It is unsurprising that personalisation has not been without its critics (see, for example, Ferguson, 2008; Rogowski, 2010b). Importantly, personalisation did not emerge from within social work or service users but from Demos, the New Labour think-tank. It was linked to the notion of consumerism, and in so doing there was a real danger of an abdication of state responsibility, with the so-called empowerment of individuals actually amounting to their *abandonment*. This is because (so-called) choice and control should not be promoted at the expense of safety and dignity, with 'cash for care' seeming to be the overriding concern rather than any genuine move to personalisation. The changes were continued evidence of an ideological adherence to the market economy, including themes of individualisation, responsibilisation and the transfer of risk from the state to the individual (Ferguson, 2007). There was an uncritical acceptance of the marketisation of social work and social care, together with the neglect of issues such as poverty and inequality. Also included was the flawed conception of the people who used social work services, the potentially stigmatising view of welfare dependency and the potential for promoting, rather than challenging, the deprofessionalisation of social work. In short, the philosophy of personalisation is not one that social workers should accept uncritically.

Moreover, following the global financial and economic crisis, Demos went on to argue that personalisation could be used to combat cuts in public spending. It added that the question of how public services could meet people's needs at a lower cost would be the most pressing public policy issue for the next decade. Although personalisation may be sold on the basis that it provides 'choice' and 'independence', the underlying policy agenda is more about reducing expenditure by maximising the care provided by family, friends and neighbours, thereby minimising the need for state-funded support. Indeed, some argued 'there is strong value-for-money evidence' for such an approach, one that meant there was 'a compelling business case' for encouraging its development (see Hunter and Ritchie, 2007, p 36).

In short, it was dependence on the state that was to be discouraged while independence should be celebrated. However, this so-called independence amounts to being dependent on the market together with all the insecurities and anxieties this brings (Leonard, 1997). From this, public policy means shaping the choices people make about their lives so as to reduce the risk they will make expensive demands on public services. Individuals will have to take more responsibility in finding their own solutions, including assessing and managing the risks of their own behaviour. This includes being liable for managing their own care within clear financial and service constraints, and even identifying their own resources that could be deployed in this endeavour. It is not hard to see that this is where consumerism and in turn personalisation comes in, with self-reliance and responsibility being to the fore rather than collective provision.

But surely you cannot reconstruct people who rely on social work/social care as 'customers' or 'consumers' because most ordinary people lack the basic information to make meaningful choices. Further, even if such information and genuine choices existed, it is far from clear that choice itself is people's primary consideration; nearness, or ease of access, to the particular service concerned is likely to be the major factor. We should surely step back and question the view that personalisation should increasingly be the backbone on which social care is to be built and provided. Being blunt, it should not be up to the individual parents/carers or older disabled young person to sort out their own problems and difficulties even if some, in many ways limited, help and advice is provided.

Conclusion

As suggested earlier, social work with disabled children and families has never had the 'cachet' associated by practising with other children and families service users groups. However, this should not detract from the fact that although it is a complex and demanding field of practice, one that is immensely interesting and rewarding, and one that raises a number of important ethical and moral dilemmas.

Then there are the challenges arising from current austerity measures and the growing influence of personalisation. After all, one only has to recall what has happened to social work with older people – it is now dominated by the care management and the personalisation agenda more generally. This has led to practitioners focusing on routinised bureaucracy being completed quickly, while simultaneously there has been discouragement of the counselling and interpersonal aspects of social work (something which, of course, applies to all social work). In addition, we have increasingly seen such tasks being carried out by people who are not qualified social workers. More fundamentally, responsibility for meeting need is being left to the parents/carers of disabled children or older disabled young people as the state retreats from the provision of services for the collective good. Such individuals are left to pursue their own interests as they see best, notwithstanding the difficulties that can be caused in the process. Despite all of this, possibilities for critical social work in this area remain.

There is a need to move away from a social work role that, for instance, is restricted to matters narrowly concerned with the personal care provided to disabled children. Instead the responsibility has to involve helping and supporting disabled people, including disabled children and their families, more holistically in all areas of their lives (Sapey, 2009). For example, and as I have attempted to show in this chapter, it is not enough to 'signpost' people to services or agencies such as housing or the Department for Work and Pensions while merely addressing issues of the child's basic care. Advocacy in relation to benefits and housing may well be required. Indeed, a holistic perspective lends itself to seeing the social model of disability as the appropriate model for social workers to adopt, which is certainly the view of disabled people. For instance, Connors and Stalker (2003, p 137) point out that the social model 'seems to fit well with ... [disabled] children's accounts of their everyday lives.' Their research indicates that disabled children are aware of their *impairment* as well as their *disability*, the latter referring to *barriers to being* such as the thoughtless or hostile attitudes and behaviour of others, as well as *barriers to doing*, of the material, structural and institutional kind. These are some of the areas that a critical practice can focus on, one example shown above in relation to Michael's schooling.

The social model also helps to highlight that if a family has a disabled child, the whole family can experience unequal opportunities and outcomes, including the financial hardship, stress and anxiety referred to earlier (Dowling and Dolan, 2001). This is why critical social work has to give attention to such material factors as poverty and inadequate housing, again, as indicated in the case of Michael.

Overall, we need a society that is ready to accept and value the difference, and the ensuing celebration of diversity, inherent in disability. Disabled children and families need to encounter social workers who, while not losing sight of the commonalities between people, are willing to acknowledge the positives that can arise with difference, notwithstanding the problems encountered within wider society. The implications of this for those who work with disabled children and families are significant and require a social work that aims towards the transformative societal goal of valuing difference and diversity, while not devaluing commonalities.

Key points

Disability is a social construct and there are a range of different understandings and models of disability, all of which have an impact on social work policies and practice.

For critical social work, the social model of disability is the most appropriate. It draws on the views of disabled people and enables practitioners to better understand the position of disabled people in society.

The critical social worker is not an expert on 'disability' but a professional able to support disabled children and families to determine and act on what they want and need. This involves knowledge and understanding of relevant legislation and policy, and balancing the rights and wishes of the disabled child with the parents'/carers' need for support.

Critical social work involves overcoming structural, institutional, cultural, professional and personal barriers that devalue difference and impairment.

Further reading

Connors, C. and Stalker, K. (2003) *The views and experiences of disabled children and their siblings*, London: Jessica Kingsley Publishers. This remains a useful examination of how disabled children and their siblings feel and experience relationships with professionals and the wider world.

Needham, C. (2011) *Personalising public services: Understanding the personalisation narrative*, Bristol: The Policy Press. A text that provides an excellent account of personalisation as it affects social care, arguing for a critical understanding of the major tenets behind the agenda.

Oliver, M., Sapey, B. and Thomas, P. (2012) *Social work with disabled people* (4th edn), Basingstoke: Palgrave Macmillan. A key text examining the relationship between the social model of disability and social work policies and practice.

Thomas, C. (2007) *Sociologies of disability and illness: Contested ideas in disability studies and medical sociology*, Basingstoke: Palgrave Macmillan. A comprehensive account of how disability has been theorised within disability studies and medical sociology.

Note
[1] This, and the other case studies in this chapter, are adapted from Clawson (2011).

9

Conclusion:
Critical social work and its future

> [Critical] social work has greater ambitions [than meeting national
> guidelines and targets, and delivering 'joined-up' government], because
> it seeks growth and empowerment as human beings for the people
> we serve, development and social progress for the communities we
> work in and greater justice and equality in the societies to which we
> contribute. It is not that every act of social work will achieve such
> large goals, but these values help to guide us in using our judgement
> about what is best. (Payne et al, 2009, p 4)

Neoliberalism has left us with a situation whereby nation states have become
'market states', having little concern with collective provision or social justice,
instead merely wanting to extend 'opportunities' to all so that individuals can
take care of their own needs and responsibilities. It involves the embracement of
the free market economy and has a very narrow and restricted notion of what
the possibilities of societal advancement could be. Such possibilities involve the
collective meeting of everyone's basic needs in a society where the overriding goal
is social justice and equality, rather than self-interest and self-responsibility. This
view of the future may be idealistic, even Utopian, because the rich and powerful,
by acting through the state, endeavour, usually with success, to determine the
direction society takes. This direction is, of course, one that favours their interests
and desires. But surely all is not lost. As Ruth Levitas (for example, 2001, 2012,
2013: forthcoming) persuasively argues, Utopian thinking certainly has its merits.
For instance, from a Marxist perspective there have been times when the working
class, through trade unions, have obtained concessions from the ruling class (Bailey
and Brake, 1975a), the development of the welfare state being a prime example.
Despite its imperfections, the welfare state can be seen as being one of the peaks
of human civilisation, although sadly the balance of class forces changed under
the Thatcher years, leading to its gradual dismantling. This situation continues,
as does the neoliberal project, even if, as is argued in this chapter, it is perhaps
beginning to stall.

Pierre Bourdieu (1998) speaks out against the new myths of our time, especially
those associated with neoliberalism, and offers a passionate defence of the public
interest. He points out that the withdrawal of the state from many areas of social
life in recent decades has produced growing despair and alienation in the most
deprived sections of the population. The dismantling of public welfare in the name
of private enterprise, flexible markets and global competitiveness is increasing

the misery of those who have suffered most. In his sharp, uncompromising and convincing attack on neoliberalism and those who champion it, Bourdieu stands up for the interests of the powerless, and helps to give a voice to those individuals, groups and social movements whose views are rarely heard in the dominant media. This is an example of precisely what critical social work with children and families has to try and do.

All public sector workers have been denigrated over recent decades and, as far as social work is concerned, perhaps we have seen the 'rise and fall' of the profession (Rogowski, 2010b). As we have seen throughout this book, what remains of social work is a limited version of previous possibilities; social workers have been reduced to working speedily to ration services and carry out risk assessment/management. To the extent that there is any face-to-face practice with service users, as far as children and families are concerned, the controlling aspect dominates. As Butler and Drakeford (2001, p 17) put it, under New Labour 'the function of social work is predominantly to ensure that difficult and troublesome individuals are made to accept prevailing social norms', which is part of a 'tendency to align social work with authoritarian, rather than libertarian policies.' Such comments are surely no less relevant when it comes to the Coalition government's approach. As we have seen, this authoritarian and controlling role is evident in relation to the various children and families user groups referred to throughout this book. However, a more sanguine view of the possibilities for social work can be taken, one where practice does not *have* to take a neoliberal form, especially at a time when the neoliberal project seems to be faltering.

In looking at critical social work and its future, there are two points I want to emphasise. First, coinciding with Bourdieu's thesis, there was, and continues to be, an increased interest in feminist-based ethics of care (Robinson, 1999, 2010; Williams, 2001; Held, 2006; Mahon and Robinson, 2010; Barnes, 2012). Second, as a result of the ongoing global financial and economic crisis, there are serious doubts about the neoliberal project, and questions are beginning to be asked about what is to come 'after [neo]liberalism' (Robinson, 2010). Such thinking helps provide a basis for the future of critical social work, a practice that emphasises the caring side of the profession and aims for a future based on social justice and equality. This chapter begins by elaborating on these notions, as well as a radical/critical social policy, prior to looking at the future for critical social work with children and families.

Ethics of care

When it comes to ethics of care, Fiona Williams (1989, 2001) provides a succinct discussion of some of the major issues. In brief, a welfare state should have a number of aims in mind, but the most important seem to be the following: reversing the misery of those in poverty, providing protection and security from social and economic risks, and providing citizenship. Important aspects of this approach are the state having an important role in addressing the health, education, employment, housing and social needs of citizens, at least to a basic minimal level. New Labour and the current Coalition government, however, have made much of distancing, even retreating, from such goals. Rather than collective means of alleviating social and economic problems as they affect individuals, it is individuals who are supposed to manage their own lives, if necessary relying on friends, relatives or charity when required. Such an (essentially right-wing) ideological view sees an ethic of *paid work* as being the means for citizens to achieve in these areas, but the argument here is that, at the very least, this view needs to be balanced by a political ethics of *care* (Williams, 2001).

The ethic or principle of paid work has been central to welfare reforms over recent decades and particularly the last 15 years, including those reforms produced by the Coalition government. The argument centres on the financial imperative to get people, including lone parents and disabled people, 'off welfare' and into work. Another line of reason rests on the moral imperative to turn people into better citizens because of the positives associated with paid work. These are presented as including a number of themes, with paid work being seen as: the first responsibility of citizenship; the route out of dependency into independency and economic self-sufficiency; a solution to poverty; the way individuals connect to wider society; the role model that mothers and fathers offer children; and the way society is bound together. One could read this, for instance, as recognition of education and training needs, along with the rights of those whose access to paid work has been historically marginalised, such as women and disabled people. On the other hand, and perhaps more to the point, the changes have been aimed at making more people dependent on the market and less of a burden on the taxpayer; it is a move towards expecting people to 'sort their own life out', the value of self-responsibility being central rather than the emphasis being on collective provision, through the state, for all.

Despite the dominance of the work ethic, care has become an increasingly important analytic referent in social policy, as well as becoming increasingly significant in various policy-relevant debates following the legacy of the New Right and during the current neoliberal consensus. One has only to recall the discourses in relation to the 'mixed economy of care', community care, the treatment of looked-after/children in care, what constitutes good parenting, the care of older people, and the need to recognise care responsibilities in employment-based 'work–life' balance. In one way or another all this focuses on what care means, its uses and abuses, what it costs, how it is supported, and how and who delivers it. The key argument is that policies associated with care have the potential to be innovative but, most importantly, they can be used to create greater equality, provided that the political values that support policies are made clear.

There have been tensions between an ethics of care and an ethics of social justice, with some seeing them as gendered binaries, female and male respectively (Sevenhuijsen, 1998; Tronto, 2010). However, another way of viewing the situation is to see that the ethics of care can influence public democratic practices and our understanding of citizenship; care is not just a moral concept but also a political concept that can help rethink humankind as interdependent beings. Care, therefore, is not merely a parochial concern of women or, as it were, those 'at the bottom of the economic pile', but a central concern of human life, which is precisely why political and social institutions need to reflect this. It cannot be simply counter-posed to justice; rather, it is a social process engendering important elements of citizenship (Sevenhuijsen, 1998). The universalist paradigm taken up here means that the moral qualities involved in care – attentiveness, responsibility, competence and responsiveness – should be seen as civic virtues, with care thereby providing a lens through which to make judgements about collective commitments and individual responsibilities.

There are two other aspects to consider – care in relation to disability and to 'race' (see Williams, 2001, pp 478-86). First, the disability movement challenges an ethics of care simply because disabled people do not want care but the means to be independent. Care in this context can be disabling and this is an important point. However, this needs to be balanced by the fact that the ethics of care advocated here operates within an equality paradigm and against the historical inequalities in care relationships. In relation to the second aspect, 'race' and care, the racialised context of care means that the organisation and delivery of services need to take account of culturally specific needs, accessibility and entitlement differences. This has to go hand in hand with taking into account the ways in which changing regimes of care reconstitute existing divisions of labour. Finally, migration affects care relations in a number of ways; witness, for instance, the increase in women working outside the home which is a worldwide phenomenon, and the globalisation of both migration and capital that is reshaping the mixed economy of care. Such developments mean that arguments for a political ethics of care are as important among international policy-making bodies as they are among nation states.

A political ethics of care

Williams (2001) goes on to outline eight issues for an ethics of care, all of which warrant brief elaboration here. First, care is a meaningful activity that binds us all, in that everyone is involved, whether this is the care of oneself and/or others. Second, in giving and receiving care we learn the civic virtues of responsibility, tolerance for human limitations and frailties, and acceptance of diversity, all suggesting that it is part of genuine citizenship. The third issue is that an ethics of care demands interdependence as the basis of human interaction, with independence being about the capacity for self-determination rather than the expectation of individual self-sufficiency. Fourth, moral worth is attributed to the key positive caring dimensions of caring relationships such as dignity and the quality of human interaction, whether based on blood, kinship, sexual intimacy, friendship, collegiality, contract or service. Asking the question who is benefiting and who is not from existing care policies is the fifth issue, emphasising a stance antithetical to inequalities in care giving and receiving, whether related to gender in particular but also class, 'race', age, sexuality and religion among others. Challenging the false dichotomy of carer and cared for, and the relations of power in this, is the sixth issue. This means that those who have traditionally been without a voice in the social processes of care – for instance, disabled and older people, children and unpaid carers – have to be fully included, thereby recognising the importance of an inclusive citizenship. Seventh, quality, affordability, accessibility, flexibility, choice and control are the keys to service provision. Finally, care is not only personal but also an issue of public and political concern whose social dynamics operate at local, national and transnational levels.

We now come to the strategies to balance the ethics of work with the ethics of care. Over recent years there has been a new political discourse of the *work–life balance*, and Williams rightly argues that it provides a space in which to argue for an ethics of care, including thinking about time and space differently. Rather than care needs being fitted into the requirements of work, people's work–life needs can be viewed within three different but connected areas of their lives (Yeandle, 1999). First, there is *personal time and space*: what do we need for the care of self and maintenance of body, mind and soul? This includes mobility, relationships and relaxation. Second is *care time and space*: what do we need to properly care for others? This includes child and adult care provision, home care services, cleaning, laundry and food services, raising standards and rewards for paid carers, and state support for residential care. These would be underpinned by accessibility, affordability, quality, user control and so on; they would be complemented by the removal of disabling barriers around space, time, organisations and the environment, and a commitment to a caring, enabling environment such as safe and accessible public spaces and safe, accessible and affordable transport. Finally, there is *work time and space*: what do we need to enable us to gain economic self-sufficiency and balance these other areas? This includes paid maternity and paternity leave, paid carers' leave for women and men, job-sharing, work-based nurseries and breakfast/holiday clubs, decent universal pensions, and so forth. A 'care' culture would replace male breadwinning times and cultures, and this would prioritise the relational in people's lives.

All these areas are interlinked and they will have different emphases for different people. Some may find relationships at work key to their personal well-being, while others will want quality time with their children to provide the revitalisation qualities that are inherent in personal time. The important point, moreover, is to prioritise the opportunities to give and to receive care, and to normalise responsibilities for giving care and support as well as needs for receiving care and support. Such a stance goes a long way to balance the fixation with the ethics for work, but how realistic is it in these current neoliberal times? This is one of the questions to which I now turn.

After neoliberalism?

Following the catastrophe of the financial and economic crisis and resulting double-dip recession, the major political parties have started talking about the need to move towards a 'moral' and 'responsible' capitalism. Both Prime Minister David Cameron and Labour leader Ed Miliband have made significant speeches to this effect, and their remarks are reminiscent of former Prime Minster Ted Heath's comments about the 'unacceptable face of capitalism' during the early 1970s. Such politicians' voices chime with the anti-globalisation/capitalism protests that began in the late 1990s in Seattle and other cities, and have been ongoing ever since. Most recently there was the Occupy movement in London, New York and other cities. These popular protests were rightfully concerned about inequality, corporate greed and social injustice. More specifically, issues relate to neoliberalisation subverting nations' ability for self-determination, it having a disastrous environmental impact in terms of exhausting natural resources, and it leading to the increased exploitation of people.

Talk of morality and being responsible in relation to capitalism raises significant questions, particularly as to who the responsibility is supposed be to. Is it merely to shareholders and those few individuals at the top of global financial and business enterprises, or consumers and wider society? Then again, some might see mention of 'morality' and 'responsibility' in relation to capitalism as an oxymoron; although you may be able to find examples of 'caring' capitalists, the essence of the system is exploitative simply because it is aimed at creating maximum profits. Further, while some of the wealth might 'trickle down' to those at the bottom of society, the overall result is vast increases in inequality. Such issues, highlighted by the behaviour of bankers and the financial sector as a whole, led to the continuing global economic crisis and, have resulted in a questioning of the neoliberal project. Carolyn Noble and Mark Henrickson (2011), for example, pose the question 'After neoliberalism, new managerialism and postmodernism: what next for social work?' in an editorial for the *Journal of Social Work*. Fiona Robinson (2010) asks a similar question, 'after liberalism in world politics?' She points out that in October 2009 the London School of Economics and Political Science hosted a conference on international relations titled 'After Liberalism', this theme being emphasised in panel titles such as 'Liberalism and its Discontents' and 'RIP Neoliberalism: 1979-2009'. And Paul Michael Garrett (2010a, p 340) refers to 'faltering neoliberalization'. It is, of course, important to be cautious in heralding the demise of neoliberalism simply because neoliberal ontological categories and normative dispositions have been remarkably resilient during and since the current neoliberal debacle. However, the important point is that at the very least questions are beginning to be asked about the global dominance of neoliberal ideology.

During the 1980s the Thatcher and Reagan governments in the UK and US ushered in neoliberal, free market policies (see Chapter 3). Following the demise of the Soviet Union in 1991 there was an increased rhetorical and policy commitment to the values of neoliberalism, including the need to encourage the globalisation process. Fukuyama's (1993) *The end of history* was the credo for pursuing and achieving pro-neoliberal policies around the world. The West, through organisations such as the International Monetary Fund, The World Bank and World Trade Organization, foisted 'structural adjustment' and 'stabilisation' policies on various nation states that favoured multinational corporations, while simultaneously social provision for health, education and welfare had to be scaled back (Robinson, 2010). Witness what is presently happening to Greece and other southern European countries as a result of the Euro-zone crisis – public spending on welfare is being cut and public services are being privatised.[1]

There are at least two significant problems with such neoliberal 'solutions' (Noble and Henrickson, 2011). The first is that it is futile to view the unfettered free market as being able to somehow replace the state and provide for the needs of its citizens. Over the last three decades poverty and immiseration have increased in many countries, and the market has not been able to provide services or meet the needs of people like a robust welfare state once did (Harvey, 2007; Penna and O'Brien, 2009). Second, the deregulation of the market, of national politics and social life, turned to disaster in 2007/08 when the system of economic control by the capitalist class imploded and the state had to bail out collapsing financial markets and institutions. Capital accumulation across borders and cultures was supposed to enrich the global world, but it has been, and this is certainly putting it mildly, found wanting. Even before the financial collapse, millions of people in the developing world were falling deeper into debt and poverty, while people in the developed world were losing their homes, jobs and the safety-net of a decent welfare state. This resulted in feelings of anxiousness and insecurity for many or, in the title words of Jock Young's (2007) book, they were experiencing 'the vertigo of late modernity'.

At the beginning of this book, as well as the introduction to this chapter, we saw how Bourdieu bemoaned the effects of neoliberalism on the majority of people in the world, and similar concerns arise from a Foucaultian perspective. Lazzarato (2009), for instance, laments how neoliberalism has transformed society into an 'enterprise society' based on the market, competition, inequality, and the privileging of the individual. His complex but informative work looks at neoliberalism in action, showing how market capitalism has 'promoted insecurity, inequality and individualisation as part of ensuring the conditions for power to exercise a hold over conduct' (2009, p 110). To the extent that there is a concern with inequality, a government of the market based on competition and enterprise has to ensure that everyone is in a state of 'equal inequality'. This has involved the creation of a new form of individual, the subject who is 'an entrepreneur of himself/herself' and who is made to fit into a society that has been remade as the 'enterprise society'. The strategies of insecurity, inequality and individualisation have been used as part of a neoliberal social policy to undermine the principles and practices of mutualisation and redistribution inherent in the previous social democratic era when the welfare state was created. This neoliberal social policy is, therefore, an 'individual social policy' as opposed to a 'socialist social policy' that is based on the collectivisation and socialisation of social expenditure. It is one that not only promotes the growth of enterprise and the universalisation of the idea of enterprise, it must also transform its own services into enterprises, into sites of accumulation and profit. In the UK, for example, as we have seen, private companies are increasingly playing a role in health, education and the workfare schemes of job centres. Closer to home, as far as social work is concerned, there has been long-standing private sector involvement in adult and children's residential care, adults' home care and children's fostering. The obvious charge is that such ventures have, as their overriding goal, the need to make a profit, meaning that the needs of service users are subordinated to this imperative. More recently we have seen moves to encourage social workers to form their own practices rather than being employed directly by local authorities (Le Grand, 2007), although again there are concerns about the profit motive along with other pitfalls, all of which have been well elaborated (see Unison, 2011). Finally, we must note that the overall aim of neoliberal politics is the restoration of the power of capital to determine the distribution of wealth and to establish 'enterprise' as the dominant form. This may lead to the individual being at the mercy of the market, as well as being destructive of social bonds and the conditions for social cohesion, but it is supposed to be a price worth paying to ensure the 'enterprise society' prevails.

Although academics, global protest movements and perhaps public opinion more generally are questioning neoliberalism[2] and all it entails, what is less evident is a clear indication of what would fill the void on the way to, and after, its downfall? In short, what will, or should, take neoliberalism's place, and how do we get there? The answer to such questions has always been a problem for critics of current societal arrangements, whether they are unreconstructed Marxists, feminists, anti-racists or those (including postmodernists) concerned with managing the diversity of identities and the resulting myriad of claims and counter-claims for disability and cultural rights, sexual choices, religious freedoms and so forth. It ought to go without saying that there is no blueprint as to how a future society should be organised other than it should include such notions of social justice and equality for *all*. Reference has been made to a 'socialist social policy', this being the means to achieve such goals, but, in keeping with the issues and concerns in this book, I prefer the term radical/critical social policy, and it is to this that I now turn.

Towards a radical/critical social policy

As indicated in Chapter 6, radical/critical social policy engages with the age-old project of modernity, namely, emancipation, of ensuring all of humankind's needs are met, and ensuring social justice and equality (Rogowski, 2010a). Drawing on Marxism and aspects of feminism, anti-racism and postmodernism, there are two moral obligations to consider, namely, commitments to difference and to solidarity (Leonard, 1997). An obligation to difference means a responsibility to otherness, to the diversity of subjects, communities and cultures, and recognition of the value of the 'other'. It is in tension with the obligation to solidarity, of mutual interdependence. They must be continually balanced against each other because an unrestrained emphasis on difference leads to cultural exclusiveness, restricted identities or intense individualism, while unrestricted solidarity can lead to domination and homogenisation. It leads to policies and practices that recognise individual difference but that engage in discourses on the similarities between subjects confronting problems of, for example, identity or material survival, similarities that may be embedded in common experiences of class, gender and 'race' as well as other identities.

Furthermore, if one thinks about future policy, there are two ways of doing this (Levitas, 2001; see also 2011). First, and most common, is the method of extrapolation, the identification of key trends in the present and their projection forwards. The concern is with what is probable and possible, perhaps desirable, moving in small steps from where we are. It is rooted in the present, accepting the contours of present society, global capitalism/neoliberalism, the inequalities of the market and so on. The concern is with recapitulation as much as projection and extrapolation. Second, however, and radically, is the Utopian method that enjoins us to first think about where we want to be and how to get there.

As indicated, work and the work ethic are central themes to the current neoliberal consensus. There has been no attempt to build a consensus in favour of redistribution, reducing inequality, more progressive taxation or collective protection against risk. New Labour and the Coalition government's vision of the good society is a meritocracy where people do paid work, capitalism is allowed to run its course and there is no need to worry about incomes at the top. The rich deserve their wealth and are not resented, with the poor having abolished themselves by working in places such as McDonald's and call centres.

The point of the Utopian method, however, is that we stop and think where we are trying to get to, and for radical/critical theorists a starting point is the (admittedly problematic) concept of human need – what is necessary for a decent livelihood and decent life for all (Doyal and Gough, 1991). For example, Gorz (1999) argues for a break in the wage relation and a move beyond a wage-based society, advocating a basic income for all. A combination of basic income, decent public services and ecologically sustainable urban regeneration would make 'inclusion' a more meaningful term because it would entail greater equality. It is not reinventing and extending redistributive policies of social democracy (although that would be no bad thing), not even rethinking what constitutes work, but abandoning the work ethic itself – work can no longer be central to individual life projects. This resonates with Jordan's (2010) call for a basic or citizen's income so as to achieve improvements in social justice and equality.

A neglected area, however, and one that can be counter-posed to the work ethic, is the feminist-based ethics of care discussed above. An important point is that care ethics disrupt the dominant individual and society dichotomy by denying the ontological distinction between individuals and society, instead providing a view of creating ties rather than building bridges between individuals and society

(Sevenhuijsen, 2000; Robinson, 2010). As we saw, care ethics emphasises the universality of the need to give and to receive care, and critiques the near-universal undervaluing of the practices and labour of care and those who perform them. Significantly, ethics of care is a critique that reveals:

> ... how hidden dependencies support political economies, as well as how the social constructions of gender and race are constitutive of the value we place on caring practices, and how these assessments affect dominant understandings of 'autonomy', 'equality', 'labour' and 'citizenship'. (Robinson, 2010, p 137)

Furthermore, practices of care are the basic substance of morality; recognition of responsibilities to particular others and an understanding of the nature of those responsibilities are the first steps to be taken, followed by sustained attention to people as relational subjects who are both givers and receivers of care.

Bearing these comments in mind, there are two somewhat obvious questions that need addressing. The first is, how could all the changes outlined be afforded? Obviously, redistribution is one answer, across the life cycle and/or between groups of wage earners. Additionally, much more could certainly be demanded from the transnational corporations, with nation states acting collectively rather than competitively to limit flows of capital and to stop colluding with the fiction that neoliberal globalisation is a natural process (Monbiot, 2000). These might be transitional demands, as the kind of society eventually envisaged is incompatible with neoliberalism, but if acted on and implemented, this would enable the real needs of the service users mentioned throughout this book to be met.

The second question arises from the fact that to pursue much of the above, the power and resources of the state are needed. But how can a weakened state, as a result of the power of international capital, and deeply implicated in the political economy of neoliberalism, serve such an emancipatory purpose? In the context of the economic power of capital and with established political parties bending over backwards to work at its behest, prospects look bleak. However, perhaps a search for solidarity on basic economic and social issues while retaining a commitment to diversity is a way forward (Leonard, 1997). The new social movements focusing on identity politics, local community action and single issue alliances could become an organised solidarity based on a common interest in the development of policies that benefited all identities. Then there are the anti-capitalist/globalisation protests, along with the Occupy protests to consider; they are perhaps practical examples of an organised solidarity beginning to happen. Utopian as it may seem, such movements could lead to the establishment of a new kind of political party, one where member organisations join together not to obliterate their separate identities, but to express them, at least in part, through solidarity. Such a party could be described as a 'confederation of diversities' (Leonard, 1997, p 177), one that might well implement policies on the lines outlined, thereby contributing to equality and social justice for all.

A less Utopian social policy?

Perhaps in less Utopian terms, it is possible to make a compelling case against the pessimistic analysis of neoliberals that the welfare state must be cut back and that better alternatives are the market and self-interest. While this policy direction neglects the poor and vulnerable, there is an alternative one proposed by Alan Walker and colleagues based on the work of Peter Townsend, which would lead to a less fractured, more socially just society (Walker et al, 2011). The key elements of this manifesto for social justice are: an adequate income, sufficient to allow people to live decently and with dignity, in work, out of work, in childhood and in old age; a concerted attack on damaging social divisions in society – based, for example, on class, 'race', gender, and location – which result in exclusion, ill health and premature death; a universal child benefit and a universal basic pension paid at a level that enables full participation in society; a new welfare state at the heart of British life, aimed at nurturing the self-realisation of everyone, providing support when needed across the life course, and actively preventing poverty, inequality, ill health and exclusion; and an international welfare state in which rich nations redistribute large portions of their income to the poorest.

The manifesto does not simply state the case for social justice and list demands for policy action; it demonstrates the affordability of these basic demands. First, it rebuts the claim of the Coalition government that Britain is broke, and shows that the debt threat has been blown out of proportion; for instance, the size of the public sector is not out of step with other major European countries with more successful economic records. It also highlights alternative sources of revenue so as to avoid public spending cuts, such as closing tax loopholes and taxing vacant housing. Second, it points out that social justice in Britain depends on a fair tax system. At present the top 0.1 per cent of taxpayers benefit by more than £50,000 each from tax reliefs, and their pre-tax incomes are 31 times the average and their tax reliefs 86 times the average. Such a tax system can hardly be said to be fair and just.

Above all, the manifesto for social justice is realistic and realisable if policy makers reject inequality and choose to promote opportunities for every person in this country to live a decent and fulfilled life. So, having looked at what might come after neoliberalism in social policy terms, this brings me to a crucial part of the book: the future of critical social work with children and families.

The future of critical social work with children and families

As Paul Michael Garrett (2012) points out, it remains difficult to imagine the future(s) of social work although, significantly, it cannot be detached from the global economic crisis that erupted in 2007 as a result of three decades of neoliberalism. In the years to come, practice might not be unambiguously progressive and may simply be rooted in a defence of professional privilege, one that leads to the often authoritarian and negative neoliberal practice of present.

On the other hand, it may be grounded in a set of values and code of ethics that are potentially oppositional to neoliberalism. In either case, social work may have to be prepared for a 'long war' as neoliberalisation continues to try and enforce change that might take years, even decades, to become embedded. Even before the crisis Clarke (2004, pp 25-6) showed how there were:

> …[neoliberal] attempts to create new settlements – to fix meanings, to institutionalize them in new political-cultural formations and to naturalize them as necessary, inevitable and the best way of 'doing welfare'.

Such welfare discourses relate to how social work needs to be 'modern', entailing the current restricted and controlling aspects of welfare and social work services (Garrett, 2009b). In brief, the neoliberal aspiration is to try and create, within each individual worker and new entrant to the field, a new sense of professional milieu or habitus conducive to neoliberalisation (see also Bourdieu and Wacquant, 1992). Put more colloquially, it is about changing hearts and minds so as to facilitate the neoliberal project.

As I argued in *Social work: The rise and fall of a profession?* (Rogowski, 2010b), and echoing comments in the introduction to this book, there is a key problem that confronts social work and hinders its future. In spite of previous comments about the possibility of values/ethics in opposition to neoliberalism, and about what might lie 'after neoliberalism', the problem is that in the 'post-socialist' era (Fraser, 1997) all major parties in the UK, along with most of the governments and the main political parties in the developed (and increasingly the developing) world, accept a consensus or, more appropriately, a global ideology that continues to see neoliberalism (or, in more overtly Marxist terms, global capitalism) as the only way forward. This involves a social policy and resultant welfare state dominated by an economic agenda aimed at achieving maximum possible entry to the labour market to offset present social welfare costs and future health and pension costs (Spratt, 2008). This is despite the financial crisis and resulting global recession which in turn reflect all that is wrong with neoliberalisation. To the extent that Western governments have responded to the difficulties, it has amounted to propping up the system that is the root of all the problems. The dominance of neoliberalism largely remains, and the economic and political system this entails might emerge from the crisis largely unscathed. This is the reason why we have surely seen *both* the changing face of social work and arguably its fall. Here I elaborate a little more on this somewhat gloomy view (drawing on Rogowski, 2010b), prior to outlining some more optimistic, and yet hopefully realistic, possibilities.

The belief in free markets and limited state intervention remains intact, with resulting policies affecting developments in welfare and social work. In brief, 'market rule' dominates and focuses on the value of consumption, this in turn assuming people are *not* first and foremost citizens with rights, as well as responsibilities; rather they are simply consumers. But do we really want a society consisting of individual consumers responsible for satisfying their own needs by making economical choices in the marketplace? If this is the case, it produces a highly individualised vision of society, one that disregards issues of social justice and equality for all (Holland et al, 2007; Newman and Clarke, 2009). Again we come back to notions of self-reliance and 'standing on one's own feet', rather than more altruistic values such as cooperation and mutual support associated with collectivism.

The impact of such 'market rule' and neoliberalisation has led to the managerialism that besets social work. This involves controlling social workers and resources, ensuring risk is assessed and managed, and ensuring parents are made self-responsible for the care of their children with ever more decreasing help and support from the state via social work. In such a situation the future of social work remains uncertain, and one is tempted to say that there is unlikely to be a return to what can be considered its heyday of the 1970s, and even into the 1980s. The caring and supportive side of state social work does not fit in with the neoliberal ideology that emphasises people having to take responsibility for their own lives. Any element of 'care' might well be limited to being more of a navigator, helping users choose what service they require; it amounts to being simply a middleman/woman, in an increasingly business-oriented enterprise, aiming to satisfy customers' needs. Using current jargon, 'signposting' might be the future of social work. To the extent that a more substantial role might remain, it will be the authoritarian, controlling side, something that has increasingly been in evidence over recent decades. It may well be the case that eventually it will no longer be a unified profession; after all it was not long ago that there were calls to have separate degrees for those working with children and those with adults.

In future there may be opportunities for less qualified support, care and other workers – quasi-social workers if you will – to carry out what were social work responsibilities and roles. However, such workers will have less knowledge and understanding about the real situation of the people they are dealing with and their own position in the process of managing and controlling people who are essentially casualties of current societal arrangements. From its very beginnings, social work has attempted to challenge the status quo, and to do this knowledge and understanding is required. It is precisely because of this knowledge and understanding, which was gleaned from genuine attempts to develop a profession, that social work has been able to highlight inequalities and oppressions in present, neoliberal, society. It is also because of this that social work has increasingly come under attack and, more recently under New Labour, has actually been sidelined and largely ignored, at least until the 'Baby Peter' tragedy.

Perhaps all that can be expected over the coming years is that social workers will become even more the acceptable face of the state in saying that no or minimal services can be offered. Going further, as Dominelli (2009b, p 23) puts it, one scenario is that 'Growing inequalities, housing shortages, rising food and fuel prices and the threat of unemployment can combine to confine social work interventions to the dustbin of history as irrelevant or parasitic.' That is, of course, unless practitioners find new responses and 'resources for hope' to both current and forthcoming challenges. Similarly, Cree (2009) points out social work is at the crossroads and can either fight to hold onto its nascent professional status in the face of the encroachment of other professional groupings and managerialism, or, in effect, retreat and accept the status quo.

Students or newly qualified social workers might find the foregoing analysis somewhat disheartening, while more experienced practitioners and academics are likely to find a ring of truth. Whatever view is taken, I do not want to leave the reader with such a gloomy scenario. There are more positive views of the situation; one only has to bear in mind the earlier discussion about ethics of care and what is to come after neoliberalism. Then there is the actual practice outlined with various service user groups in the earlier chapters. Indeed, having got the somewhat pessimistic possible future prospects out of the way, let us now look at more positive possibilities, something that I have attempted to do previously (see, for example, Rogowski, 2011b).

In the first place, however, some overburdened practitioners argue that critical social work might be all well and good at a theoretical level, but how do you put such ideas into day-to-day practice? This arises because there can be a gap between radical/critical theory and practice, and it is certainly true that the 'old' radical strategies of group and community work no longer form a significant part of social work in the UK. Even so, the opportunities for such critical practice that remain need to be taken as otherwise the way is left clear for those who support the status quo. In particular, it is important to avoid seeing social work in terms of simply moral policing, the social control aspect, with more emphasis instead being given to the caring side, one that is concerned with social change and justice.

Nowadays, critical practice may have to amount to the previously mentioned 'quiet challenges' (White, 2009) and resistance to managerial and business-oriented discourses and practice (see, for example, Chapter 6 in relation to young offenders). Such challenges have similarities to the small-scale acts of resistance of 'deviant social work' (Carey and Foster, 2011). One example is just to ignore managerial 'advice', and to continue to work in real partnership with users on the issues of concern. Pursuing this and, for example, delaying the return of paperwork often means that by the time the manager is doing their 'checking', they have forgotten what their original 'advice' was, by now simply wanting to process the case as quickly as possible. When it comes to more specific cases, let us look at what critical practice might entail.

First, disaffected teenage young people can be hard to reach and engage with. A social worker could be faced with a 15-year-old young man with a disrupted care background. He might be challenging in terms of not going to school, being disruptive when there, and often going missing from home. Drug and alcohol misuse are other issues. He refuses to engage with social workers because, at the instigation of managers, they keep changing, or his case is closed. Faced with this, it is important that the young man's views are fully reflected in the various assessments and other reports, together with the need for practitioners to persevere, to be available and to be honest and consistent in their dealings with him. Admittedly, this can be a difficult task given that managers want to process cases speedily and with as little recourse to the public purse as possible. But attempts can be made and can be successful despite the difficulties, which resonates with arguments about the importance of relationship-based practice (Ruch et al, 2010).

A second example is that of a teenage girl who is continually absconding, staying out overnight, sometimes for days at a time. She also associates with other girls who then 'hang around' with or who are targeted by teenage and older young men who befriend and sexually exploit them. Again, in reports written for child exploitation meetings, instead of focusing on inadequate parenting, in effect blaming, often single-parent mothers doing their best in difficult circumstances, the practitioner could advocate for a more progressive response such as groupwork with the young woman concerned and her female friends, even though few social workers are currently allowed to use this method. This could, use an empowering model (for example, Mullender and Ward, 1991), focussing on the issues and concerns, but with an emphasis on young women learning from each other's experiences. The activities of the young women could be related to current society which, despite changes influenced by feminist thought, is still dominated by men.

A third example concerns a single parent and her two teenage children who recently moved into the area from another local authority. The mother had been diagnosed with bipolar disorder and her son with ADHD. She was on probation following an assault offence. In the previous local authority, the children had been subject to child protection/safeguarding plans because of domestic violence/abuse, which subsequently saw them 'downgraded' to being children 'in need', and then as children with 'additional needs', thus requiring an assessment under the Common Assessment Framework (CAF). Following the family's move, she telephoned children's services asking for financial assistance pending her benefits being sorted out. An initial assessment indicated that the children's needs were being met, that they were not at any risk, and that financial assistance was indeed needed to tide them over. However, a manager refused the financial assistance, merely saying a 'child in need' meeting needed to be convened with a view to a CAF being drawn up. The social worker felt differently and helped the mother write a letter of complaint. The mother also said she did not feel the necessity for a CAF and the social worker backed her up, as well as advocating on her behalf regarding benefits. In the end, the manager agreed on financial payments pending the benefits situation being resolved, also agreeing that a CAF, after all, would be superfluous.

In relation to child protection/safeguarding, following tragedies such as Victoria Climbié and 'Baby Peter', it is too easy for practitioners to fall into the trap of seeing themselves solely as the 'hard cops' of the welfare state. This is largely because of the role they have been forced into in the current neoliberal world, as a result often merely involving intrusive questioning, gathering information and in so doing, inspecting families' homes and lifestyles. All too often this is carried out *not* with the aim of finding out what help and support is needed to provide reasonable care of the children, but with a view to defending the organisation's reputation if things go wrong. Instead, social workers should work with children and families on the basis that they are potential allies in dealing with the issues under consideration. For instance, in a case of neglect (see, for example, Daniel et al, 2011), you could have young children arriving at school late or not at all, often dirty, ill-clad and hungry, because their single-parent mother is often hungover from repeated alcohol misuse and has been unable to get up. A neoliberal social work approach would be to simply tell her to change her lifestyle or face the consequences of child protection procedures and care proceedings. A more critical social work approach, however, would work on the issues of concern but in a more collaborative/partnership-oriented way by listening to, and wherever possible, acting on, the mother's and children's view of the situation. This would include spending time with the family, delving into the reasons for her drinking, her and her children's worries and anxieties and so on. Financial and housing problems, for example, might be factors. Linking the family members with, and if necessary accompanying them to, appropriate local groups and agencies dealing with their particular issues might be needed. Advocating on behalf of their situation might also be required. All this takes time, and could well be frowned upon by managers who merely want to quickly process such cases, but nonetheless, the resilient practitioner will find ways around this and create some space.

'Old' radical social work concerns with politicisation and consciencisation, for example, can still play a part, despite postmodernism assertions that challenge the basis of over-arching 'truths'. It is still possible to work with users on an individual basis with the aim of developing an understanding of the underlying causes of the problems and difficulties they face, namely, the neoliberal system we currently live in.

As well as practitioners working on an individual basis with users in progressive, radical/critical ways, there is also a role for collective action. This means acting with, for example, the British Association of Social Workers and the nascent College of Social Work so as to ensure a stronger professional identity. Then there is the Social Work Action Network, the radical/critical campaigning organisation that aims to develop strategies to resist managerialism. There is also the Global Agenda for Social Work and Social Development which which was presented to MPs in the House of Commons during March 2012. This offers a vision, inspiration and framework for social work internationally, one developed by the International Association of Schools of Social Work, the International Federation of Social Work and the International Council on Social Welfare (de Chenu et al, 2012). It looks at how social work can address social rights and the anti-social effects of globalisation, particularly the growth of inequalities in and between countries. As argued throughout this book, countries with larger inequalities, such as the UK, generate the worst measures of child well-being, poor outcomes in terms of health and social issues, and increased mental illness. The Global Agenda questions the increased emphasis on markets in welfare as well as neoliberalism itself because it exacerbates rather than redresses inequalities. Trade unions, of course, can and do assist in such collective processes, as do political parties and broader social groupings. The anti-globalisation movement is significant because of its ability to bring together disparate groups – trade unionists, environmentalists, peace campaigners, feminists, socialists and many others – to challenge the neoliberal world. Such 'unity in diversity' (Leonard, 1997, p 177) provides ways forward in challenging and resisting neoliberalisation.

Conclusion

Over the New Labour years the capacity of social work to be a force for progressive policy and social change was significantly eroded, and such a situation continues under a Conservative-led Coalition government. Current policies, involving massive public expenditure cuts and changes to social security, the NHS and education, have major implications for the ways in which services are delivered and experienced by individuals (Bochel, 2011). The shape of welfare services more generally is also continuing to change, with a smaller role for the state and a larger role for the private sector and potentially for social enterprises and the voluntary sector – the so-called 'Big Society'.[3] All this has an impact on social work, ultimately meaning social workers will have to put up with pressure to 'get more for less'; more and quicker paper/computer work being completed with fewer, and increasingly less qualified, staff. It involves less help, via collective provision through the state, for children and families who will increasingly have to rely on their own resources and contacts. Sadly, it is a return to Victorian times and the beginnings of professional social work.

Following Stepney (2006 p 1289) social work in the UK has been 'rebranded and reshaped' within a 'modernised' welfare state, only to become politically 'compromised and compliant' in the process; it has been '"the dog that didn't bark" even when its soul appeared to be stripped out'. Arguably the result is that in many ways, practising critical social work is 'mission impossible'. Or again, Jordan (2004) argues that emancipatory social work, rather than being an opportunity, can be an oxymoron in the current individualist age. However, the argument throughout this book is that this is not the whole story because, despite the many challenges, critical practice is possible and has the potential to combine

> the role of protection with prevention, whilst embodying possibilities for critical reflection and change. Further, it offers practitioners a means for critical engagement with the issues that lie at the root of injustice and exclusion so as to develop a more emancipatory approach, whilst resisting pressures for more enforcement and control. (Stepney 2006, p 1289)

It is about being aware of, and dealing with, the practices of power and resistance at a time when social work is increasingly embedded in the 'corporate era' (Davies and Leonard, 2004).

As Dominelli (2010, p 172) puts it, what is needed is a 'politics of practice', individual work with users as well as acting collectively with others so as to challenge inegalitarian social relations. This 'politics of practice' involves recognition, representation and redistribution. Recognition focuses on the strengths of service users. Representation helps individuals and communities to represent their views and aspirations to the 'powers that be'. And redistribution is about ensuring that resources, in both the UK and globally, are distributed equitably. Notions of mutuality, reciprocity and solidarity, all of which can be associated with an ethics of care and what may come 'after neoliberalism', are to the fore, rather than such neoliberal notions of self-interest, self-responsibility and not least, 'freedom'. In particular, it should be emphasised that the neoliberal version of 'freedom' is a bastardised version of the word, fundamentally being about the freedom of the powerful to exploit the weak, and the rich to exploit the poor (Monbiot, 2011). This leads to economic and social casualties and, as always, these are the people social work has to deal with.

In brief, critical social work is needed to challenge managerial-dominated, often authoritarian, neoliberal social work. It involves a practice that works towards a more socially just and equal world 'after neoliberalism'. The need to is to work towards 'social reform and for structural transformations as a precondition for human welfare' (Davies and Leonard, 2004, p 160).

Key points

Future developments in relation to social work with children and families need a critical response to counter the authoritarian, controlling aspects of practice that often dominate in the current neoliberal and managerial climate.

Feminist-based ethics of care provide an example of future Utopian possibilities, which are in tune with critical social work's emancipatory social justice and equality-based ambitions.

Neoliberalism has seemingly stalled, providing an opportunity for more Utopian reconstitutions of society whereby all humankind's basic needs are met and their full potentials realised.

Further reading

Barnes, M. (2012) *Care in everyday life: An ethic of care in practice*, Bristol: The Policy Press. This book provides a thorough analysis of care ethics and their centrality to understanding human life and social policy.

Garrett, P.M. (2012) 'The future of social work', in M. Grey, J. Midgley and S.A. Webb (eds) *The Sage handbook of social work*, London: Sage Publications. This provides some interesting thoughts on the future of social work, in particular its critical aspects, and manages to retain a sense of optimism for the profession's future.

Levitas, R. (forthcoming) *Utopia as method: The imaginary reconstitution of society*, Basingstoke: Palgrave Macmillan. This is sure to be a fascinating and informative book, one that helps prefigure a future more socially just and equal world.

Notes

[1] This echoes Naomi Klein's work which shows how catastrophes or 'social shocks' can be exploited by the powerful for political motives to force through economic restructuring so as to aid the neoliberal cause; it amounts to 'disaster capitalism' (Lavalette, 2011b).

[2] Perhaps surprisingly, although there is undoubted public anger against bankers and the financial system more generally, this does not seem to be directed against the neoliberal project and the free market economy as a whole. The roles of education and the media are key here, tending to focus on promoting neoliberalism as the only way society can be organised. To the extent that there are social ills/problems they are blamed on, for instance, the bloated public sector ('jobs-worths'), those dependent on welfare ('scroungers') and immigrants who are 'taking our jobs' and 'forcing wages down'. The 'Broken Britain' narrative of David Cameron also seems to have some purchase, notwithstanding that one of the key neoliberal values is competition, which has a destructive rather than a unifying effect by systematically undoing the cohesion that society constructs. On the whole, rather than look up and focus on structural issues in society such as the vast inequalities of wealth and power, most people tend to look down and blame/scapegoat others for their own precarious predicament. There is much to be said about 'divide and rule' being used by those with power.

[3] An important component of the 'Big Society' is, of course, charity and perhaps this is most obviously seen in the alarming growth of food banks. It is not only such as the sick, old and unemployed that are being forced into using them, but many of the working poor too; a sad comment on current societal arrangements.

References

Abel-Smith, B. and Townsend, P. (1966) *The poor and the poorest*, London: Bell & Sons.

Adams, R. (1996) *Social work and empowerment*, London: Macmillan.

Bailey, R. and Brake, M. (eds) (1975a) *Radical social work*, London: Edward Arnold.

Bailey, R. and Brake, M. (1975b) 'Introduction: social work in the welfare state', in R. Bailey and M. Brake (eds) *Radical social work*, London: Edward Arnold, pp 1-12.

Banks, S. (2001) *Ethics and values in social work* (2nd edn), London: Palgrave.

Barclay Report (1982) *Social workers: Their roles and tasks*, London: Bedford Square Press.

Barnes, C., Mercer, G. and Shakespeare, T. (2005) *Exploring disability: A sociological introduction*, Oxford: Polity Press.

Barnes, M. (2012) *Care in everyday life: An ethic of care in practice*, Bristol: The Policy Press.

Bateman, N. (2000) *Advocacy skills for health and social care professionals*, London: Jessica Kingsley Publishers.

Bateman, T. (2011) '"We now breach more kids in a week than we used to in a whole year": the punitive turn, enforcement and custody', *Youth Justice*, vol 11, no 2, pp 115-33.

BBC (2011a) *News*, 4 February.

BBC (2011b) *Question Time*, 27 October.

BBC (2011c) *News*, 15 November.

Beasley, C. (1999) *What is feminism? An introduction to feminist theory*, London: Sage Publications.

Beck, U. (1992) *Risk society: Towards a new modernity*, London: Sage Publications.

Becker, H.S. (1963) *Outsiders: Studies in the sociology of deviance*, London: Macmillan.

Becker, H.S. (1967) 'Whose side are we on?', *Social Problems*, vol 14, no 3.

Bell, S. (2011) *The Guardian*, 21 January.

Beresford, P. and Croft, S. (1993) *Citizen involvement: A practical guide for change*, Basingstoke: Macmillan.

Berger, P. and Luckmann, T. (1971 [1966]) *The social construction of reality*, Harmondsworth: Penguin.

Berry, J.W. (1988) 'Acculturation and psychological adaptation among refugees', in D. Miserez et al, *Refugees: The trauma of exile, the humanitarian role of the Red Cross and Red Crescent*, Dordrecht: Martinus Nijhof.

Blagg, H. and Smith, D. (1989) *Crime, penal policy and social work*, Harlow: Longman.

Blair, T. (1998) *The third way*, Fabian Pamphlet 558, London: Fabian Society.

Blond, P. (2010) *Red Tory: How left and right have broken Britain, and how we can fix it*, London: Faber & Faber.

Bochel, H. (ed) (2011) *The Conservative Party and social policy*, Bristol: The Policy Press.

Bokhari, F. (2008) 'Falling through the gaps: Safeguarding children trafficked into the UK', *Children & Society*, vol 22, no 3, pp 201-11.

Bokhari, F. (2012) 'Separated children in the UK: Policy and legislation', in E. Kelly and F. Bokhari (eds) *Safeguarding children from abroad: Refugee, asylum seeking and trafficked children in the UK*, London: Jessica Kingsley Publishers, pp 20-36.

Bostock, L. (2003) *Effectiveness of childminding registration and its implications for private fostering*, SCIE Position Paper No 1, London: Social Care Institute for Excellence.

Bottoms, A. (1995) 'The philosophy and politics of punishment and sentencing', in C. Clarkson and R. Morgan (eds) *The politics of sentencing reform*, Oxford: Oxford University Press.

Bourdieu, P. (1998) *Acts of resistance: Against the new myths of our time*, Cambridge: Polity Press.

Bourdieu, P. and Wacquant, L. (1992) *An invitation to reflexive sociology*, Cambridge: Polity Press.

Bradshaw, J. (ed) (2011) *The well-being of children in the UK*, Bristol: The Policy Press.

Brake, M. and Bailey, R. (eds) (1980) *Radical social work and practice*, London: Edward Arnold.

Broad, B. (2005) *After the Act: Implementing the Children (Leaving Care) Act 2000*, Leicester: de Montfort University.

Broadhurst, K. (2009) 'Safeguarding children through parenting support: How does every parent matter?', in K. Broadhurst, C. Grover and J. Jamieson (eds) *Critical perspectives on safeguarding children*, Chichester: Wiley-Blackwell, pp 111-30.

Broadhurst, K., Grover, C. and Jamieson, J. (eds) (2009) *Critical perspectives on safeguarding children*, Chichester: Wiley-Blackwell.

Broadhurst, K., Hall, C., Wastell, D. et al (2010b) 'Risk, instrumentalism and the humane project in social work: Identifying the informal logics of risk management in children's statutory services', *British Journal of Social Work*, vol 40, no 4, pp 1046-64.

Broadhurst, K., Wastell, D., White, S. et al (2010a) 'Performing initial assessment: Identifying the latent conditions for error at the front door of local authority children's services', *British Journal of Social Work*, vol 40, no 2, pp 352-70.

Bullock, R., Courtney, M., Sinclair, I. and Thorburn, J. (2006) 'Can the corporate state parent?', *Adoption and Fostering*, vol 30, no 4, pp 6-19.

Butler, I. and Drakeford, M. (2001) 'Which Blair Project: Communitarianism, social authoritarianism and social work', *Journal of Social Work*, vol 1, no 1, pp 7-19.

CAB (Citizens' Advice Bureau) (2002) *CAB clients' experiences of the NASS*, London: CAB Publications.

Calhoun, C. (1995) *Critical social theory*, Oxford: Blackwell.

Callinicos, A. (1999) *Social theory: A historical introduction*, Cambridge: Polity Press.

Carey, M. and Foster, V. (2011) 'Introducing "deviant" social work: Contextualising the limits of radical social work whilst understanding (fragmented) resistance in the state social work labour process', *British Journal of Social Work*, vol 41, no 3, pp 576-93.

CEOP (Child Exploitation and Online Protection Centre) (2010) *Strategic threat assessment: Child trafficking in the UK*, London: CEOP.

Channel 4 (2011) *Main News*, 9 November.

Charles, M. and Wilton, J. (2004) 'Creativity and constraint in child welfare', in M. Lymbery and S. Butler (eds) *Social work ideals and practice realities*, Basingstoke: Palgrave Macmillan, pp 179-99.

Clarke, J. (2004) *Changing welfare, changing states: New directions in social policy*, London: Sage Publications.

Clarke, J. and Newman, J. (1997) *The managerial state*, London: Sage Publications.

Clarke, J. and Newman, J. (2012) 'The alchemy of austerity', *Critical Social Policy*, vol 32, no 3, pp 299-319.

Clawson, R. (2011) 'Social work with disabled children and adults', in K. Wilson, G. Ruch, M. Lymbery and A. Cooper et al, *Social work: An introduction to contemporary practice*, 2nd edn, Harlow: Pearson, pp 566-92.

Cleaver, H. and Walker, S. (2004) 'From policy to practice: The implementation of a new framework for social work assessment of children and families', *Child and Family Social Work*, vol 9, pp 81-90.

Cohen, S. (1975) 'It's all right for you to talk: Political and sociological manifestos for social action', in R. Bailey and M. Brake (eds) *Radical social work*, London: Edward Arnold, pp 76-95.

Cohen, S. (1985) *Visions of social control*, Cambridge: Polity Press.

Cohen, S. (2001) *Immigration controls, the family and the welfare state*, London: Jessica Kingsley Publishers.

Cohen, S. (2002) 'The local state of immigration controls', *Critical Social Policy*, vol 22, no 3, pp 518-43.

Cohen, S. (2003) *No one is illegal: Asylum and immigration control past and present*, Stoke-on-Trent: Trentham Books.

Cohen, S., Humphries, B. and Mynott, E. (eds) (2002) *From immigration to welfare controls*, London: Jessica Kingsley Publishers.

Colley, H. and Hodkinson, P. (2001) 'Problems with Bridging the Gap: the reversal of structure and agency in addressing social exclusion', *Critical Social Policy*, vol 21, no 3, pp 335-59.

Community Care (2012a) 'Privatisation of CAHMS by Richard Branson in Devon', 22 March (www.communitycare.co.uk).

Community Care (2012b) 'Fear over plans to "slaughter" child protection guidance', 28 March (www.communitycare.co.uk).

Connors, C. and Stalker, K. (2003) *The views and experiences of disabled children and their siblings*, London: Jessica Kingsley Publishers.

Contact a Family (2012) 'Statistics' (www.caf.org.uk).

Cook, D. (2006) *Criminal and social justice*, London: Sage Publications.

Cook, P. (2000) *Final report on disabled children and abuse: Research project funded by Children in Need*, Nottingham: Ann Craft Trust.

Cooke, P. and Standen, P.J. (2002) 'Abuse and disabled children: Hidden needs?', *Child Abuse Review*, vol 11, pp 1-18.

Cooper, J. (20011a) 'Child protection volunteers help children and save money study finds', *Community Care*, 29 November.

Cooper, J. (2011b) 'Mental health cuts put services for younger children under pressure', *Community Care*, 29 September.

Corrigan, P. and Leonard, P. (1979) *Social work practice under capitalism*, London: Macmillan.

Crawley, H. (2010) 'No one gives you a chance to say what you're thinking', *Area*, vol 42, no 2, pp 162-9.

Crawley, H. and Kelly, E. (2012) 'Asylum, age disputes and the process of age assessment', in E. Kelly and F. Bokhari (eds) *Safeguarding children from abroad: Refugee, asylum seeking and trafficked children in the UK*, London: Jessica Kingsley Publishers, pp 55-68.

Cree, V. (2009) 'The changing nature of social work', in R. Adams, L. Dominelli and M. Payne (eds) *Social work: Themes, issues and critical debates* (3rd edn), Basingstoke: Palgrave Macmillan, pp 26-56.

Crow, B. (2011) 'Letter', *The Times*, 13 November.

Crow, L. (1996) 'Including all of our lives: Renewing the social model of disability', in J. Morris (ed) *Encounters with strangers, feminism and disability*, London: Women's Press.

Dalrymple, J. and Burke, B. (2006) *Anti-oppressive practice: Social care and the law* (2nd edn), Buckingham: Open University Press.

Daniel, B. (2012) 'Foreword', in E. Kelly and F. Bokhari (eds) *Safeguarding children from abroad: Refugee, asylum seeking and trafficked children in the UK*, London: Jessica Kingsley Publishers, pp 7-8.

Daniel, B., Taylor, J. and Scott, J. with Derbyshire, D. and Neilson, D. (2011) *Recognizing and helping the neglected child: Evidenced-based practice for assessment and intervention*, London: Jessica Kingsley Publishers.

Davies, L. and Leonard, P. (eds) (2004) *Social work in a corporate era: Practices of power and resistance*, Aldershot: Ashgate.

DCSF (Department for Children, Schools and Families) (2007) *Care matters: Time for change*, London: DCSF.

DCSF (2009) *Safeguarding disabled children: Practice guidance*, London: The Stationery Office.

Deacon, A. (2002) *Perspectives on welfare*, Buckingham: Open University Press.

Deakin, N. (1987) *The politics of welfare*, London: Methuen.

Dearling, A. and Skinner, A. (eds) (2002) *Making a difference: Practice and planning in working with young people in community safety and crime prevention programmes*, Lyme Regis: Russell House.

de Beauvoir, S. (1964) *The second sex*, London: Bantum Books.

de Chenu, L., Sims, S. and Williams, J. (2012) 'Getting to know the global agenda', *Professional Social Work*, March, pp 24-5.

DES (Department for Education and Skills) (2004) *Every Child Matters: Change for children*, London: The Stationery Office.

DES (2006a) *Care matters: Looked-after children*, London: The Stationery Office.

DES (2006b) *Children looked after in England 2005-6*, London: DES.

DES (2007) *Aiming high for disabled children: Better support for families*, London: DES.

DfEE (Department for Education and Employment) (2001) *Sure Start: Making a difference for children and families*, London: DfEE.

DH (Department of Health) (1995) *Child protection: Messages from research*, London: HMSO.

DH (1999) *National priorities guidance for children's services*, London: The Stationery Office.

DH (2000a) *Framework for the assessment of children in need and their families*, London: The Stationery Office.

DH (2000b) *Carers and Disabled Children's Act 2000*, London: The Stationery Office.

DH (2002) *Meeting the needs of disabled children*, London: The Stationery Office.

DH and DES (2004) *National service framework for children, young people and maternity services*, London: The Stationery Office.

Disability Allowance (2011) *Welfare Reform Bill 2011* (www.disabilityalliance.org/ibchanges5.htm).

Dixon, J. (2010) 'Supervision, ethics and risk', *British Journal of Social Work*, vol 40, no 8, pp 2398-413.

Dominelli, L. (1997) *Anti-racist social work*, Basingstoke: Macmillan.

Dominelli, L. (2002a) *Feminist social work theory and practice*, Basingstoke: Palgrave Macmillan.

Dominelli, L. (2002b) *Anti-oppressive social work theory and practice*, Basingstoke: Palgrave Macmillan.

Dominelli, L. (2009a) 'Anti-oppressive practice: The challenges of the twenty-first century', in R. Adams, L. Dominelli and M. Payne (eds) *Social work: Themes, issues and critical debates* (3rd edn), Basingstoke: Palgrave Macmillan, pp 49-64.

Dominelli, L. (2009b) 'Repositioning social work', in R. Adams, L. Dominelli and M. Payne (eds) *Social work: Themes, issues and critical debates* (3rd edn), Basingstoke: Palgrave Macmillan, pp 13-25.

Dominelli, L. (2010) *Social work in a globalising world*, Cambridge: Polity Press.

Dominelli, L. and McCleod, E. (1989) *Feminist social work*, Basingstoke: Macmillan.

Dorling, D. (2010) *Injustice: Why social inequality persists*, Bristol: The Policy Press.

Dowling, M. and Dolan, L. (2001) 'Disabilities: inequalities and the social model', *Disability & Society*, vol 16, no 1, pp 21-36.

Doyal, L. and Gough, I. (1991) *A theory of human need*, London: Macmillan.

Eagleton, T. (2011) *Why Marx was right*, New Haven, CT: Yale University Press

Ely, P. and Denney, D. (1987) *Social work in a multi-racial society*, Aldershot: Gower.

Engels, F. (1973 [1892]) *The condition of the working class in England*, Moscow: Progress Publishers.

European Commission (2010) *Communication from the Commission to the European Parliament and the Council: Action plan on unaccompanied minors (2010-14)*, SEC (2010) 534, Brussels: European Commission.

Farnsworth, K. (2011) 'From economic crisis to a new age of austerity: the UK', in K. Farnsworth and Z. Irving (eds) *Social policy in challenging times: Economic crisis and welfare systems*, Bristol: The Policy Press, pp 251-70.

Farrington, D. and Langan, P. (1992) 'Changes in crime and punishment in England and America in the 1980s', *Justice Quarterly*, vol 9, pp 5-46.

Fell, P. and Hayes, D. (2007) *What are they doing here? A critical guide to asylum and immigration*, Birmingham: Venture Press.

Ferguson, H. (2011) *Child protection practice*, Basingstoke: Palgrave Macmillan.

Ferguson, I. (2007) 'Increasing user choice or privatizing risk? The antinomies of personalisation', *British Journal of Social Work*, vol 37, no 3, pp 387-403.

Ferguson, I. (2008) *Reclaiming social work: Challenging neoliberalism, promoting social justice*, London: Sage Publications.

Ferguson, I. (2011) 'Why class (still) matters', in M. Lavalette (ed) *Radical social work today: Social work at the crossroads*, Bristol: The Policy Press, pp 115-34.

Ferguson, I. and Lavalette, M. (2009) *Social work after Baby P: Issues, debates and alternative perspectives*, Liverpool: Liverpool Hope University Press.

Ferguson, I. and Woodward, R. (2009) *Radical social work in practice: Making a difference*, Bristol: The Policy Press.

Finch, N. (2012) 'Return of separated children to counties of origin', in E. Kelly and F. Bokhari (eds) *Safeguarding children from abroad: Refugee, asylum seeking and trafficked children in the UK*, London: Jessica Kingsley Publishers, pp 119-34.

Firestone, W.A. (1990) 'Accommodation: Towards a paradigm-praxis dialectic', in E.G. Guba (ed) *The paradigm dialogue*, London: Sage Publications.

Fook, J. (2002) *Social work: Critical theory and practice*, London: Sage Publications.

Fook, J. (2004) 'Critical reflection and transformative possibilities', in L. Davies and P. Leonard (eds) *Social work in a corporate era*, Aldershot: Ashgate.

Fook J. (2012) Social Work: a critical approach to practice London: Sage Publications

Fook, J. and Gardner, F. (2007) *Practising critical reflection*, Maidenhead: Open University Press.

Franklin, A. and Sloper, P. (2006) 'Participation of disabled children and young people in decision making within social services departments: A survey of current and recent activities in England', *British Journal of Social Work*, vol 36, no 5, pp 723-41.

Fraser, D. (2002) *The evolution of the welfare state*, London: Palgrave Macmillan.

Fraser, N. (1997) *Justice interruptus: Critical reflections on the post-socialist condition*, London: Routledge.

Freire, P. (1972) *Pedagogy of the oppressed*, Harmondsworth: Penguin.

French, S. (1994) 'What is disability?', in S. French (ed) *On equal terms: Working with disabled people*, Oxford: Butterworth-Heinemann.

Friedman, M. (1962) *Capitalism and freedom*, Chicago, IL: University of Chicago Press.

Fukuyama, F. (1993) *The end of history and the last man*, Harmondsworth: Penguin.

Garrett, P.M. (2002) 'Getting a grip: New Labour and the reform of the law on adoption', *Critical Social Policy*, vol 22, no 2, pp 174-202.

Garrett, P.M. (2003) *Remaking social work with children and families: A critical discussion of the 'modernisation' of social care*, London: Routledge.

Garrett, P.M. (2005) 'Social work's electronic turn: Notes on the deployment of information and communication technologies in social work with children and families', *Critical Social Policy*, vol 25, no 4, pp 529-53.

Garrett, P.M. (2008) 'Thinking with the Sardinian: Antonio Gramsci and social work', *European Journal of Social Work*, vol 11, no 3, pp 237-50.

Garrett, P.M. (2009a) 'The case of Baby P: Opening up spaces for the debate on the "transformation" of children's services?', *Critical Social Policy*, vol 29, no 3, pp 533-47.

Garrett, P.M. (2009b) *Transforming children's services: Social work, neoliberalism and the 'modern' world*, Maidenhead: Open University Press.

Garrett, P.M. (2009c) 'The "whalebone" in the (social work) corset? Notes on Gramsci and social work educators', *Social Work Education*, vol 28, no 5, pp 461-75.

Garrett, P.M. (2010a) 'Examining the "Conservative revolution": neoliberalism and social work education', *Social Work Education*, vol 29, no 4, pp 340-355.

Garrett, P.M. (2010b) 'Creating happier children and more fulfilled social workers: Neoliberalism, privatisation and the reframing of leftish critiques in Britain', *Journal of Progressive Human Services*, vol 21, no 1, pp 83-101.

Garrett, P.M. (2010c) 'Marx and "modernization": Reading *Capital* as social critique and inspiration for social work resistance to neoliberalization', *Journal of Social Work*, vol 9, no 2, pp 199-221.

Garrett, P.M. (2012) 'The future of social work', in M. Grey, J. Midgley and S.A. Webb (eds) *The Sage handbook of social work*, London: Sage Publications, pp 631-45.

Garret P. M. (2013) *Social work and social theory*, Bristol: The Policy Press.

Gelsthorpe, L. and Morris, A. (1994) 'Juvenile justice 1945-1992', in M. Maguire, R. Morgan and R. Reiner (eds) *The Oxford handbook of criminology*, Oxford: Oxford University Press.

George, V. and Wilding, P. (1993) *Welfare and ideology*, Hemel Hempstead: Harvester Wheatsheaf.

Ghate, D. and Hazel, N. (2002) *Parenting in poor environments: Stress, support and coping*, London: Jessica Kingsley Publishers.

Giddens, A. (1994) *Beyond left and right*, Cambridge: Polity Press.

Giddens, A. (1998) *The third way*, Cambridge: Polity Press.

Giddens, A. (2000) *The third way and its critics*, Cambridge: Polity Press.

Goldson, B. (ed) (1999) *Youth justice: Contemporary policy and practice*, Aldershot: Ashgate.

Goldson, B. (2000) *The new youth justice*, Lyme Regis: Russell House.

Goldson, B. (2006) 'Penal custody: Intolerance, irrationality and indifference', in B. Goldson and J. Muncie (eds) *Youth crime and youth justice: Critical issues*, London: Sage Publications.

Goldson, B. (2007) 'New Labour's youth justice: A critical assessment of the first two terms', in G. McIvor and P. Raynor (eds) *Developments in social work with offenders*, London: Jessica Kingsley Publishers.

Goldson, B. and Muncie, J. (eds) (2006) *Youth crime and justice*, London: Sage Publications.

Goodman, S. and Trowler, I. (eds) (2012) *Social work reclaimed: Innovative frameworks for child and family work practice*, London: Jessica Kingsley Publishers.

Gorz, A. (1999) *Reclaiming work: Beyond the wage-based society*, Cambridge: Polity Press.

Gough, I. (1979) *The political economy of the welfare state*, London: Macmillan.

Grady, P. (2004) 'Social work responses to accompanied asylum seeking children', in D. Hayes and B. Humphries (eds) *Social work, immigration and asylum: Debates, dilemmas and ethical issues for social work and social care*, London: Jessica Kingsley Publishers, pp 132-50.

Green, R. (2002) *Mentally ill parents and children's welfare*, London: NSPCC.

Grover, C. (2009) 'Child poverty', in K. Broadhurst, C. Grover and J. Jamieson (eds) *Critical perspectives on safeguarding children*, Chichester: Wiley-Blackwell, pp 55-72.

Habermas, J. (1981a) *The theory of communicative action. Vol 1: Reason and the rationalization of society*, London: Heinemann.

Habermas, J. (1981b) *The theory of communicative action. Vol 2: Lifeworld and system*, Cambridge: Polity Press.

Habermas, J. (1987) *The philosophical discourse of modernity*, Cambridge, MA: MIT Press.

Hagell, A. and Newburn, T. (1994) *Persistent young offenders*, London: Policy Studies Institute.

Haines, K. (2009) 'Youth justice and young offenders', in R. Adams, L. Dominelli and M. Payne (eds) *Critical practice in social work*, Basingstoke: Palgrave Macmillan, pp 293-302.

Hall, C., Peckover, S. and White, S. (2008) 'How practitioners use ICT in social care work', *Community Care*, 15 May, pp 26-7.

Hammersley, M. and Atkinson, P. (1995) *Ethnography: Principles and practice*, London: Routledge.

Hanmer, J. and Statham, D. ([1988] 1999) *Women and social work: Towards a more women-centred practice*, Basingstoke: Macmillan.

Harris, J. (2003) *The social work business*, London: Routledge.

Harris, J. and White, V. (eds) (2009) *Modernising social work: Critical considerations*, Bristol: The Policy Press.

Harvey, D. (2007) *A brief history of neo-liberalism*, Oxford: Oxford University Press.

Harvey, L. (1990) *Critical social research*, London: Hyman Unwin.

Hayek, F.A. (1982) *Law, legislation and liberty: A new statement of the principles of the liberal principles of justice and political economy*, Vols 1-3, London: Routledge & Kegan Paul.

Hayes, D. (2004) 'History and context: The impact of immigration control on welfare delivery', in D. Hayes and B. Humphries (eds) *Social work, immigration and asylum: Debates, dilemmas and ethical issues for social work and social care practice*, London: Jessica Kingsley Publishers, pp 11-28.

Hayes, D. and Humphries, B. (eds) (2004a) *Social work, immigration and asylum: Debates, dilemmas and ethical issues for social work and social care*, London Jessica Kingsley Publishers.

Hayes, D. and Humphries, B. (2004b) 'Conclusion', in D. Hayes and B. Humphries (eds) *Social work, immigration and asylum: Debates, dilemmas and ethical issues for social work and social care*, London: Jessica Kingsley Publishers, pp 217-25.

Healy, K. (2000) *Social work practices: Contemporary perspectives on change*, London: Sage Publications.

Held, V. (2006) *The ethics of care: Personal, political and global*, Oxford: Oxford University Press.

Heller, R., Jamrozik, K. and Weller, D. (2004) 'Suspected child abuse: False positives and false negatives', *Medical Journal of Australia*, vol 181, no 5.

Henderson, P. and Thomas, D. (2002) *Skills in neighbourhood work* (3rd edn), London: Routledge.

Hill, M. and Hopkins, P. (2009) 'Safeguarding children who are refugees or asylum seekers: Managing multiple scales of legislation and policy', in K. Broadhurst, C. Grover and J. Jamieson (eds) *Critical perspectives on safeguarding children*, Chichester: Wiley-Blackwell, pp 229-46.

HM Government (2005) *Controlling our borders: Making migration work for Britain*, London: The Stationery Office.

HM Government (2006) *Working together to safeguard children*, London: The Stationery Office.

HM Government (2007a) *Building on progress: Public services*, London: Cabinet Office.

HM Government (2007b) *Putting people first: A shared vision and commitment to the transformation of adult social care*, London: Cabinet Office.

HM Government (2010) *Working together to safeguard children: A guide to inter-agency working to safeguard and promote the welfare of children*, London: The Stationery Office.

Hobsbawm, E. (2011) *How to change the world: Tales of Marx and Marxism*, London: Little Brown.

Holland, D., Nonini, S., Lutz, C., Bartlett, L., Frederick-McGlathery, M., Gulbranson, T. and Murillo, E. (2007) *Local democracy under siege: Activism, public interests and private politics*, New York: New York University Press.

Holman, B. (2002) *The unknown fostering: A study of private fostering*, Lyme Regis: Russell House.

Home Office (1997) *No more excuses: A new approach to tackling youth crime in England and Wales*, London: The Stationery Office.

Home Office (2002) *Secure borders, safe haven: Integration with diversity in modern Britain*, London: Home Office.

Home Office (2008) *Better outcomes: The way forward. Improving the care of unaccompanied asylum seeking children*, London: Home Office.

Home Office/DH (Department of Health)/DES (Department of Education and Science)/Welsh Office (1991) *Working together under the Children Act 1989: A guide to arrangements for interagency co-operation for the protection of children from abuse*, London: HMSO.

Howe, D. (1992) 'Child abuse and the bureaucratisation of social work', *Sociological Review*, vol 40, no 3, pp 491-508.

Hudson, B. (2003) *Justice in the risk society*, London: Sage Publications.

Hughes, L. and Owen, H. (2009) *Good practice in safeguarding children: Working effectively in child protection*, London: Jessica Kingsley Publishers.

Humphries, B. (2002) 'From welfare to authoritarianism: The role of social work in immigration control', in S. Cohen, B. Humphries and E. Mynott (eds) *From immigration controls to welfare controls*, London: Routledge, pp 126-40.

Humphries, B. (2004) 'An unacceptable role for social work: Implementing immigration policy', *British Journal of Social Work*, vol 34, no 1, pp 93-107.

Hunt, L. (2011) 'Parents who feel "set up to fail"', *Community Care*, 29 September, pp 20-1.

Hunter, S. and Ritchie, P. (eds) (2007) *Co-production and personalisation in social care: Changing relationships in the provision of social care*, London: Jessica Kingsley Publishers.

IFS (Institute for Fiscal Studies) (2010) *Economist* (www.ifs.org.uk/budgets/budgetjune2010/chote.pdf).

IND (Immigration and Nationality Directorate) and ADSS (Association of Directors of Social Services) (2004) *Age assessment joint working protocol between the Immigration and Nationality Directorate of the Home Office (IND) and Association of Directors of Social Services (ADSS) for UK local government and statutory childcare agencies*, London: IND and ADSS.

Ishola, P. (2012) 'Identification of separated children in the UK', in E. Kelly and F. Bokhari (eds) *Safeguarding children from abroad: Refugee, asylum seeking and trafficked children in the UK*, London: Jessica Kingsley Publishers, pp 37-54.

Jameson, F. (1992) *Postmodernism or the cultural logic of late capitalism*, London: Verso.

Jamieson, J. (2009) 'In search of youth justice', in K. Broadhurst, C. Grover and J. Jamieson (eds) *Critical perspectives on safeguarding children*, Chichester: Wiley-Blackwell, pp 189-210.

Jones, C. (1999) 'Social work: Regulation and managerialism', in M. Exworthy and S. Halford (eds) *Professionalism and the new managerialism in the public sector*, Buckingham: Open University Press, pp 37-49.

Jones, C. (2004) 'The neoliberal assault: Voices from the frontline of British social work', in I. Ferguson, M. Lavalette and E. Whitemore (eds) *Globalisation, global justice and social work*, London: Routledge, pp 95-106.

Jordan, B. (2001) 'Tough love: Social work, social exclusion and the Third Way', *British Journal of Social Work*, vol 31, pp 527-46.

Jordan, B. (2004) 'Emancipatory social work: Opportunity or oxymoron?', *British Journal of Social Work, vol 34*, no 1, pp 5-1.

Jordan, B. (2007) *Social work and well-being*, Lyme Regis: Russell House.

Jordan, B. (2008) *Welfare and well-being: Social value in public policy*, Bristol: The Policy Press.

Jordan, B. (2010) *Why the Third Way failed: Economics, morality and the origins of the 'Big Society'*, Bristol: The Policy Press.

Jordan, B. (2012) Personal communication.

Jordan, B. and Parton, N. (eds) (1983) *The political dimensions of social work*, Oxford: Basil Blackwell.

Joseph, J. (2006) *Marxism and social theory*, Basingstoke: Palgrave Macmillan.

Kelly, E. and Bokhari, F. (2012a) 'Introduction', in E. Kelly and F. Bokhari (eds) *Safeguarding children from abroad: Refugee, asylum seeking and trafficked children in the UK*, London: Jessica Kingsley Publishers, pp 9-20.

Kelly, E. and Bokhari, F. (eds) (2012b) *Safeguarding children from abroad: Refugee, asylum seeking and trafficked children in the UK*, London: Jessica Kingsley Publishers.

Kidane, S. (2001) *Food, shelter and half a chance: Assessing the needs of unaccompanied asylum-seeking and refugee children*, London: British Association for Adoption and Fostering.

Kilbrandon Report (1964) *Children and young people in Scotland*, Edinburgh: HMSO

Kincaid, J. (1973) *Poverty and equality in Britain*, London: Pelican.

King, P. (2011) *The new politics: Liberal conservatism or the same old Tories?*, Bristol: The Policy Press.

Laing, R.D. (1965) *The divided self*, Harmondsworth: Penguin.

Lambie, G. (2011) 'The historical context of the global financial crisis: From Bretton Woods to the debacle of neoliberalism', in J. Richardson (ed) *From recession to renewal: The impact of the financial crisis on public services and local government*, Bristol: The Policy Press, pp 25-50.

Laming, Lord (2003) *The Victoria Climbié Inquiry*, London: The Stationery Office.

Langan, M. and Lee, P. (eds) (1989) *Radical social work today*, London: Unwin Hyman.

Lavalette, M. (ed) (2011a) *Radical social work today: Social work at the crossroads*, Bristol: The Policy Press.

Lavalette, M. (2011b) 'Introduction', in M. Lavalette (ed) *Radical social work today: Social work at the crossroads*, Bristol: The Policy Press, pp 1-10.

Lavalette, M. and Ioakimidis, V. (eds) (2011) *Social work in extremis: Lessons for social work internationally*, Bristol: The Policy Press.

Layard, R. (2005) *Happiness: Lessons from a new science*, London: Penguin.

Lazzarato, M. (2009) 'Neoliberalism in action: Inequality, insecurity and the reconstitution of the social', *Theory, Culture and Society*, vol 26, no 6, pp 109-33.

Ledwith, M. (2011) *Community development: A critical approach* (2nd edn), Bristol: The Policy Press.

Le Grand, J. (2007) *Consistent care matters: Exploring the potential of social work practices*, London: Department for Education and Skills.

Le Grand, J. and Estrin, S. (eds) (1989) *Market socialism*, Oxford: Clarendon Press.

Leonard, P. (1978) 'Introduction to the series', in P. Corrigan and P. Leonard, *Social work practice under capitalism: A Marxist approach*, London: Macmillan.

Leonard, P. (1984) *Personality and ideology: Towards a materialist understanding of the individual*, London: Macmillan.

Leonard, P. (1997) *Postmodern welfare: Reconstructing an emancipatory project*, London: Sage Publications.

Levitas, R. (2001) 'Against work: A Utopian incursion into social policy', *Critical Social Policy*, vol 21, no 4, pp 449-65.

Levitas, R. (2011) *The concept of Utopia* (revised 3rd edn), Oxford: Peter Lang.

Levitas R. (2012) 'The Just's umbrella: Austerity and the big society in Coalition policy and beyond' *Critical Social Policy*, vol 32, no 3, pp 320-42.

Levitas, R. (2013, forthcoming) *Utopia as method: The imaginary reconstitution of society*, Basingstoke: Palgrave Macmillan.

Lipsky, M. (2010 [1980]) *Street-level bureaucracy: Dilemmas of the individual in public service* (2nd edn), New York: Russell Sage.

Lister, R. (2000) 'Strategies for social exclusion: Promoting social cohesion or social justice?', in P. Askonas and A. Stewart (eds) *Social inclusion: Possibilities and tensions*, London: Macmillan.

Littlechild, B. (1997) 'Young offenders: Punitive policies and the rights of children', *Critical Social Policy*, vol 17, no 4, pp 73-92.

London-Edinburgh Weekend Return Group (1980) *In and against the state*, London: Pluto Press.

Lonne, B., Parton, N., Thomson, J. and Harries, M. (2008) *Reforming child protection*, London: Routledge.

Lymbery, M. and Butler, S. (eds) (2004) *Social work ideals and practice realities*, Basingstoke: Palgrave Macmillan.

Lymbery, M. and Postle, K. (2010) 'Social work in the context of adult social care in England and the resultant implications for social work education', *British Journal of Social Work*, vol 40, no 8, pp 2502-22.

Macleod, M. and Saraga, E. (1994) 'Child sexual abuse: Challenging the orthodoxy', in M. Loney (ed) *The state or the market?* (2nd edn), London: Sage Publications.

McAra, L. (2006) 'Welfare in crisis? Key developments in Scottish youth justice', in J. Muncie and B. Goldson (eds) *Comparative youth justice*, London: Sage Publications, pp 127-46.

Mahadevan, J. (2012) 'Young asylum seekers being left homeless and hungry', *Children and Young People Now* (www.markallengroup.com).

Mahon, R. and Robinson, F. (eds) (2010) *The ethics and social politics of care: Transnational perspectives*, Vancouver: University of British Columbia.

Marcuse, H. (1964) *One dimensional man*, London: Routledge & Kegan Paul.

Marshall, T.H. (1996 [1950]) *Citizenship and social class*, London: Pluto Press.

Masters, G. and Smith, D. (1998) 'Portia and Persephone revisited: Thinking about feelings in criminal justice', *Theoretical Criminology*, vol 2, no 1, pp 5-27.

Marx, K. and Engels, F. (1967 [1848]) *The Communist manifesto*, Harmondsworth: Penguin.

Marx, K. and Engels, F. (1970 [1845-46]) *The German ideology*, London: Lawrence & Wishart.

Masocha, S. and Simpson, M.K. (2011) 'Xenoracism: Towards a critical understanding of the construction of asylum seekers and its implications for social work practice', *Practice: Social Work in Action*, vol 23, no 1, pp 5-18.

Maughan, B., Collishaw, C. and Goodman, R. (2004) 'Time trends in adolescence', *Journal of Child Psychology and Psychiatry*, vol 45, no 8, pp 1350-62.

Meltzer, N. and Gatward, R. with Goodman, R. and Ford, T. (2000) *Mental health and adolescents in Britain*, London: Office for National Statistics.

Miliband, R. (1973 [1969]) *The state in capitalist society: The analysis of the western system of power*, London: Quartet Books.

Miliband, R. (1977) *Marxism and politics*, Oxford: Oxford Paperbacks.

Miliband, R. (1994) *Socialism for a sceptical age*, Cambridge: Polity Press.

Miller, D. (2003) *"Disabled children and abuse": It doesn't happen to disabled children*, London: NSPCC.

Mishra, R. (1999) *Globalisation and the welfare state*, Cheltenham: Edward Elgar.

Mitchell, W. and Sloper, P. (2002) *Quality services for disabled children*, Research Works 2002-02, York: Social Policy Research Unit, University of York.

Monbiot, G. (2000) *Captive state: The corporate takeover of Britain*, London: Macmillan.

Monbiot, G. (2011) 'This bastardised libertarianism makes "freedom" an instrument of oppression', *The Guardian*, 19 December.

Morgan, R. (2006) *Being fostered: A national of the survey views of foster children, foster carers and birth parents about foster care*, London: Commission for Social Care Inspection.

Morgan, R. and Newburn, T. (2007) 'Youth justice', in M. Maguire, R. Morgan and R. Reiner (eds) *The Oxford handbook of criminology* (4th edn), Oxford: Oxford University Press, pp 1024-60.

Morris, K., Barnes, M. and Mason, P. (2009) *Children, families and social exclusion: New approaches to prevention*, Bristol: The Policy Press.

Mullaly, R.P. (2003) *Structural social work: Ideology, theory and practice* (2nd edn), Oxford: Oxford University Press.

Mullender, A. and Ward, D. (1991) *Self-directed groupwork: Users taking action for empowerment*, London: Whiting and Birch.

Muncie J. (1999) *Youth and crime: A critical introduction*, London: Sage.

Muncie, J. (2006) 'Governing young people: Coherence and contradiction in contemporary youth justice', *Critical Social Policy*, vol 26, no 4, pp 770-93.

Muncie, J. (2008) 'Adulteration', in B. Goldson (ed) *Dictionary of youth justice*, Cullompton: Willan.

Muncie, J. (2009) *Youth and crime* (3rd edn), London: Sage Publications.

Munro, E. (2008) *Effective child protection* (2nd edn), London: Sage Publications.

Munro, E. (2011) *The Munro Review of child protection: Final report*, London: Department of Education.

Nairn, A. (2011) *Child well-being in the UK, Spain and Sweden: The role of inequality and materialism*, UNICEF.

NAO (National Audit Office) (2006) *Sure Start children's centres*, London: The Stationery Office.

Newman, J. and Clarke, J. (2009) *Publics, politics and Power: Remaking the public in public services*, London: Sage Publications.

Noble, C. and Henrickson, M. (2011) 'Editorial: After neoliberalism, new managerialism and postmodernism: What next for social work?', *Journal of Social Work*, vol 11, no 2, pp 128-31.

O'Brien, M. and Penna, S. (1998) *Theorising welfare: Enlightenment and modern society*, London: Sage Publications.

Okitikpi, T. (ed) (2011) *Social control and the use of power in social work with children and families*, Lyme Regis: Russell House.

Oliver, M. (1990) *The politics of disablement*, London: Macmillan.

Oliver, M. (1996) *Understanding disability: From theory to practice*, London: Macmillan.

Oliver, M. and Sapey, B. (2006) *Social work with disabled people* (3rd edn), Basingstoke: Palgrave Macmillan.

Oswain, M. (1998) 'An historical perspective', in C. Robinson and K. Stalker (eds) *Growing up with disability*, London: Jessica Kingsley Publishers, pp 29-43.

Page, R. (2009a) 'Conservative governments and the welfare state since 1945', in H. Bochel, C. Bochel, R. Page and R. Sykes (eds) *Social policy: Themes, issues and debates* (2nd edn), Harlow: Pearson Longman, pp 110-33.

Page, R. (2009b) 'Labour governments and the welfare state since 1945', in R. Page, *Social policy: Themes, issues and debates* (2nd edn), Harlow: Pearson Longman, pp 134-62.

Parton, N. (1985) *The politics of child abuse*, London: Macmillan.

Parton, N. (2008) 'Changes in the form of knowledge in social work: From the "social" to the "informational"?', *British Journal of Social Work*, vol 38, no 2, pp 253-69.

Parton, N. (2011) 'Child protection and safeguarding in England: Changing and competing conceptions of risk and their implications for social work', *British Journal of Social Work*, vol 41, no 5, pp 854-75.

Parton, N. (2012: forthcoming) 'The Munro Review of child protection: An appraisal', *Journal of Social Work*.

Payne, M. (2005) *Modern social work theory* (3rd edn), Basingstoke: Palgrave Macmillan.

Payne, M., Adams, R. and Dominelli, L. (2009) 'On being critical in social work', in A. Adams, L. Dominelli and M. Payne (eds) *Critical practice in social work* (2nd edn), Basingstoke: Palgrave Macmillan, pp 1-16.

Pearce, H. (2012) 'Safe accommodation for separated children', in E. Kelly and F. Bokhari (eds) *Safeguarding children from abroad: Refugee, asylum seeking and trafficked children in the UK*, London: Jessica Kingsley Publishers, pp 69-84.

Pearson, G. (1973) 'Social work as the privatised solution of public ills', *British Journal of Social Work*, vol 3, no 2, pp 209-27.

Peckover, S., Broadhurst, K., White, S., Wastell, D., Hall, H. and Pithouse, A. (2011) 'The fallacy of formalisation: Practice makes process in the assessment of risks to children', in H. Kemshall and B. Wilkinson (eds) *Good practice in assessing risk: Current knowledge, issues and approaches*, London: Jessica Kingsley Publishers, pp 84-101.

Pemberton, C. (2011a) 'Councils pressurise foster carers to become special guardians to save cash', *Community Care*, 20 October (7).

Pemberton, C. (2011b) 'Contact a Family survey reveals plight of families with disabled children', *Community Care*, 7 December.

Penketh, L. (2000) *Tackling institutional racism*, Bristol: The Policy Press.

Penna, S. and O'Brien, M. (2009) 'Neoliberalism', in M. Gray and S. Webb (eds) *Social work theory and methods*, London: Sage Publications, pp 109-18.

Pierson, J. (2010) *Tackling social exclusion* (2nd edn), Abingdon: Routledge.

Pithouse, A. and Broadhurst, K. (2009) 'The Common Assessment Framework: Effective innovation for children and young people with "additional needs" or simply more technical hype?', in K. Broadhurst, C. Grover and J. Jamieson (eds) *Critical perspectives on child safeguarding*, Chichester: Wiley-Blackwell, pp 73-92.

Pitts, J. (1988) *The politics of juvenile crime*, London: Sage Publications.

Pitts, J. (2000) 'The new youth justice and the politics of electoral anxiety', in B. Goldson (ed) *The new youth justice*, Lyme Regis: Russell House.

Pitts, J. (2001) 'Korrectional karaoke: New Labour and the "zombification" of youth justice', *Youth Justice*, vol 1, no 2, pp 3-12.

Postle, K. (2001) 'The social side is disappearing: I guess it started with us being called care managers', *Practice: Social Work in Action*, vol 13, no 1, pp 13-26.

Powell, M. (ed) (1999) *New Labour, new welfare state?*, Bristol: The Policy Press.

Powell, M. (ed) (2002) *Evaluating New Labour's welfare reforms*, Bristol: The Policy Press.

Powell, M. (ed) (2008) *Modernising the welfare state: The Blair legacy*, Bristol: The Policy Press.

Pratt, J. (2007) *Penal populism*, Abingdon: Routledge.

Prideaux, S. (2001) 'New Labour, old functionalism: The underlying contradiction of welfare reform in the US and the UK', *Social Policy & Administration*, vol 35, no 1, pp 85-115.

Pritchard, C. and Williams, R. (2010) 'Comparing possible child abuse related deaths in England and Wales with the major developed countries 1974-2006', *British Journal of Social Work*, vol 20, no 2, pp 1700-18.

Pruit, D. (2000) *Adolescence: Emotional, behavioural, and cognitive development from early adolescence through the teen years*, London: Harper Paperbacks.

Quinton, D. (2004) *Supporting parents: Messages from research*, London: Jessica Kingsley Publishers.

Ransome, P. (2010) *Social theory for beginners*, Bristol: The Policy Press.

Rees, G. and Stein, M. (2011) 'Children and young people in and leaving care', in J. Bradshaw (ed) *The well-being of children in the UK*, Bristol: The Policy Press, pp 175-90.

Rees, S. (1991) *Achieving power*, Sydney: Allen & Unwin.

Reinharz, S. (1992) *Feminist methods in social research*, Oxford: Oxford University Press.

Roberts, Y. (2005) 'When love is not enough', *The Guardian*, 17 August.

Robinson, F. (1999) *Globalizing care: Ethics, feminist theory and international relations*, Boulder, CO: Westview Press.

Robinson, F. (2010) 'After liberalism in world politics? Towards an international political theory of care', *Ethics and Social Welfare*, vol 4, no 2, pp 130-44.

Rogowski, S. (2000/01) 'Young offenders: Their experience of offending and the youth justice system', *Youth and Policy*, vol 70, pp 52-70.

Rogowski, S. (2003/04) 'Young offenders: Towards a radical/critical social work practice', *Youth and Policy*, vol 82, pp 60-73.

Rogowski, S. (2006) 'Young offending: The lives, views and experiences of three "typical" young offenders', *Youth and Policy*, vol 91, pp 41-57.

Rogowski, S. (2008) 'Social work with children and families: Towards a radical/critical practice', *Practice: Social Work in Action*, vol 20, no 1, pp 17-28.

Rogowski, S. (2010a) 'Young offenders: Towards a radical/critical social policy', *Journal of Youth Studies*, vol 13, no 2, pp 197-211.

Rogowski, S. (2010b) *Social work: The rise and fall of a profession?*, Bristol: The Policy Press.

Rogowski, S. (2011a) 'Managers, managerialism and social work with children and families: The deformation of a profession?', *Practice: Social Work in Action*, vol 23, no 3, pp 157-67.

Rogowski, S. (2011b) 'Social work with children and families: Challenges and possibilities in the neo-liberal world', *British Journal of Social Work* 42, no 5, pp 921-40.

Rogowski, S. (2011c) 'Why no change is risky?', *Professional Social Work*, November, pp 14-15.

Rojek, C., Peacock, G. and Collins, S. (1988) *Social work and received ideas*, London: Routledge.

Roy, R., Young, F. and May-Chahal, C. (2009) 'Looked after children and young people in residential care', in R. Adams, L. Dominelli and M. Payne (eds) *Critical practice in social work*, Basingstoke: Palgrave Macmillan, pp 270-79.

Ruch, G., Turney, D. and Ward, A. (eds) (2010) *Relationship-based social work: Getting to the heart of the matter*, London: Jessica Kingsley Publishers.

Sales, R. (2002) 'The deserving and the undeserving? Refugees, asylum seekers and welfare in Britain', *Critical Social Policy*, vol 22, no 3, pp 456-78.

Sales, R. and Hek, R. (2004) 'Dilemmas of care and control: The work of an asylum seeking team in London', in D. Hayes and B. Humphries (eds) *Social work, immigration and asylum: Debates, dilemmas and ethical issues for social work and social care*, London Jessica Kingsley Publishers, pp 59-76.

Sapey, B. (2009) 'Engaging with the social model of disability', in P. Higham (ed) *Post-qualifying social work practice*, London: Sage Publications, pp 89-102.

Sayer, T. (2008) *Critical practice in working with children*, Basingstoke: Palgrave Macmillan.

Seebohm Report (1968) *Report of the Committee on Local Authority and Allied Social Services*, Cmnd 2703, London: HMSO.

SEU (Social Exclusion Unit) (1999) *Bridging the gap: New opportunities for 16-18 year olds*, London: The Stationery Office.

SEU (2003) *A better education for children in care*, London: Office of the Deputy Prime Minister.

Sevenhuijsen, S. (1998) *Citizenship and the ethics of care*, London: Routledge.

Sevenhuijsen, S. (2000) 'Caring in the Third Way: The relational between obligation, responsibility and care in Third Way discourse', *Critical Social Policy*, vol 20, no 1, pp 5-37.

Shakespeare, T. (2006) *Disability rights and wrongs*, Abingdon: Routledge.

Shaw, C. and de Sousa, S. (2012) 'Living with unrelated adults: Private fostering', in E. Kelly and F. Bokhari (eds) *Safeguarding children from abroad: Refugee, asylum seeking and trafficked children in the UK*, London: Jessica Kingsley Publishers, pp 85-99.

Simmonds, J. (2008) 'Foreword: Direct work with children – Delusion or reality', in B. Luckock and M. Lefevre (eds) *Direct work: Social work with children and young people in care*, London: British Association for Adoption and Fostering.

Sinclair, M. (2010) *How to cut public spending (and still win an election)*, London: Biteback.

Small, J. with Goldstein, P. (2000) 'Ethnicity and placement: Beginning the debate', *Fostering and Adoption*, vol 24, no 1, pp 15-24.

Smith, D. (1995) *Criminology for social work*, Basingstoke: Macmillan.

Smith, D. (ed) (2004) *Social work and evidenced-based practice*, London: Jessica Kingsley Publishers.

Smith, D. (2006) 'Youth crime and justice: Research, evaluation and "evidence"', in B. Goldson and J. Muncie (eds) *Youth crime and justice*, London: Sage Publications, pp 78-91.

Smith, R. (2001) 'Foucault's law: The Crime and Disorder Act 1998', *Youth Justice*, vol 1, no 2, pp 17-29.

Smith, R. (2006) 'Actuarialism and early intervention in contemporary youth justice', in B. Goldson and J. Muncie (eds) *Youth crime and justice*, London: Sage Publications, pp 92-109.

Smith, R. (2007) *Youth justice: Ideas, policy and practice*, Cullompton: Willan.

Smith, R. (2008) *Social work with young people*, Cambridge: Polity Press.

Social Work Task Force (2009) *Building a safe, confident future*, London: General Social Care Council.

Spratt, T. (2008) 'Possible futures for social work with children and families in Australia, the United Kingdom and the United States', *Child Care in Practice*, vol 14, no 4, pp 413-27.

Squires, P. (2006) 'New Labour and the politics of anti-social behaviour', *Critical Social Policy*, vol 26, no 1, pp 144-68.

Squires, P. (ed) (2008) *ASBO nation: The criminalisation of nuisance*, Bristol: The Policy Press.

Stafford, A., Parton, N., Vincent, S. and Smith, C. (2012) *Child protection systems in the United Kingdom: A comparative analysis*, London: Jessica Kingsley Publishers.

Stein, M. (2004) *What works for young people leaving care?*, Barkingside: Barnardo's.

Stein, M. (2006) 'Wrong turn', *The Guardian*, 6 December.

Stephen, D. (2009) 'Time to stop twisting the knife: A critical commentary on the rights and wrongs of criminal justice responses to problem youth in the UK', *Journal of Social Welfare and Family Law*, vol 31, no 2, pp 193-206.

Stephenson, M., Giller, H. and Brown, S. (2007) *Effective practice in youth justice*, Cullompton: Willan.

Stepney, P. (2006) 'Mission impossible: Critical practice in social work', *British Journal of Social Work*, vol 36, no 8, pp 1289-307.

Stepney, R. and Ford, S. (2000) *Social work models, methods and theories*, Lyme Regis: Russell House.

Stewart, J., Smith, D., Stewart, G. and Fullwood, C. (1994) *Understanding offending behaviour*, Harlow: Longman.

Sykes, R. (2009) 'Globalisation, welfare and social policy', in H. Bochel, C. Bochel, R. Page and R. Sykes (eds) *Social policy: Themes, issues and debates* (2nd edn), Harlow: Pearson Longman, pp 486-508.

Teater B. and Balwin M. (2012) Social Work in the Community: Making a difference Bristol: Policy Press

Thompson, N. (2003) *Anti-discriminatory practice* (3rd edn), Basingstoke: Palgrave Macmillan.

Thorpe, D. (1994) *Evaluating child protection*, Buckingham: Open University Press.

Thorpe, D. (1995) 'Some implications of recent child protection research', *Representing Children*, vol 8, no 3, pp 45-56.

Thorpe, D., Smith, D., Greenwood, C. and Paley, J. (1980) *Out of care: The community support of juvenile offenders*, London: Allen & Unwin.

Timmins, N. (1996) *The five giants: A biography of the welfare state*, London: HarperCollins.

Titmuss, R.M. (1965) *Income distribution and social change*, London: Allen & Unwin.

Tolmac, J. and Hodes, M. (2004) 'Ethnic variation among adolescent psychiatric in-patients with psychotic disorders', *British Journal of Psychiatry*, vol 184, May, pp 428-31.

Tronto, J. (2010) 'A democratic ethics of care and global care workers: Citizenship and responsibility', in R. Mahon and F. Robinson (eds) *The ethics and social politics of care: Transnational perspectives*, Vancouver: University of British Columbia Press.

UK Children's Commissioners (2008) *UK Children's Commissioners Report to the UN Committee on the Rights of the Child*, London/Belfast/Edinburgh/Colwyn Bay: 11 Million/NICCY/SCCYP/Children's Commissioner for Wales.

UN (United Nations) (1989) *Convention on the Rights of the Child*, New York: UN General Assembly.

UNHCR (United Nations High Commissioner for Refugees) (1951) *Convention relating to the Rights of Refugees*, Geneva: UNHCR.

UNICEF (United Nations Children's Fund) (2007) *Child poverty in perspective: An overview of child well-being in rich countries*, Report Card 7, Florence: UNICEF Innocenti Research Centre.

Unison (2009) *Still slipping through the net? Front-line staff assess children's safe-guarding progress*, London: Unison.

Unison (2010) *Not waving but drowning: Paperwork and pressure in adult social work services*, London: Unison.

Unison (2011) *Mutual benefit? Should mutuals, co-operatives and social enterprises deliver public services?*, London: Unison.

UPIAS (Union of Physically Impaired Against Segregation) (1976) *Fundamental principles of disability*, London: UPIAS.

Utting, W. (1997) *People like us: The report of the review of the safeguards for children living away from home*, London: Department of Health/Welsh Office.

Wacquant, L. (2009) *Punishing the poor: The neoliberal government of social insecurity*, Durham, NC and London: Duke University Press.

Wade, J., Biehal, N., Farrelly, N. and Sinclair, I. (2011) *Caring for abused and neglected children: Making the right decisions for reunification or long term care*, London: Jessica Kingsley Publishers.

Walker, A., Sinfield, A. and Walker, C. (eds) (2011) *Fighting poverty, inequality and injustice: A manifesto inspired by Peter Townsend*, Bristol: The Policy Press.

Walker, S. (2004) 'Community work and psycho-social practice: Chalk and cheese or birds of a feather?', *Journal Social Work of Practice*, vol 18, no 2, pp 161-75.

Walker, S. (2011) *The social worker's guide to child and adolescent mental health*, London: Jessica Kingsley Publishers.

Webb, S.A. (2010) '(Re) assembling the Left: The politics of redistribution and recognition in social work', *British Journal of Social Work*, vol 40, no 8, pp 2364-79.

Wells, M. and Hoikkala, S. (2004) 'A comparison of two European resettlement programmes for young separated refugees', in D. Hayes and B. Humphries (eds) *Social work, immigration and asylum: Debates, dilemmas and ethical issues in social work and social care*, London: Jessica Kingsley Publishers, pp 178-200.

Westcott, H. (1998) 'Disabled children and child protection', in C. Robinson and K. Stalker (eds) *Growing up with disability*, London: Jessica Kingsley Publishers, pp 129-42.

White, S., Hall, C. and Peckover, S. (2009) 'The descriptive tyranny of the Common Assessment Framework: Technologies of categorization and professional practice in child welfare', *British Journal of Social Work*, vol 39, no 7, pp 1197-217.

White, S., Westell, D., Broadhurst, K. and Hall, C. (2010) 'When policy o'erleaps itself: The "tragic tale" of the integrated children's system', *Critical Social Policy*, vol 30, no 3, pp 405-29.

White, V. (2009) 'Quiet challenges: Professional practice in modernised social work', in J. Harris and V. White (eds) *Modernising social work: Critical considerations*, Bristol: The Policy Press, pp 129-44.

Whyte, B. (2009) *Youth justice in practice: Making a difference*, Bristol: The Policy Press.

Wild, J. (2012) 'Too much, too young', *Professional Social Work*, February, pp 24-5.

Wilkinson, R. and Pickett, K. (2010) *The spirit level: Why equality is better for everyone*, Harmondsworth: Penguin.

Williams, F. (1989) *Social policy: A critical introduction*, Cambridge: Polity Press.

Williams, F. (2001) 'In and beyond New Labour: Towards a new political ethics of care', *Critical Social Policy*, vol 21, no 4, pp 467-93.

Wilson, K., Ruch, G., Lymbery, M., Cooper, A. et al (2011) *Social work: An introduction to contemporary practice* (2nd edn), Harlow: Pearson.

Wolverhampton SCB (Safeguarding Children's Board) (2011) *Serious case review – Child J*, Wolverhampton SCB.

Wootton, B. (1959) *Social science and social pathology*, London: Allen & Unwin.

Yeandle, S. (1999) 'Supporting employed carers: New jobs, new services?', ESRC Seminar Series: The Interface between Public Policy and Gender Equality, CRESR, Sheffield Hallam University.

Young, J. (1999) *The exclusive society*, London: Sage Publications.

Young, J. (2007) *The vertigo of late modernity*, London: Sage Publications.

Index

DATE DUE
